Reviewing Basic Grammar

A GUIDE TO WRITING SENTENCES AND PARAGRAPHS

SEVENTH EDITION

Mary Laine Yarber

Robert E. Yarber

Emeritus, San Diego Mesa College

PEARSON

Longman

New York • San Francisco • Boston
London • Toronto • Sydney • Tokyo • Singapore • Madrid
Mexico City • Munich • Paris • Cape Town • Hong Kong • Montreal

Acquisitions Editor: Melanie Craig

Senior Supplements Editor: Donna Campion

Production Manager: Stacey Kulig

Project Coordination, Text Design, and Electronic Page Makeup: Thompson Steele, Inc.

Cover Design Manager: Wendy Ann Fredericks

Cover Designer: Joseph DePinho

Cover Art: © Brand X Pictures

Manufacturing Buyer: Lucy Hebard

Printer and Binder: R. R. Donnelley and Sons

Cover Printer: Phoenix Color Corporation

Please visit us at www.ablongman.com

ISBN 0-321-39607-3 (student edition)

ISBN 0-321-43612-1 (annotated instructor's edition)

2 3 4 5 6 7 8 9 10—DOH—09 08 07 06

Brief Contents

Detailed Contents

Preface

Like its predecessors, this seventh edition of *Reviewing Basic Grammar: A Guide to Writing Sentences and Paragraphs* is designed for students who need to hone their skills in grammar and basic writing before taking a freshman English course. With its sympathetic tone, its focus on basics of grammar and usage, and its scaffolded approach to writing, *RBG7* will help students become confident, effective, and interesting writers.

Approach

Reviewing Basic Grammar: A Guide to Writing Sentences and Paragraphs, seventh edition, has been guided by the following principles:

- Emphasis on the essentials of sentence structure, grammar, and punctuation, while avoiding technical terminology, is important in teaching grammar and basic writing skills.
- Inclusion of writing and writing assignments that are meaningful and reflect students' interests and concerns are important because grammar and usage cannot be taught in a vacuum.
- Presentation of concise, clear, and interesting material for both students and instructors and of abundant exercises and opportunities for evaluation is important.
- Recognition of the ethnic and cultural diversity of today's student body is important.

Organization

Chapter 1 stresses the importance of acceptable usage and grammar and their relationship with effective writing. The chapter also contains an introduction to writing paragraphs and includes a section on writing on the computer.

Building on the overview of writing paragraphs addressed in Chapter 1, subsequent chapters present writing topic sentences, methods to assure coherence by using various organizational patterns, the use of transitions within the paragraph, and strategies for paragraph development. Each chapter presents a complete and concise examination of the common problems of basic usage, followed by a sequential study of paragraph writing. The result is a thorough and seamless coverage of the fundamentals of usage and writing that will prepare the student for the challenges of a freshman English course.

Among the topics addressed in the text are the following:

- Sentence fragments, comma-splices, and fused sentences
- Subject-verb agreement
- Pronoun-antecedent agreement
- Subject and object forms of pronouns
- Use of adjectives and adverbs
- Use of indefinite pronouns such as *anyone, someone, neither,* and *none*
- Verbs and tense
- Punctuation, possessives, numbers, and capitals
- Avoidance of sexism in the use of pronouns

Features New to the Seventh Edition

- **Increased Emphasis on Simplified but Clear Explanations and Terms.** The text provides clear and understandable explanations. Similarly, it avoids confusing or difficult terms like *subject complement* and *predicate nominative.*
- **New In-Chapter Exercises.** Additional opportunities for practice and review based on topics of student interest are provided throughout the book.
- **New Chapter Review Tests.** Identical in format and difficulty, chapter review tests provide the student with feedback that alerts him or her to those areas of the chapter that need to be reviewed. An additional chapter review test for each chapter is featured on the companion Website.
- **Increased Integration of Grammar and Sentence Writing.** This edition of *Reviewing Basic Grammar* correlates the acquisition of grammar skills with sentence writing in a series of exercises that conclude each chapter.
- **Increased Emphasis on the Needs of the ESL Student.** Students whose first language is not English often need additional help, and each chapter contains a Language Tip box. In addition, "A Checklist for the ESL Writer" in the Appendix furnishes more detailed assistance.
- **Expanded *Instructor's Manual/Test Bank.*** The *Instructor's Manual/Test Bank* now includes two versions of chapter tests and final examinations.

Enduring Features

- **Clear Explanations, Examples, and Exercises.** The grammar and usage sections of each chapter provide clear explanations and examples, as well as exercises in a variety of formats—including sentence completion, multiple choice, sentence generation, and editing.

- **Student Paragraphs and Paragraphs by Professional Writers.** Examples written by students and those by popular, professional writers illustrate the various rhetorical patterns introduced in each chapter.
- **Writing Tips.** Boxed, readily identifiable writing tips are included on such practical matters as using the proper format for papers, selecting the best dictionary, and building one's vocabulary.
- **Computer Activity.** A boxed computer activity is included in each chapter and can be easily adapted to any word-processing program.
- **Review Tests.** Two review tests, identical in format and difficulty, conclude the grammar and usage section of each chapter.
- **Writing Paragraphs.** Each chapter concludes with a section on writing paragraphs. The section instructs on such topics as writing effective thesis sentences and organizing paragraphs.
- **Answers.** Answers to even-numbered exercises are included at the end of the text so that students may evaluate their work as they move through the chapters.
- **A Checklist for the ESL Writer.** A checklist in the Appendix that includes cross-references to the chapters in the text addresses the most troublesome and confusing problems encountered by students whose first language is not English. To supplement this appendix, qualified adopters of this book may obtain *ESL Worksheets* (ISBN 0-321-01955-5) by contacting their Longman representative. Written by Jocelyn Steer, a recognized authority on the teaching of English to ESL students, the worksheets provide extra practice in the areas that usually require additional attention.
- **Companion Website.** A Website that includes a wealth of additional exercises, gradable quizzes, an additional chapter review test, extensive material on spelling, e-mail capabilities, summaries, and interactive activities accompanies this text for no additional cost to the student. Visit this online resource at **http://www.ablongman.com/yarber**.

The Teaching and Learning Package

Each component of the teaching and learning package for *Reviewing Basic Grammar: A Guide to Writing Sentences and Paragraphs*, seventh edition, has been crafted to ensure that the course is a rewarding experience for both instructors and students.

The *Instructor's Manual/Test Bank*, free to adopters, provides the following teaching aids:

- Answers to the chapter review exercises.
- Two tests on grammar and usage for Chapters 2–11 (Forms A and B). The tests are identical in format and difficulty. An answer key is included.
- Two cumulative final examinations on grammar and usage (Forms A and B). The examinations are identical in format and difficulty, and an answer key is included.

■ Exercises that supplement the Appendix, "A Checklist for the ESL Writer," for those students who need additional review.

The *Reviewing Basic Grammar* companion Website is free to students and instructors who use this text. With quizzes, summaries, bonus review tests, and interactive activities, this rich Website provides students with additional opportunities to practice the skills they have learned in the textbook. The Website can be accessed by going to **http://www .ablongman.com/yarber**.

The Longman Developmental English Package

In addition to the book-specific supplements discussed above, many other skills-based supplements are available for both instructors and students. All of these supplements are available either free or at greatly reduced prices.

For Additional Reading and Reference

The Dictionary Deal. Two dictionaries can be shrink-wrapped with this text at a nominal fee. *The New American Webster Handy College Dictionary* is a paperback reference text with more than 100,000 entries. *Merriam-Webster's Collegiate Dictionary*, eleventh edition, is a hardback reference with a citation file of more than 14.5 million examples of English words drawn from actual use. For more information on how to shrink-wrap a dictionary with your text, please contact your Longman sales representative.

Penguin Quality Paperback Titles. A series of Penguin paperbacks is available at a significant discount when shrink-wrapped with this text. Some titles available are Toni Morrison's *Beloved*, Julia Alvarez's *How the Garcia Girls Lost Their Accents*, Mark Twain's *Huckleberry Finn*, *Narrative of the Life of Frederick Douglass*, Harriet Beecher Stowe's *Uncle Tom's Cabin*, Dr. Martin Luther King, Jr.'s *Why We Can't Wait*, and plays by Shakespeare, Miller, and Albee. For a complete list of titles or more information, please contact your Longman sales consultant.

Penguin Academics: *Twenty-Five Great Essays, Fifty Great Essays,* **and** *One Hundred Great Essays,* **edited by Robert DiYanni.** These alphabetically organized essay collections are published as part of the "Penguin Academics" series of low-cost, high-quality offerings intended for use in introductory college courses. All essays were selected for their teachability, both as models for writing and for their usefulness as springboards for student writing. For more information on how to shrink-wrap one of these anthologies with your text, please contact your Longman sales consultant.

100 Things to Write About. This 100-page book contains 100 individual assignments for writing on a variety of topics and in a wide range of formats, from expressive to analytical. Ask your Longman sales representative for a sample copy. 0-673-98239-4

Newsweek **Alliance.** Instructors may choose to shrink-wrap a 12-week subscription to *Newsweek* with any Longman text. The price of the subscription is 59 cents per issue (a total of $7.08 for the subscription). Available with the subscription is a free "Interactive Guide to *Newsweek*"—a workbook for students who are using the text. In addition, *Newsweek* provides a wide variety of instructor supplements free to teachers, including maps, Skills Builders, and weekly quizzes. For more information on the *Newsweek* program, please contact your Longman sales representative.

Electronic and Online Offerings

The Longman Electronic Newsletter. Twice a month during the spring and fall, instructors who have subscribed receive a free copy of the Longman Developmental English Newsletter in their e-mailbox. Written by experienced classroom instructors, the newsletter offers teaching tips, classroom activities, book reviews, and more. To subscribe, send an e-mail to **BasicSkills@ablongman.com.**

The Longman Writer's Warehouse. This innovative and exciting online supplement is the perfect accompaniment to any developmental writing course. Created by developmental English instructors specially for student writers, the Writer's Warehouse covers every part of the writing process. Also included are journaling capabilities, multimedia activities, diagnostic tests, an interactive handbook, and a complete instructor's manual. The Writer's Warehouse requires no space on your school's server; rather, students complete and store their work on the Longman server, and are able to access it, revise it, and continue working at any time. For more details about how to shrink-wrap a free subscription to the Writer's Warehouse with this text, please consult your Longman sales representative. For a free guided tour of the site, visit **http:// longmanwriterswarehouse.com.**

The Writer's ToolKit Plus. This CD-ROM offers a wealth of tutorial, exercise, and reference material for writers. It is compatible with either a PC or Macintosh platform and is flexible enough to be used either occasionally for practice or regularly in class lab sessions. For information on how to bundle this CD-ROM free with your text, please contact your Longman sales representative.

For Instructors

Electronic Test Bank for Writing. This electronic test bank features more than 5,000 questions in all areas of writing, from grammar to paragraphing, through essay writing, research, and documentation. With this easy-to-use CD-ROM, instructors simply choose questions from the electronic test bank, then print out the completed test for distribution. CD-ROM: 0-321-08117-X Print version: 0-321-08486-1

Competency Profile Test Bank, Second Edition. This series of sixty objective tests covers ten general areas of English competency, including fragments; comma-splices and run-ons; pronouns; commas; and capitalization. Each test is available in remedial, standard, and advanced versions. Available as reproducible sheets or in computerized versions. Free to instructors. Print version: 0-321-02224-6

Diagnostic and Editing Tests and Exercises, Seventh Edition. This collection of diagnostic tests helps instructors assess students' competence in Standard Written English for purpose of placement or to gauge progress. Available as reproducible sheets or in computerized versions, and free to instructors. Print version: 0-321-19647-3. CD-ROM: 0-321-19645-7

ESL Worksheets, Third Edition. These reproducible worksheets provide ESL students with extra practice in areas they find the most troublesome. A diagnostic test and posttest are provided, along with answer keys and suggested topics for writing. Free to adopters. 0-321-07765-2

Longman Editing Exercises. Fifty-four pages of paragraph editing exercises give students extra practice using grammar skills in the context of longer passages. Free when packaged with any Longman title. 0-205-31792-8 Answer key: 0-205-31797-9

80 Practices. A collection of reproducible, ten-item exercises that provide additional practices for specific grammatical usage problems, such as comma-splices, capitalization, and pronouns. Includes an answer key. Free to adopters. 0-673-53422-7

CLAST Test Package, Fourth Edition. These two 40-item objective tests evaluate students' readiness for the CLAST exams. Strategies for teaching CLAST preparedness are included. Free with any Longman English title. Reproducible sheets: 0-321-01950-4

TASP Test Package, Third Edition. These twelve practice pretests and posttests assess the same reading and writing skills covered in the TASP examination. Free with any Longman English title. Reproducible sheets: 0-321-01959-8

Teaching Online: Internet Research, Conversation, and Composition, **Second Edition.** Ideal for instructors who have never surfed the Net, this easy-to-follow guide offers basic definitions, numerous examples, and step-by-step information about finding and using Internet resources. Free to adopters. 0-321-01957-1

The Longman Instructor Planner. This all-in-one resource for instructors includes monthly and weekly planning sheets, to-do lists, student contact forms, attendance rosters, a gradebook, an address/phone book, and a mini almanac. Ask your Longman sales representative for a free copy. 0-321-09247-3

For Students

Researching Online, **Fifth Edition.** A perfect companion for a new age, this indispensable new supplement helps students navigate the Internet. Adapted from *Teaching Online,* the instructor's Internet guide, *Researching Online* speaks directly to students, giving them detailed, step-by-step instructions for performing electronic searches. Available free when shrink-wrapped with this text. 0-321-09277-5

Ten Practices of Highly Successful Students. This popular supplement helps students learn crucial study skills, offering concise tips for a successful career in college. Topics include time management, test-taking, reading critically, stress, and motivation. 0-205-30769-8

The Longman Student Planner. This daily planner for students includes daily, weekly, and monthly calendars, as well as class schedules and a mini almanac of useful information. It is the perfect accompaniment to a Longman reading or study skills textbook and is available free to students when shrink-wrapped with this text. 0-321-04573-4

The Longman Writer's Journal. This journal for writers, free with any Longman English text, offers students a place to think, write, and react. For an examination copy, contact your Longman sales consultant. 0-321-08639-2

The Longman Writer's Portfolio. This unique supplement provides students with a space to plan, think about, and present their work. The portfolio includes an assessing/organizing area (including a grammar diagnostic test, a spelling quiz, and project planning worksheets), a before- and during-writing area (including peer review sheets, editing checklists, writing self-evaluations, and a personal editing profile), and an after-writing area (including a progress chart, a final table of contents, and a final assessment). Ask your Longman sales representative for ISBN 0-321-10765-9

State-Specific Supplements

[For Florida Adoptions] ***Thinking Through the Test,*** **by D.J. Henry.** This special workbook, prepared specially for students in Florida, offers ample skill and practice exercises to help students prep for the Florida State Exit Exam. To shrink-wrap this workbook free with your textbook, please contact your Longman sales representative. Available in two versions: with answers and without answers. Also available: two laminated grids (one for reading, one for writing) that can serve as handy references for students preparing for the Florida State Exit Exam.

[For New York Adoptions] Preparing for the CUNY-ACT Reading and Writing Test, edited by Patricia Licklider. This booklet, prepared by reading and writing faculty from across the CUNY system, is designed to help students prepare for the CUNY-ACT exit test. It includes test-taking tips, reading passages, typical exam questions, and sample writing prompts to help students become familiar with each portion of the test.

[For Texas Adoptions] ***The Longman TASP Study Guide,*** **by Jeanette Harris.** Created specifically for students in Texas, this study guide includes straightforward explanations and numerous practice exercises to help students prepare for the reading and writing sections of the Texas Academic Skills Program Test. To shrink-wrap this workbook free with your textbook, please contact your Longman sales representative.

The Longman Series of Monographs for Developmental Educators

Ask your Longman sales consultant for a free copy of these monographs written by experts in their fields.

#1: *The Longman Guide to Classroom Management.* Written by Joannis Flatley of St. Philip's College, the first in Longman's new series of monographs for developmental English instructors focuses on issues of classroom etiquette, providing guidance on dealing with unruly, unengaged, disruptive, or uncooperative students. Ask your Longman sales representative for a free copy. 0-321-09246-5

#2: *The Longman Guide to Community Service-Learning in the English Classroom and Beyond.* Written by Elizabeth Rodriguez Kessler of California State University, Northridge, this is the second monograph in Longman's series for developmental educators. It provides a definition and history of service-learning, as well as an overview of how service-learning can be integrated effectively into the college classroom. 0-321-12749-8

Acknowledgments

We continue to be grateful to the many instructors at colleges and universities throughout the country who have expressed their pleasure with previous editions of this book.

We are happy to acknowledge the contributions of Nancy Freihofer and Mandy Sladen of Thompson Steele, Inc. to the preparation and editorial layout of this edition of *Reviewing Basic Grammar*.

Mary Laine Yarber wishes to thank her colleagues and friends for valuable feedback and encouragement: Ed Blitz, Laurel Ann Bogen, Randall and Roberta Denis, Tassie Hadlock-Piltz, Jennifer Jadovitz, Suzi Woodruff Lacey, Steve Lattimore, Stephen R. Martinez, Ann McKechnie, Thomas Meurer, Mira Pak, Solace Pineo, Robin and Courtney Reid, Cheri Clew Ryan, Jeffrey and Bernice Skorneck, Daryl Solomon, Susan Strom, Shelley Triggs, Carol Wrabel, and Erich Yost. She also thanks her father and co-author, Robert Yarber, and her family—Mary Winzerling Yarber, Don and Sylvia Yarber, Elizabeth Reeves Sparks, and William Winzerling—for their encouragement and humor. She writes in memory of treasured colleagues Jessica Kaplan and Ronald Mills-Coyne.

Robert E. Yarber is pleased to acknowledge, as in previous editions, the contributions of his daughter and co-author, Mary Yarber. Her knowledge, energy, and wit, as well as her concern for her students, are obvious throughout the book and in the classroom. He continues to appreciate the contributions of his wife, Mary Winzerling Yarber, who is a writer and master teacher and who also served as a referee when needed during the revision of this book.

Finally we would like to thank the following reviewers for sharing their insights and suggestions:

Jonathan Alexander, University of Cincinnati
Sylvia Boyd, Phillips Community College of the University of Arkansas
Robin Cosgrove, University of Minnesota, Duluth
Holly L. French, Bossier Parish Community College
Andrew Hoffman, San Diego Mesa College
Carolyn Kershaw, Allegheny Community College
John Kopec, Boston University
Martha Knight, Bossier Parish Community College
Tom Lajeunesse, University of Minnesota, Duluth
Jane Maher, Nassau Community College
Rebecca Smith Mann, Guilford Technical Community College
Karen Mason, Bossier Parish Community College
Sam Rogal, Illinois Valley Community College
Faye Schuett, Schoolcraft College
Lynne Sharpe, North Seattle Community College
Alice Sink, High Point University
William Wilson, Palm Beach Community College
Holly Young, Arkansas State University at Beebe.

MARY LAINE YARBER
ROBERT E. YARBER

GETTING STARTED: COMPUTERS, GRAMMAR, SENTENCES, AND PARAGRAPHS

CHAPTER PREVIEW

In this chapter, you will learn about:

- The importance of standard English
- Why writing is important
- Writing with the computer
- Writing sentences
- Writing paragraphs: An overview

Standard English: Who Needs It?

The English language is spoken and written by almost five hundred million people around the world. In Europe, which is uniting rapidly and which has at least fifteen languages, English is increasingly used to communicate. In Asia, English is spoken and written in both business and social settings as a result of American business and cultural influences.

In the United States, there is a growing link between a worker's writing skills and his or her earning power. The Information Age has made e-mail, text-messaging, Web posts, and other kinds of electronic writing vital to a surging number of businesses; employees who cannot present themselves well in these ways often receive lower positions and pay than they would like. Because of this new focus on written communication in business and other job fields, many employers now ask applicants to answer at least some of their interview questions in writing. E-mails, reports, proposals, summaries, text messages, Web site postings, and letters are typically required in today's work world. And they must be not only factually accurate but also free of serious mistakes in grammar, spelling, and punctuation.

Even before you begin your career, strong English skills are crucial. Almost every class that you will take in college requires writing of some kind. You will be expected to write exams, reports, essays, and term papers that are well organized, logical, and convincing and that follow the principles of **standard written English.**

Fortunately, you already know and unconsciously follow most of the principles of standard written English. The chapters that follow in this book will build on that knowledge. Standard written English is the kind of English that you find in reports, books, newspapers, and articles and that you hear spoken by news announcers on television or radio and by your instructors in classrooms. In informal conversations, of course, you can ignore many of the principles of standard written English. Most **slang,** for example, is perfectly acceptable to many speakers of American English. But if such expressions appear in writing, they can get in the way of the writer's ideas and distract the reader.

The clothes you wear while working on your car or painting your room would not be appropriate for a job interview. Nor would the expressions you use with your friends be appropriate when you speak to a traffic judge whom you are trying to impress. To be a good writer, therefore, you will be expected to follow the principles of standard written English— in other words, to use language that is right for the job. If your writing does not follow those principles—if it is filled with errors in grammar, spelling, and punctuation—it will confuse and mislead your reader. It could even convince him or her that you and your ideas should not be taken seriously.

Preparing to Write A Collaborative Checklist

Discuss these questions with other students in your class.

1. Do you find yourself in situations in which writing is important? Explain.
2. What ritual do you follow before you write? Do you like to have music on? Drink coffee? Do you sharpen your pencils, clean your room, or play a computer game? Describe the routine you follow in order to get started.
3. Good writers read. What do you read regularly? Which magazines, books, or newspapers? Who are your favorite authors, or what are your favorite types of books?
4. Bring to class an example of writing by a professional reporter or author whom you like. What do you like about it? Read the example to the class and see if others like it. If they do not, examine their reasons.
5. What are your strengths as a writer? Try to be specific: mention things like ideas, vocabulary, organization, or any other aspect of your writing that does not present problems for you.
6. What are your weaknesses as a writer? Again, try to be specific: mention things like getting started, weak vocabulary, poor spelling, shortage of ideas, and so on.
7. Bring to class some of your own writing that you like. Read it to the class (or have someone else read it). What are their reactions?

> ## Writing Tips   According to the Dictionary ...
>
> The dictionary is a learning tool that you will use in your college classes and for the rest of your life. A dictionary contains much more than definitions. It tells you the history of a word and how it is spelled, hyphenated, and pronounced. Traditional favorites of college students and instructors include *The American Heritage College Dictionary, Merriam-Webster's Collegiate Dictionary,* and *The Random House College Dictionary.* Ask your instructor for more suggestions.

For these reasons, the following chapters will give you a quick review of the parts of speech and then deal with the most serious kinds of errors that writers make. But do not get the idea that the avoidance of errors equals good writing. You will also need practice in writing sentences and paragraphs that are interesting, coherent, and correct.

Writing with the Computer

Until recent years, writing a composition of any length meant taking notes, writing one or more drafts while revising and correcting at each stage, and typing a final copy. Weakness in content, mistakes in grammar, and even typographical errors were sometimes ignored because the author did not want to type another copy. Now, however, the act of writing has changed because of the introduction of computers. Increasing numbers of writers believe that composing on a computer makes the revising and editing process much easier and more efficient.

The chief advantage is that the computer allows you to rewrite, correct, change, and revise selected portions of your paper without retyping the whole paper. The parts that you do not change remain in their original form and do not have to be retyped. As you can imagine, computers allow and encourage writers to revise their manuscripts more easily and quickly than the traditional way.

Just as there are different writing styles among those who use a pen or typewriter, so there are differing practices among computer users. Some writers work directly at the keyboard and compose until they have completed their first draft. Then they revise and edit until they have made all of their modifications and changes. Others write their first draft by hand and then use the computer to prepare their final copy. Still others write at the keyboard, print a copy, and then revise with pen or pencil; they then go back to the computer for further alterations.

Regardless of the composing style that you adopt, you should not become discouraged at your first attempts to use a computer. As you master it, you will learn that you can move or delete words, sentences, paragraphs, or entire pages; change words, phrases, or sentences; correct punctuation, mechanics, and misspelled words; and copy part or all of the paper to use for other purposes.

In addition to revising and editing, the computer has other uses. In the preparation and formatting of a paper, you can change spacing and margins, incorporate boldface, italicize words and titles, center material on a page, and close any spaces left by deletions and substitutions.

The effect of using a computer will be obvious as you become familiar with its features. The most obvious is that revision is easier: by merely pressing a few keys or moving the mouse, you can shift words, sentences, and entire paragraphs. By putting down ideas as they come to you, you will be less worried about forgetting important points and more likely to draft quickly. After you have written a draft, you can incorporate additional material, and because you can get a clean copy whenever you want after making changes, you will probably revise and edit more than if you had to retype continually.

Using the computer will not make you a good writer. You will still need to arrange your ideas in the most effective and logical order, develop and plan your paragraphs carefully, and use the most appropriate word choice and sentence structure. But for the last, important stage of the writing process—revising and editing—the computer can be an invaluable tool.

Writing Sentences

In each of the following chapters you will be asked to write original sentences that apply the grammatical skills you will have learned in the chapter. Editing exercises are also included, and each will ask you to correct and revise sentences in accordance with these skills.

EDITING EXERCISE

The sentences below contain some of the most common errors in usage. Rewrite each sentence in standard written English. To help you recognize the errors, you can refer to the chapter indicated after each sentence.

1. Sean bought a motorcycle for his wife with an electric starter. (Chapter 10)

2. Because the sidewalk was covered with ice, I walked very careful to avoid falling. (Chapter 10)

3. The prospect of moving to a warmer climate delighted his wife and he. (Chapter 6)

4. Rappelling is a method of descent used by mountain climbers it employs double ropes rather than picks and shoe cleats. (Chapter 9)

5. Each of the band members had signed their name on the concert program. (Chapter 7)

6. An old-fashioned remedy for a cough, made by mixing honey, lemon, and hot water. (Chapter 9)

7. After running in the marathon, Jackie laid down and rested. (Chapter 5)

8. As a freshman in college, Mario had broke three records as a member of the basketball team. (Chapter 5)

9. Osteoporosis is caused by loss of bone mass and strength, it affects twenty-five percent of women over age sixty. (Chapter 9)

10. Han and myself were assigned the task of washing dishes after the dinner. (Chapter 6)

11. The survivors of the automobile accident said that a heavy downpour of rain had made it real difficult to see the freeway. (Chapter 10)

12. Football is one of the sports that is becoming popular in Europe. (Chapter 4)

13. The bankruptcy of many large corporations has frightened many investors, they are afraid of losing their life savings. (Chapter 9)

14. The president has spoke to the American people and to Congress about his tax reform proposal. (Chapter 5)

15. Maria was disappointed to learn that who you know sometimes is as important as what you know in the business world. (Chapter 6)

16. A piece of the rudder, weighing hundreds of pounds and falling from the airplane as it lifted off the runway. (Chapter 9)

17. One of the principal agricultural products of Idaho are potatoes. (Chapter 4)

18. The salesman, who sells the most automobiles next month, will receive a trip to Hawaii as his prize. (Chapter 11)

19. The guitar player walked out on the stage and begins to play selections from her new album. (Chapter 5)

20. Barking loudly and straining at its leash, the mail carrier tried to befriend the dog. (Chapter 10)

The Paragraph: An Overview

Most of the writing that you will be asked to do in college will be in the form of paragraphs. A **paragraph** consists of several related sentences that deal with a single topic, or an aspect of a topic. Paragraphs may stand alone, as in the case of responses to questions on examinations. Usually, however, paragraphs are parts of longer pieces of writing, such as essays, reports, and term papers. In such cases paragraphs help your reader by breaking down complicated ideas into manageable parts and relating each part to the main idea or thesis of your composition.

Regardless of whether it is freestanding or part of a larger unit, a well-organized paragraph has three characteristics:

- ■ A good paragraph is *unified:* all of its sentences are related to one main idea.
- ■ A good paragraph is *coherent:* the thoughts proceed logically from sentence to sentence.
- ■ A good paragraph is *developed:* it contains enough information to convey the idea of the paragraph in a reasonably thorough way.

In the following chapters you will practice writing paragraphs that are unified, coherent, and developed. As mentioned above, a *unified* paragraph is one about a single idea or topic. The sentence that states the paragraph's topic is the **topic sentence,** and the topic is developed and supported by the specifics in the sentences that follow or precede it. In Chapter 2 you will learn to recognize topic sentences and to write your own paragraphs with topic sentences.

Good paragraphs are *coherent.* This means that the sentences are in the right order with the right connecting words so that the reader is not confused. Chapters 3–6 will introduce you to ways to make your paragraphs coherent so that your thoughts will be easy to follow— from sentence to sentence and from paragraph to paragraph.

In addition to being unified and coherent, good paragraphs are *developed.* They contain details and material that fulfill the promise made to the reader in the topic sentence. Several methods of paragraph development are available to you, and they are presented in Chapters 7–11.

Introductory and Concluding Paragraphs

The first and last paragraphs of your essay are important. The introduction creates the first impression and therefore must be effective. The conclusion is your last chance to influence or impress your readers and to leave them with a sense of completion.

Some writers write the introduction first, but others prefer to write it after the rest of the essay has been written. Similarly, some write the conclusion first, using it as a kind of final destination point to aim for as they write. Regardless of when the introduction and conclusion are written, they are vital parts of the essay.

Introductions

A good introduction to an essay performs several jobs. The most obvious is to introduce the subject that you will develop and to pave the way for the thesis statement or controlling idea of the essay. The introduction should also catch the readers' interest, making them want to read on. A good introduction informs readers of the writer's intention and suggests the tone of the essay, indicating whether it will be humorous, angry, or serious.

Here are some suggestions for writing introductions. Paragraphs that follow are student examples.

Begin with a Direct Statement of Your Topic and Thesis

■ Every January, millions of American men and women huddle around their television sets to watch football's Super Bowl. Although typical viewers would probably tell you they're watching the game because they admire the players' abilities or a certain team, they are actually watching the game because it fulfills several of their unconscious needs and desires.

Begin with a Personal Anecdote

■ I was fifteen when my father was transferred to an American base in Japan and our entire family was moved from our home in Texas. Because there would not be an opening in the base school for a semester, and because my parents did not want me to lose any school time, I was enrolled in the nearby public school in Osaka. From that experience I learned the importance of tolerance and understanding of others whose skin, culture, or language might be different. I also learned what it means to be a member of a minority.

Computer Activity

Create a folder that will contain each of the computer activities for our text. Each activity will take the form of a stand-alone document created on your computer.

When you create a new document, give it an appropriate name, using your SAVE AS command.

On the first line of the document, enter a document/subject title and the date, or follow the naming style your instructor advises.

For Chapter 1, list the benefits that you hope to gain from reviewing basic grammar and paragraph writing.

If your class has a projector for displaying computer screens, display and discuss your comments with your classmates, or exchange your file with a classmate for discussion.

Begin with a Question

■ What are the chances of a chemical or biological attack by terrorists on one of our major American cities? How many people would survive? Would such an attack make living conditions impossible for the survivors? These and similar questions are being asked by our government as well as by ordinary citizens as a result of recent terrorist attacks throughout the world.

Begin with a Quotation

■ "To be or not to be; that is the question." Every year an increasing number of people are answering those words of Hamlet's by taking their own lives. Suicide is a major cause of death among Americans under the age of twenty-five.

Begin with an Imaginary Scene or a "What If?" Situation

■ Can you imagine living your life without being able to see or hear anyone or anything? As if that were not bad enough, imagine not being able to speak. You would feel totally isolated and cut off from the world. That is how Helen Keller felt, before she met her teacher, Anne Mansfield Sullivan.

Begin with a Surprising Statement

■ Staying up all night to study before a final exam is one of the most harmful and least productive ways to prepare for a test. Although hundreds of thousands of college students might believe otherwise, psychologists and college counselors say that a good night's rest is actually more helpful than spending the time cramming.

Conclusions

The conclusion of your essay, like its introduction, can fulfill several purposes. It can summarize your main points or restate your thesis (avoiding the same words or expressions that were used throughout the essay). It can suggest a sense of "closure" by referring to a quotation or fact used in the introduction. Some introductions ask the reader to do something—to take some action, consider another alternative, or think more deeply about an issue or problem. Other introductions speculate on the future by predicting what will happen as a result of the situation described in the essay.

Your conclusion should be in proportion to the length of the body of the essay. For a short paper, a few sentences are enough. For longer papers, one or two paragraphs would be appropriate. Regardless of length, your conclusion should convey to the reader a sense of completion.

Some suggestions for writing conclusions, with examples from student papers, follow.

End with a Summary of Your Main Points

■ These steps should be reviewed before the actual interview. A neat, organized résumé will let your prospective employer see your qualifications at a glance. A clear idea of the salary you expect gives both you and your interviewer a starting point for a discussion of wages. A businesslike, serious approach to the interview indicates your attitude toward the position. These steps are the best way to prepare for an interview.

End with a Restatement of Your Thesis

■ The facts, as we have seen, do not justify a belief in the existence of life in outer space. Despite the influence of Hollywood, the conditions necessary for life found on Earth cannot be duplicated anywhere else in the universe. Man is unique, and to think otherwise is to ignore the evidence.

End with a Fact or Quotation Used in the Introduction

■ "All men are created equal" does not mean that all men and women are identical. What the writers of our Declaration of Independence meant is that individuals should be given their rights as unique human beings and respected for their common humanity.

End by Asking Your Audience to Do Something

■ There will be no improvement in our schools until there is a change of attitude in the home. Insist that your children attend classes regularly. Ask them about their assignments and homework. Spend some time every day reading to your children and listening to them read. Stress the importance of punctuality, neatness, and accuracy. By your attitude and behavior you will show that you value education and believe in the importance of the schools.

End with a Prediction

■ If gun control legislation is not passed, the consequences will be tragic for America. As the ownership of guns increases, violence will escalate. Crime involving handguns will multiply, and this country will become an armed camp. Vigilante groups will roam the streets. But there is still time to stop this madness. All it takes is courage on the part of our legislators.

WRITING PARAGRAPHS

This assignment calls for you to write a paragraph of at least six sentences on the topic of your choice. Remember that all of your sentences in the paragraph should deal with a single topic. After you have finished your first draft, look it over for ways to improve it. Will the paragraph be clear and interesting to your reader? Does your paragraph contain any sentences that stray from your topic? Does it have any errors in spelling, usage, or punctuation? Your instructor may ask you to exchange your first draft with another student in your class for his or her suggestions.

EXERCISE A

A. *Describe one of the following:*

- *your favorite hideaway when you want to "get away from it all"*
- *your impressions of a recent movie, concert, or television program*

B. *Tell what happened the last time you had an unpleasant encounter with a person in authority. For example, it may have been an argument with a traffic cop, a dispute with your parents, or a run-in with your boss.*

EXERCISE B

Write an opening paragraph that might begin an informal essay on one of these topics. Use one of the methods discussed in this chapter.

- *our immigration laws*
- *the military draft*
- *the right of the government to spy on its citizens*
- *the importance of courses in music and the arts*
- *the efficiency of the Postal Service*
- *women's athletics in college*
- *the need for a computer in college*
- *ethnic restaurants*
- *the health care system in our country*
- *the homeless in America*

Write a concluding paragraph that might be appropriate for an informal essay on one of these topics. Use one of the methods discussed in this chapter.

- *women and the "glass ceiling"*
- *adjusting to dormitory life*
- *violence in the media*
- *a graduation requirement that you want to be dropped*
- *the availability of credit cards for college students*
- *America's most popular sport*
- *the warming of the planet*
- *the benefits of having a pet*
- *college fraternities and sororities*
- *the advantages of knowing a foreign language*

Writing Tips In the Beginning . . .

Unless your instructor says otherwise, your assignments don't need title pages. Instead, provide a simple heading on your first page. Starting one inch from the top of the page, key or type (or write) your name flush with the left margin. Below it, key or type your instructor's name, the course number, and the date. Double-space each line. Double-space twice more, indent five spaces (one-half inch), and begin your paper.

CHAPTER 2

THE PARTS OF SPEECH: A REVIEW

CHAPTER PREVIEW

In this chapter, you will learn about:

- The eight parts of speech: A review
  Nouns
  Pronouns
  Verbs
  Adjectives
  Adverbs
  Prepositions
  Conjunctions
  Interjections
- Writing paragraphs: The topic sentence and unity
  in the paragraph

Internet, *blog, googling, text-messaging, cyberspace*—These are just a few of the many words from the world of computers that have entered the English language. Although our language has more than a half-million words, it is constantly adding thousands of new ones from every field of human activity. Despite their number, all of these words—long or short, familiar or strange—can be divided into only eight categories: the eight parts of speech. When you learn to recognize the parts of speech, you will be on your way to understanding how the English language works, and you can talk about it intelligently and precisely. Even more important, you will be able to identify the tools that will help you to write clear, interesting, and correct sentences and paragraphs and to become a more confident writer. Our study of grammar and usage continues, therefore, by examining the parts of speech.

The Noun

We will start with the noun because every English sentence either contains one or is about one. A **noun** *is a word that names something—a person, a place, a thing, or an idea.*

■ student, Idaho, coffee maker, envy

Some nouns refer to a general class of persons, places, or things. They are called **common nouns,** and they are not capitalized unless they are used to begin a sentence.

■ comedian, state, automobile, war, era

Some nouns refer to specific persons, places, or things. They are called **proper nouns,** and they are always capitalized.

■ Ali G., Florida, Porsche Boxster, Vietnam War, Information Age

As you will see in later chapters, nouns are important because they can work as several parts of the sentence.

The Pronoun

We could not get along without nouns. But occasionally, in order to avoid repetition, we use other words in place of nouns. The words that we substitute for nouns are called **pronouns.**

■ As Paul began to take Paul's biology exam, Paul tried to ignore the beeping sound coming from a cellular phone behind Paul.

This sentence is obviously monotonous because of its overuse of *Paul.* We can improve it by using pronouns.

■ As Paul began to take *his* biology exam, *he* tried to ignore the beeping sound coming from a cellular phone behind *him.*

Tip **for Spotting Nouns**

If you can put a word in the slot in the following sentence, it is a noun.

"A (or An) _____ is remarkable."

Examples: An *elephant* is remarkable.
A *rainbow* is remarkable.

The pronouns in this sentence are *his*, *he*, and *him*, and their **antecedent** (the word to which they refer) is *Paul*. Here is another sentence with pronouns and an antecedent.

■ **The runner waved to her fans as she ran the victory lap around the track, and the crowd cheered her.**

What are the pronouns in this sentence? What is their antecedent?

Unlike a noun, a pronoun does not name a specific person, place, thing, or idea. You will learn more about pronouns and their uses in Chapters 6 and 7. Meanwhile, you should try to recognize the most common pronouns.

Common Pronouns	
I, me, my, mine	we, us, our, ours
you, your, yours	they, them, their, theirs
he, him, his	anybody, everybody, somebody
she, her, hers	everyone, no one, someone
it, its	something, some, all, many, any
who, whose, whom	each, none, one, this, that, these, those, which, what

EXERCISE 2-1

Underline the nouns and circle the pronouns.

1. Although hundreds of computer scientists have contributed to the rise of personal computers, (none) is more famous or controversial than Bill Gates.
2. Gates is the chairman of Microsoft, (whose) software is the world's best seller.
3. (He) was born in 1955 in Seattle, Washington, and raised with two sisters.
4. (Their) father was an attorney and (their) mother was a schoolteacher.
5. Gates became interested in computers in grade school and soon began programming (them.)
6. As a freshman at Harvard University, (he) befriended Steve Ballmer, (whom) (he) later hired as chief executive officer at Microsoft.
7. Gates was still a college teen when (he) wrote *Basic*, a programming language for the world's first personal computer.
8. (His) family must have been stunned when (they) learned that Bill had decided to drop out of Harvard in (his) junior year.
9. (He) and a friend, Paul Allen, started a company in 1975; (its) sole product was software.

10. (They) believed that (you), (your) classmates, and (everyone) else would eventually need computers at <u>home</u> and at <u>work</u>.
11. <u>Gates</u> and <u>Allen</u> wanted to make <u>software</u> (that) (anybody) could learn to use, even if (he) or (she) had no <u>training</u> in <u>computing</u>.
12. Not (everyone) says (that) the <u>software</u> is as easy and reliable as (it) could be, though.
13. <u>Critics</u> of the <u>programs</u> say (that) (they) are easily damaged or destroyed by Internet <u>viruses</u> and sudden, unexplained <u>stoppages</u>.
14. (Others) say (that) <u>Microsoft</u> bullies (its) <u>competitors</u>, making (it) difficult for (anyone) else to become the next software <u>pioneer</u>.
15. Nevertheless, when <u>magazines</u> publish <u>lists</u> of (our) wealthiest and most admired <u>citizens</u>, <u>Bill Gates</u> is usually mentioned.

The Verb

Every sentence that you speak or write contains a verb. Sometimes the verb is only implied; usually, however, it is stated. When you can recognize and use verbs correctly, you have taken a big step toward being a better speaker and writer.

A **verb** is a part of speech that expresses action or a state of being and thereby tells us what a noun or pronoun does or what it is. If the verb tells us what a noun or pronoun does, it is an **action verb.**

- Roberta *paints* beautiful landscapes, which she hides in her attic.
- Neil Armstrong *landed* on the moon in 1969.
- Huang *attends* medical school in California.

If the verb expresses a state of being rather than action, it is a **linking verb.** Linking verbs do not express action; instead, they connect a noun or pronoun with a word or group of words that describe or rename the subject.

- The subject of tonight's debate *is* prayers in public school. (*Subject* is linked by the verb *is* to *prayers,* a word that renames it.)
- I.Q. tests *are* unreliable predictors of academic success, according to many educators. (*Tests* is linked to *predictors* by the verb *are.*)
- My new speakers *sound* much better than my old ones. (*Speakers* is linked to the word that describes it—*better*—by the verb *sound.*)
- Computers were very expensive for the average family to purchase in the 1970s. (What words are linked? What word links them?)
- Belize is a small nation in Central America. (What word renames Belize? How are the two words linked?)

The most common linking verbs are formed from the verb *to be: am, are, is, was,* and *were*. Other words often used as linking verbs are *appear, become, grow, remain, seem,* and the "sense" verbs: *feel, look, smell, sound,* and *taste*.

Verbs are the only words that change their spelling to show tense. **Tense** is the time when the action of the verb occurs. Notice in the following sentences how the tense or time of the action is changed by the spelling of the verb.

- Our mayor *delivers* an annual message to the citizens of our city. (present tense)
- Last week she *delivered* her message on local television. (past tense)

You will learn more about the use of tense in Chapter 5.

To show additional differences in meaning, verbs often use helping words that suggest the time at which the action of the verb takes place and other kinds of meaning. These words are called **helping/auxiliary verbs,** and they always come before the main verb. Verbs that consist of helping verbs and a main verb are called **verb phrases.** Look carefully at the following sentences.

- I *will* bowl.
- He *had* studied.
- Zhang *did* not want lunch.

- The sisters *were* saddened.
- The child *was* photographed.
- They *might have been* selected.

Each of the verbs in the preceding sentences consists of a helping/auxiliary verb and a main verb. Here are the common helping/auxiliary verbs. You should memorize them.

Common Helping/Auxiliary Verbs	
can, could	have, has, had
may, might, must, ought	do, does, did
shall, should, will, would	am, is, are, was, were, been, be, being

Some verbs can be either helping/auxiliary verbs or main verbs. In other words, if they appear alone without a helping/auxiliary verb, they are main verbs. But if they precede a main verb, they are helping/auxiliary verbs. The following verbs can be either helping/auxiliary verbs or main verbs. You should memorize them.

Forms of *to be*:	am, is, are, was, were
Forms of *to do*:	do, does, did
Forms of *to have*:	has, have, had

Tips **for Recognizing Verbs**

An *action verb* is a word that fits in the slot in the following sentence.

"*I* (or *He* or *She* or *They*) *usually* _____."

Examples: *I usually* jog.
She usually snores.
They usually help.

A *linking verb* is a word that fits in the slot in the following sentence.

"*I* (or *He* or *She* or *They*) _____ happy."

Examples: *I* am *happy.*
He is *happy.*
They were *happy.*

Look at the following sentences carefully.

■ Victims of the earthquake *were* unable to drink the water. (*Were* is the main verb in this sentence.)

■ Victims of the earthquake *were given* food and clothing by the Red Cross. (*Were given* is a verb phrase. The main verb is *given,* and the helping/auxiliary verb is *were.*)

■ Tanya *has* a new car. (*Has* is the main verb in this sentence.)

■ She *has* already *driven* it two thousand miles. (*Has driven* is a verb phrase. The main verb is *driven,* and the helping/auxiliary verb is *has.*)

EXERCISE 2-2

If the italicized word in each sentence is an action verb, write "1"; if the italicized word is a linking verb, write "2"; if the italicized word is a helping/auxiliary verb, write "3." Use the space provided on the left.

__2__   1. Horses have *been* pets and helpers to humans for thousands of years.

__1__   2. Although a variety of breeds *exists*, there are some general traits that most horses share.

__2__   3. Most horses *are* social animals who enjoy living and moving with other horses.

__1__   4. They *observe* a hierarchy within their groups.

__3__   5. For example, young horses *will* rarely drink water from a trough until older group members have finished drinking.

___3___   6. Until a new horse's place is determined within the group, many conflicts *may* occur.

___2___   7. Horses *are* natural runners, and they race each other just for fun.

___3___   8. They are also swift learners and *can* master a number of skills to help or amuse their owners.

___2___   9. Like dogs, horses possess acute hearing and can *become* easily frightened by sudden loud noises.

___2___   10. Thanks to equally sharp eyesight, horses *are* able to see distsant leaves where another animal is scampering.

The Adjective

In your writing you will often want to modify (or describe) a noun or pronoun. The word you will use is an **adjective,** a word that modifies nouns and pronouns. Adjectives usually answer one of the following questions: *How many? What kind? Which one? What color?*

■ **How many?**   *Many* students believe that the Social Security system will be bankrupt before they are old enough to retire. (*Many* modifies *students.*)

■ **What kind?**   *Egg* bagels gave us energy for our hike. (*Egg* modifies *bagels.*)

■ **Which one?**   *This* backpack was found in the cafeteria. (*This* modifies *backpack.*)

■ **What color?**   His *purple* socks did not complement his red suit. (*Purple* modifies *socks.*)

The adjectives in the sentences above came immediately before the nouns they modified. Some adjectives, however, come after linking verbs and describe the subject of the verb. Adjectives in this position are called **predicate adjectives.** Study the sentences carefully.

■ We were surprised to learn that old pairs of American jeans in Russia are very *expensive.* (*Expensive* is a predicate adjective because it comes after a linking verb—*are*—and modifies the noun *pairs.*)

■ After waiting in the hot sun for three days, the refugees became *angry.* (*Angry* is a predicate adjective because it comes after a linking verb—*became*—and modifies the noun *refugees.*)

Possessive pronouns (pronouns that show ownership such as *my, your, her, his, our,* and *their*) are adjectives when they come before nouns. Notice the examples.

■ *our* apartment

■ *their* lunch break

■ *my* employer

Tips **for Spotting Adjectives**

1. You can add *-er* and *-est* or *more* and *most* to adjectives.

   Examples: strong, strong*er*, strong*est*
   eager, *more* eager, *most* eager

2. An adjective will fill the blank in this sentence.

   "*The* (noun) *is* _____."

   Example: The cupboard is *empty.*

3. Adjectives describe nouns and pronouns.

   Examples: The *tired* surfers paddled back to shore.
   She is *proud* of her degree in math.

4. Adjectives tell *how many, what kind, which one,* and *what color.*

   Examples: Ryan has *four* dogs, *three* cats, and *a dozen* goldfish.
   I have a *German* pen pal and an *Ecuadoran* pen pal.
   Did you eat the *last* bagel?
   White roses and *yellow* daisies dot her garden.

Demonstrative pronouns (pronouns that point out or indicate) are adjectives when they come before nouns. Notice the following examples.

- *this* building
- *that* statement

- *these* flowers
- *those* books

A special type of adjective is called the **article.** The English language contains three articles: *a, an* (used before words that begin with a vowel sound), and *the.*

- After *an* absence of sixteen years, Maricela returned to *the* city of her birth and *a* parade in her honor.

EXERCISE 2-3

A. In the space before each sentence, write the noun or pronoun that is modified by the italicized adjective.

_____animal_____	1.	A 420 million year-old millipede is the *oldest* animal known to have lived on land.
_____fossil_____	2.	The *half-inch-long* fossil has air holes, which means that it was able to breathe oxygen and live on land.
_____spider_____	3.	Before this discovery, the earliest known land dweller was a *long-legged* spider who lived twenty million years later.

_____ *life*   4. If this millipede lived on land at that time, there must have also been moss or *small* plant life for it to eat.

_____ *specimen*   5. The *tiny* specimen was found on a beach near Aberdeen, Scotland, by Mike Newman, a bus driver who holds a degree in geology.

_____ *discoverer*   6. To honor the *studious* discoverer, the specimen was named for him: Pneumodesmus newmani.

_____ *fossils*   7. Millipedes are often called *living* fossils because they have not changed significantly over millions of years.

_____ *creatures*   8. Ten thousand species of millipedes have evolved from *ancient* creatures that once lived in the sea.

_____ *name*   9. Despite their *interesting* name, millipedes do not have a thousand legs, and they are not related to centipedes (which do not have a hundred legs).

_____ *category*   10. Millipedes belong to the *same* animal category as insects, spiders, and crustaceans.

B. In the space before each sentence, write the predicate adjective that modifies the italicized noun or pronoun.

_____ *difficult*   1. *Surviving* as a single parent while attending college is often difficult.

_____ *unwise*   2. The author of a recent article stresses that *it* is unwise to dwell on your disappointment in or dislike of your child's other parent.

_____ *injurious*   3. *Feelings* of anger can be injurious to your child's relationship with you.

_____ *valuable*   4. Although you may not have a lot of money, the *time* you spend with your child is more valuable than wealth and possessions.

_____ *enjoyable*   5. *Activities* like going for a walk or a bike ride can be as enjoyable as going to a mall or a toy store.

_____ *beneficial, helpful*   6. *Friends* that you can trust are often beneficial and helpful in the raising of a child.

_____ *important*   7. Because children need stability and security, *it* is important to set up daily rituals and regular routines for your child.

_____ *fun*   8. *Discussing* your homework and school experiences with your child is often fun as you share common experiences.

_____ *vital*   9. A consistent *standard* of discipline is vital in teaching what is and is not acceptable behavior.

_____ *happy, successful*   10. Because of your influence, your *child* will become happy and successful.

The Adverb

Adverbs are words that describe or modify verbs, adjectives, and other adverbs. Study these sentences carefully.

- The huge chopper transported the soldiers *quickly.* (*Quickly* modifies the verb *transported.*)
- The *extremely* tall guard dribbled the basketball *slowly.* (*Extremely* modifies the adjective *tall,* and *slowly* modifies the verb *dribbled.*)
- The tall guard dribbled the basketball *very* slowly. (*Very* modifies the adverb *slowly.*)

Adverbs usually answer the following questions: *When? Where? How? To what extent?*

- **When?** Hector *immediately* realized that he had confused Megan with her sister. (The adverb *immediately* modifies the verb *realized.*)
- **Where?** Please wait *here.* (The adverb *here* modifies the verb *wait.*)
- **How?** The deer struggled *unsuccessfully* to escape. (The adverb *unsuccessfully* modifies the verb *struggled.*)
- **To what extent?** The state capitol building was *completely* remodeled after the election. (The adverb *completely* modifies the verb *was remodeled.*)

Adjectives and adverbs are often confused. Remember that *adjectives* describe nouns and pronouns, and that *adverbs* modify verbs, adjectives, and other adverbs. Notice the differences in the following sentences.

- Her *loud* hiccups distracted the speaker. (*Loud* is an adjective because it modifies the noun *hiccups.*)
- If you sneeze *loudly,* you will distract the speaker. (*Loudly* is an adverb because it modifies the verb *sneeze.*)

Tips for Recognizing Adverbs

1. Adverbs are words that will fit in the following slot.

   "He will meet us _____."

2. Adverbs tell *when, where, how,* and *to what extent.*

   Examples: He will meet us *later. (when)*
   He will meet us *here. (where)*
   He will meet us *punctually. (how)*
   He will meet us *briefly. (to what extent)*

Many adverbs are formed by adding *-ly* to the adjective (as in *loudly*, in the sentence above). But keep in mind that some adverbs do not end in *-ly* (*above*, *never*, *there*, *very*, and so on). On the other hand, some words that end in *-ly* are not adverbs (words such as *silly*, *friendly*, and *lovely*).

EXERCISE 2-4

A. In the space before each sentence, write the adjective, verb, or adverb modified by the italicized adverb.

twenty million   1. *Approximately* twenty million Americans attend monster truck spectaculars every year.

crash   2. Monster trucks have huge tires that enable them to scoot up a ramp, take off, and travel through the air 100 feet, 30 off the ground, then crash *dramatically* back to earth without being smashed to pieces.

Japanese   3. A common feat is to land on a car, *preferably* a Japanese import, and crush it.

popular   4. Other *very* popular events at truck shows include mud racing and dropping drivers strapped in their cars 170 feet in the air onto several vans.

derives   5. The appeal of monster trucks *probably* derives from the roar and the mud.

stems   6. It also stems *partly* from the fantasy most of us have experienced as we have been trapped in traffic, wishing we could push aside the cars around us.

have   7. The trucks *inevitably* have colorful names such as Carolina Crusher, Bearfoot, and Grave Digger, among others.

famous   8. But the *most* famous is Bigfoot, the product of Bob Chandler, the originator of the monster truck.

gross   9. Bigfoot-licensed products and souvenirs sold at truck shows gross over $300 million *annually*.

popular   10. Over seven hundred monster truck shows a year are held throughout the world, and the *most* popular drivers enjoy the kind of fame reserved for movie stars.

B. In the space before each sentence, write the adverb that modifies the italicized word or words.

often   1. Polygraphs are often *called* lie detectors, though they can detect only physiological changes.

___generally___ 2. A polygraph generally *uses* several medical devices to observe changes in a person's body functions.

___sometimes___ 3. These changes sometimes *indicate* deceptive behavior by the person taking the test.

___digitally___ 4. Gone are the days of a needle bouncing along chart paper; most polygraphs *monitor and record* physical data digitally.

___carefully___ 5. During the test, sensors are carefully *placed* in several locations on the person's body.

___slightly___ 6. Two rubber tubes, placed on the chest and stomach, *expand* slightly with each breath and note its depth.

___electrically___ 7. To monitor heart rate and blood pressure, signals are *transmitted* electrically from a plastic cuff around the person's upper arm.

___heavily___ 8. Humans *sweat* more heavily when under stress, so sensors placed on two fingertips measure the flow.

___completely___ 9. Polygraph results are not completely *reliable* because someone may show physical changes for reasons besides lying—including exhaustion, effects of medication, and even fear of the test itself.

___legally___ 10. Because of the polygraph's unreliability, private sector employers *cannot* legally *require* workers to take polygraph tests, but government agencies, including the FBI and CIA, can administer the tests to their workers and applicants.

The Preposition

Prepositions are connecting words—they do not have any meaning or content in or of themselves. They exist only to show relationships between other words. For this reason they must simply be learned or remembered. Prepositions are words like *at, by, from,* and *with* that are usually followed by a noun or pronoun (*at home, by herself, from Toledo,* and *with you*). The word following the preposition is called its **object;** the preposition and its object are called a **prepositional phrase.**

Here are some prepositional phrases. The object in each prepositional phrase is italicized. Notice that a preposition can have more than one object and that some prepositions are made up of more than one word.

- according to *authorities*
- after *the meeting*
- below *the deck*
- between *you and me*

- from *one coast* to *another*
- in addition to *requirements in science*
- through *the final week*
- together with *the director and producer*
- within *the hour*
- without *a clue*

Here are some of the most common prepositions. As noted above, some prepositions consist of more than one word.

Common Prepositions		
about	concerning	out
above	despite	out of
according to	down	outside
across	due to	over
after	during	past
against	except	regarding
ahead of	for	round
along	from	since
among	in	through
around	in addition to	to
away from	in front of	together with
because of	inside	toward
before	instead of	under
behind	into	underneath
below	like	unlike
beneath	near	until
besides	next to	up
between	of	upon
beyond	off	with
but (when it	on	within
means *except*)	onto	without
by	on account of	

Tips for Recognizing Prepositions

1. A preposition is a word that will fill the slot in the following sentence.

   "The airplane flew _____ the clouds."

   Examples: The airplane flew *above, below, beyond, under, around,* or *through* the clouds.

2. A preposition is a word that will fill the slot in the following sentence.

   "A purse was lying _____ street."

   Examples: A purse was lying *in, next to, alongside,* or *beside* the street.

   Some prepositions, of course, will not fit either sentence, and they must be learned.

Prepositional phrases may serve the same function as either adjectives or adverbs in a sentence.

- **Adjective:** News *of an impending rebellion* panicked the government. (The italicized phrase modifies the noun *news.*)
- **Adjective:** The ushers *in blue suits* quieted the crowd. (The italicized phrase modifies the noun *ushers.*)
- **Adverb:** Juan and Ashley left *during the intermission.* (The italicized phrase modifies the verb *left.*)
- **Adverb:** The president spoke *with emotion.* (The italicized phrase modifies the verb *spoke.*)

EXERCISE 2-5

Underline the prepositional phrases in each sentence; write "adv" above the phrase if it is used as an adverbial modifier, or "adj" if it is used as an adjectival modifier.

1. The first symptom of Alzheimer's disease in most older people is loss of memory.
2. Most patients are not aware of the problem and don't realize the need for an appointment with a doctor.
3. Alzheimer's disease affects the hippocampus, one of the areas of the brain.
4. The hippocampus is involved in learning something initially, and then that information is stored or processed in other areas of the brain.

5. For that reason, most Alzheimer's patients have problems with learning and remembering new things but are better at remembering old things.
    - adv. (For that reason)
    - adj. (with learning)
    - adv. (remembering old things)

6. Billions of cells make up the brain like bricks that make up a house.
    - adj. (of cells)
    - adv. (like bricks)

7. The dendrite is the part of the cell that receives information, and the axon is the part that sends information out.
    - adj. (of the cell)

8. The axons and dendrites are important to memory because they connect one brain cell to another.
    - adv. (to memory)
    - adv. (to another)

9. One of the theories held by scientists is that the axons and dendrites shrink in Alzheimer's patients.
    - adj. (of the theories)
    - adv. (by scientists)
    - in (adv.)
    - adv. (Alzheimer's patients)

10. As a result, loss of memory is one of the first effects when these connections are disrupted.
    - adv. (As a result)
    - adj. (of memory)
    - adj. (of the first effects)

The Conjunction

A **conjunction** is a word that joins words or groups of words. In a sense, conjunctions are like prepositions: they do not represent things or qualities. Instead, they merely show different kinds of relationships between other words or groups of words. There are two kinds of conjunctions you will need to recognize: coordinating and subordinating.

Coordinating conjunctions join words and word groups of equal importance or rank. You should memorize these coordinating conjunctions.

Coordinating Conjunctions						
and	so	nor	yet	but	for	or

The following sentences show how coordinating conjunctions join single words and groups of words.

■ Alexi speaks English *and* Russian fluently. (*And* links two words.)

■ Joao was born in Brazil, *but* he moved to the United States at the age of four. (*But* links two independent clauses.)

■ Do you prefer fish *or* chicken? (*Or* links two words.)

■ You should talk to a counselor, *or* you might take the wrong courses. (*Or* links two independent clauses.)

In Chapter 8 you will see how coordinating conjunctions are used in compound sentences. Incidentally, it used to be considered ungrammatical to begin a sentence with one of these words, but this "rule" is no longer observed, even by the best writers.

Some coordinating conjunctions combine with other words to form **correlative conjunctions.** The most common correlative conjunctions are *both . . . and; either . . . or; neither . . . nor;* and *not only . . . but also.* Notice the following examples.

- *Both* Ty Murray *and* Kristie Peterson are legends of professional rodeo.
- Ray will *either* go to summer school *or* work in his father's store.
- John Kennedy was *not only* the first Roman Catholic president *but also* the first president born in the twentieth century.

Subordinating conjunctions, like coordinating conjunctions, join groups of words. Unlike coordinating conjunctions, however, they join unequal word groups or grammatical units that are "subordinate." You will study subordinating conjunctions in greater detail in Chapters 8 and 9, especially with respect to complex sentences and fragments.

Some conjunctions like *after, before, for, since, but,* and *until* can also function as prepositions.

- The popularity of leisure suits declined *after* the presidency of Richard Nixon. (preposition)
- Aisha sold her truck *after* she bought a minivan. (conjunction)
- Jaime bought flowers *for* his girlfriend. (preposition)
- Jaime bought flowers, *for* he knew his girlfriend was angry. (conjunction)
- Every member of the General Assembly *but* Cuba voted for the motion. (preposition)
- Every member voted, *but* Cuba demanded a recount. (conjunction)

EXERCISE 2-6

Underline the coordinating conjunctions in the sentences below.

1. The savings-and-loan disaster cost the government millions of dollars, but the greatest loss was to the lives of investors.
2. The relationship between smoking and cancer has been long established, yet many young people continue to smoke.
3. Neither the Israelis nor the Palestinians would comment on the negotiations.
4. Because he had a car alarm and had parked in front of a church, he was surprised and angry to discover that his new Miata was either stolen or towed away.
5. Leon bought a fax machine, but he didn't know how to use it.

The Interjection

The **interjection** (or *exclamation*, as it is sometimes called) is a word that expresses emotion and has no grammatical relationship with the rest of the sentence.

Mild interjections are followed by a comma.

- *No,* it's too early.
- *Oh,* I suppose so.
- *Yes,* that would be fine.

Strong interjections require an exclamation mark.

- *Wow!* My phone bill is huge!
- *Ouch!* That hurts!
- *Fire!*
- *Yo!* I'm over here!
- *Hey!* I think I finally understand physics!

A Word of Caution

Many words do double or triple duty; that is, they can be (for instance) a noun in one sentence and a verb in another sentence. The situation is much like a football player who lines up as a tight end on one play and a halfback on another. His or her function in each play is different; and so it is with words and parts of speech. A word like *light*, for example, can be used as a verb.

- We always *light* our Christmas tree after the children are asleep.

It can also be used as an adjective.

- Many beer drinkers spurn *light* beer.

Light can also be used as a noun.

- All colors depend on *light.*

What part of speech is *light*, then? It depends on the sentence; no word exists in a vacuum. To determine the part of speech of a particular word, you must determine its function or use in the sentence.

EDITING EXERCISES

Identify the part of speech of each italicized word in the following paragraphs.

Hurricane! In much of the United States, there is no word more *frightening.* Hurricanes destroy thousands of lives and homes each year, *but* some precautions *can* help prevent death or major damage. Since doors and windows *are* vulnerable parts of your home, you must protect them. Entry doors, for example, should have at least *three* hinges and dead bolt locks with three-inch *bolts.* Because of *their* size, garage doors are *highly* vulnerable to wind damage, especially if they're wider than eight feet. Install wood *or* metal stiffeners to prevent rippling or removal. Glass doors and windows survive *better* if made of laminated glass or plastic glazing. Covering them with *plywood* shutters limits breakage *by* flying *debris.* Inspect your yard and *remove* bicycles, toys, tools, or other objects that *could* fly *into* your windows or walls. If, despite your best efforts, you *must* evacuate, make sure *your* family members have chosen a safe place to meet, such as a Red Cross *shelter.*

A quinceañera is a *young* woman's fifteenth-birthday religious *celebration* in both Mexico and the United States, and *it* symbolizes her transition *from* childhood to adulthood. In the small villages of Mexico the emphasis *is* on the *religious* nature of the ceremony. In Chicano communities in the United States, it is *often* followed by a dinner and dance in the gym *of* the local church *or* community center. Not *all* fifteen-year-olds *have* quinceañeras. Many *families* cannot afford *them.* Food for several hundred guests, *printed* invitations, flowers, paying *for* a band for dancing, *rental* of a hall, *and* hiring a professional photographer are *among* the expenses that the parents of the *young* honoree must *necessarily* assume for this occasion.

WRITING SENTENCES The Parts of Speech

This review exercise gives you a chance to show that you can recognize the parts of speech. It also lets you show your originality by writing sentences of your own. When writing your sentences, do not hesitate to review the appropriate pages in this chapter as needed.

1. Write two original sentences; in each sentence use a common noun and a proper noun. Circle the nouns.
2. Write two original sentences; in each sentence use at least one pronoun from the list on page 14. Circle the pronouns.
3. Write a sentence containing an action verb. Circle the action verb.
4. Write a sentence containing a linking verb. Circle the linking verb.
5. Write a sentence containing a helping/auxiliary verb and a main verb. Circle the helping verb.
6. Write a sentence containing a predicate adjective. Circle the predicate adjective.
7. Write a sentence containing at least one adverb. Circle the adverb.
8. Write a sentence containing at least two prepositional phrases. Circle each prepositional phrase.

Language Tips

When using nouns, verbs, and adjectives, be careful to use the following endings so that your meaning is clear.

The plural form of most nouns is formed by adding an *–s* or *–es* to the singular form.

> book/books   idea/ideas   match/matches

The singular form of a verb when used with *he/she/it* is also formed by adding an *–s* or *–es*.

> works   enjoys   washes

For more information about the plural form of nouns, see pages 79–80. For more information about other forms of the verb, see pages 286–296 in the appendix, "A Checklist for the ESL Writer."

Name _____ Date _____

REVIEW TEST 2-A
Parts of Speech

A. *Identify the parts of speech of the italicized words by using the appropriate letter in the space provided.*

a. noun   b. pronoun   c. adjective   d. adverb

___c___ 1. West Virginia has more than *one million* acres reserved for park land.

___a___ 2. The first female *pilot* of a major U.S. airline was Emily Warner, hired in 1973.

___a___ 3. Fruit juice often has more *calories* and less fiber than a piece of fruit.

___d___ 4. Americans buy more personal computers *online* than any other product.

___d___ 5. Honda and Toyota *routinely* produce the most fuel-efficient vehicles.

___b___ 6. In the same year that the American Revolution ended, *some* heard Beethoven's first compositions and read William Blake's first poems.

___c___ 7. Djibouti, a nation in Northeastern Africa, is almost entirely a *stony* desert.

___b___ 8. The first known Olympic Games took place in 776 B.C.; *they* consisted of only a 200-yard foot race.

___b___ 9. Stags, Hawks, Capitals, and Nationals—they are National Basketball Association champion teams *who* no longer exist.

___a___ 10. Since 1928, *Time* magazine has chosen an influential man or woman as Person of the Year.

B. *Identify the parts of speech of the italicized words by using the appropriate letter in the space provided.*

a. preposition   b. conjunction   c. interjection

___c___ 11. *Wow!* In the 1930s, the longest drought in U.S. history left more than fifty million acres of land barren.

___b___ 12. We hadn't heard of the first recipients of the Academy Award for acting, Janet Gaynor *and* Emil Jannings.

___c___ 13. *Watch out!* Your favorite song may be on this magazine's yearly list of America's fifty most hated songs.

___b___ 14. The seven-day week originated in ancient Mesopotamia, *but* it wasn't added to the Roman calendar until much later.

___a___ 15. There is concern that hate crimes are increasing *around* the world.

C. *Identify the italicized words by using the appropriate letter in the space provided.*
     a. action verb   b. linking verb   c. helping/auxiliary verb

___b___ 16. Smith *is* still the most common last name in the United States.

___c___ 17. Harvard University *has* received more monetary donations than any other college in recent years.

___c___ 18. Dick Rutan and Jeana Yeager *are* known for making the fastest nonstop flight around Earth.

___c___ 19. About eighty people *have* reached the highest peak on all seven continents, known as the Seven Summits.

___a___ 20. Ireland's flag *has* three simple stripes: green, white, and orange.

___c___ 21. The oldest known human ancestors *were* found in Africa.

___a___ 22. Americans *spend* about forty dollars per person for food each week.

___b___ 23. Delaware *was* the first state to join the union.

___a___ 24. The Presidential Medal of Freedom is the nation's highest civilian award; it *recognizes* exceptional service in a number of sports, arts, and academic fields.

___b___ 25. Comets *are* giant snowballs of frozen gases.

REVIEW TEST 2-B
Parts of Speech

A. *Identify the parts of speech of the italicized words by using the appropriate letter in the space provided.*

a. noun   b. pronoun   c. adjective   d. adverb

___c___   1.   Jupiter is the largest planet in our *solar* system.

___a___   2.   We agreed to meet at the *stadium* in Jacksonville.

___a___   3.   In Antarctica, there is a huge *peak* named for President Andrew Jackson.

___d___   4.   The Big Dipper is *actually* part of a larger constellation, Ursa Major.

___c___   5.   Diana's husband can narrate the career of *any* member of the New York Yankees.

___b___   6.   *We* will hold an auction to benefit the home for battered women.

___d___   7.   Rottweilers are *increasingly* popular among dog owners.

___a___   8.   One-third of all *companies* in the United States are owned by women.

___a___   9.   Actress Cameron Diaz is a *native* of San Diego.

___c___   10.   Playstation is a very *popular* video game system among all age groups.

B. *Identify the parts of speech of the italicized words by using the appropriate letter in the space provided.*

a. preposition   b. conjunction   c. interjection

___a___   11.   *Between* you and me, I thought the Braves were the better team in the Series.

___b___   12.   He's not very good at chemistry, *but* in math he is brilliant.

___a___   13.   We found the cat hiding *under* Kurt's bed.

___c___   14.   *No*, thank you, I don't care for another piece of pizza.

___b___   15.   The driver *and* four of the passengers were injured in the accident.

C. *Identify the italicized words by using the appropriate letter in the space provided.*

a. action verb   b. linking verb   c. helping/auxiliary verb

___b___   16.   William Harrison *was* president for only thirty-one days before dying of pneumonia.

___a___   17.   My father *had* a collection of all the CDs of the Grateful Dead.

  _a_   18. A beam of the sun's light *requires* eight minutes to reach Earth.

  _c_   19. Buying and opening a fast-food franchise *can* cost more than four hundred thousand dollars.

  _c_   20. Marcus *will* eat catfish only if it is from the Mississippi River.

  _b_   21. My grandfather *is* a collector of baseball cards.

  _b_   22. Proteins *are* crucial because they build, repair, and maintain the body.

  _a_   23. Artifacts from Chile show that humans *lived* in the Americas as long as 12,500 years ago.

  _c_   24. Mild burns *can be* treated by placing the area in ice water until the pain diminishes.

  _a_   25. Pedro *slept* for ten hours after running the marathon.

Go to www.ablongman.com/yarber to complete Review Test 2-C.

WRITING PARAGRAPHS

THE TOPIC SENTENCE AND UNITY IN THE PARAGRAPH

Every good paragraph deals with a single topic or aspect of a topic. The sentence that states the paragraph's topic is the **topic sentence.** It is the sentence that alerts the reader to the central idea. It also reminds the writer of that central idea so that he or she does not include sentences that wander off the topic. For this reason, the topic sentence is frequently placed at the beginning of the paragraph, although it can appear in other parts of the paragraph. Regardless of its location, the topic sentence is usually the most general sentence in the paragraph, and it is developed and supported by the specifics in the sentences that follow or precede it.

In your reading you will occasionally notice paragraphs by experienced writers that do not include a topic sentence. In such instances the topic sentence is implicit—that is, the controlling or central idea is implied because the details in the paragraph are clear and well organized. But until you become an adept writer and are certain that your paragraphs stick to one idea, you should provide each paragraph with a topic sentence.

Topic Sentence First

The following paragraph was written by Frederick Douglass, a former slave who gained fame as a gifted speaker for voting rights for African Americans in the nineteenth century. The first sentence in the paragraph is the topic sentence, and it announces the main idea in a general way: "Everybody has asked the question, and they learned to ask it early of the abolitionists, 'What shall we do with the Negro?'" The sentences that follow give examples of possible actions that Douglass says should be avoided; they explore and answer the question posed in the topic sentence. Like most well-written paragraphs, this one begins with a general point and then supports it with specific details.

■ Everybody has asked the question, and they learned to ask it early of the abolitionists, "What shall we do with the Negro?" I have had but one answer from the beginning. Do nothing with us! Your doing with us has already played the mischief with us. Do nothing with us! If the apples will not remain on the tree of their own strength, if they are wormeaten at the core, if they are early ripe and disposed to fall, let them fall! I am not for tying or fastening them on the tree in any way, except by nature's plan, and if they will not stay there, let them fall. And if the Negro cannot stand on his own legs, let him fall also. All I ask is, give him a chance to stand on his own legs! Let him alone! If you see him on his way to school, let him alone, don't disturb him! If you see him going to the dinner table at a hotel, let him go! If you see him going to the ballot-box, let him alone, don't disturb him! If you see him going into a work-shop, just let him alone—your interference is doing him a positive injury. Let him fall if he cannot stand alone!

—Frederick Douglass, "What the Black Man Wants"

The topic sentence in the above paragraph is clear. It tells the reader what to expect in the sentences that follow, and it reminds the writer of the central idea of the paragraph so that he or she is unlikely to stray from the topic.

Topic Sentence in the Middle

Sometimes the topic sentence is placed in the middle of the paragraph. In such cases the sentences that precede the topic sentence lead up to the main idea, and the sentences that follow the main idea explain or describe it.

■ There are 1,500 species of bacteria and approximately 8,500 species of birds. The car-rot family alone has about 3,500 species, and there are 15,000 known species of wild orchids. *Clearly, the task of separating various living things into their proper groups is not an easy task.* Within the insect family, the problem becomes even more com-plex. For example, there are about 300,000 species of beetles. In fact, certain species are disappearing from the earth before we can even identify and classify them.

—Wallace, *Biology: The World of Life,* p. 283

Notice that the writer begins his paragraph with examples of living things with many species. Then he announces his main idea: separating living things into their proper species is not an easy task. The rest of the paragraph gives another example and additional informa-tion to support his topic sentence.

Topic Sentence Last

Many writers lead up to the main point of a paragraph and then conclude with it at the end.

■ Is there a relationship between aspects of one's personality and that person's state of physical health? Can psychological evaluations of an individual be used to predict physical as well as psychological disorders? Is there such a thing as a disease-prone personality? *Our response is very tentative, and the data are not all supportive, but for the moment we can say yes, there does seem to be a positive correlation between some personality variables and physical health.*

—Gerow, *Psychology: An Introduction,* p. 700

In this paragraph the writer poses a series of questions about the relationship between one's personality and physical health. Then he concludes at the end of the paragraph that they are related.

EXERCISE A Locating Topic Sentences

Underline the topic sentence in each of the following paragraphs. Be ready to explain your choice.

a. Before humans learned to farm, they were nomads, moving from place to place in search of game and vegetation. Each group consisted of about thirty to fifty people. Once farming was developed, the beginnings of cities appeared. Farming provided steady sustenance, which allowed people to live in larger groups and in permanent settlements. Each group had to make rules for civil coexistence, for divisions of labor, and for trade. People began to base their identities less on family ties than on geographical or cultural ties, and they placed growing value on the interests of the larger community.

b. Reasons for the popularity of fast-food chains appear obvious enough. For one thing, the food is generally cheap as restaurant food goes. A hamburger, french fries, and a shake at McDonald's, for example, cost about one-half as much as a similar meal at a regular "sit-down" restaurant. Another advantage of the chains is their convenience. For busy working couples who don't want to spend the time or effort cooking, the fast-food restaurants offer an attractive alternative. And, judging by the fact that customers return in increasing numbers, many Americans like the taste of the food.

c. The dolphin's brain generally exceeds the human brain in weight and has a convoluted cortex that weights about 1,100 grams. Research indicates that, in humans, 600 to 700 grams of cortex is necessary for a vocabulary. Absolute weight of the cortex, rather than the ratio of brain weight to total body weight, is thought to be indicative of intelligence potential. The dolphin's forehead is oil-filled and contains complex sound-generating devices. Tests indicate that the dolphin is sensitive to sound at frequencies up to 120 kilocycles, whereas human vocal cords pulsate at 60 to 120 cycles per second with a choice of many more harmonics. These facts provide convincing argument for possible dolphin intelligence.

Focusing the Topic Sentence

Keep in mind that a topic sentence must be focused and limited enough to be discussed fully within a single paragraph. Notice the difference between the following pairs of topic sentences.

37

- **Too broad:** The United States has many museums with excellent collections of art.
- **Focused:** The St. Louis Art Museum has an outstanding collection of Expressionist paintings and prints.
- **Too broad:** Cultures vary throughout the world with respect to body language.
- **Focused:** Hand gestures that are seemingly innocent in the United States are frequently obscene or insulting in certain Latin countries.
- **Too broad:** Shakespeare's plays indicate that he was familiar with many areas of knowledge.
- **Focused:** Shakespeare's *Merchant of Venice* suggests that he was familiar with the law.

Another requirement of the topic sentence is that it must be capable of being developed. If the main idea is merely factual, it does not permit development. Notice the differences between the following sentences.

- **Factual:** St. Petersburg is a major city in Russia.
- **Revised:** St. Petersburg reminds its visitors of the Italian city of Venice.
- **Factual:** California has more than one hundred community colleges.
- **Revised:** Many California college freshmen prefer the community college for its many unique features.
- **Factual:** Some school systems in our country do not have music appreciation courses in their grade schools.
- **Revised:** Students should be introduced to the pleasures of music while still in the lower grades.

EXERCISE B Revising Topic Sentences

The topic sentences below are either too broad or too factual. Revise each so that it will make an effective topic sentence.

1. The All-Star baseball game is held every July.
2. The Great Depression of the 1930s had a series of traumatic consequences for our nation.
3. The debate over the Vietnam War has raged for many years.
4. High blood pressure increases the risk of serious illness.
5. John Lennon was born in 1940.
6. The annual Cotton Bowl is held in Dallas.
7. Many reforms have been proposed for America's public schools.

8. The real name of "Dr. Seuss," the writer, is Theodor Geisel.
9. Admission of women to the service academies began in the fall of 1976.
10. Astronomy is a fascinating subject.

The best way to be certain that your paragraphs have unity is to construct a specific, focused topic sentence and then develop it through the entire paragraph. If the paragraph sticks to what is promised in the topic sentence, it has unity. Any sentence that does not develop the topic violates the unity of the paragraph and should be omitted.

In the following paragraph, notice how the sentence in bold type introduces another idea and violates the unity of the paragraph.

■ There are many styles of martial arts, and you must do some research in order to choose the right one for your needs. First, you should decide your reasons for learning a martial art: fitness, self-defense, or tournament competition, for example. You should consider how much you are willing to spend on lessons and equipment. Before selecting a teacher, observe how he or she interacts with students. Ask about the teacher's own training and skill level. **The actor Bruce Lee held black belts in a number of martial arts.** Find out what professional associations the instructor belongs to, and verify his or her status in the martial arts community. By inquiring and asking questions, you can find a martial arts program that will bring you pleasure and physical benefits.

The topic sentence in the preceding paragraph announced the main idea: to choose the right style of martial arts for your needs, you must do some research. The fact that Bruce Lee held black belts in a number of martial arts is irrelevant and does not support the topic sentence. Therefore, the boldface sentence should be deleted from the paragraph.

Writing Tips First Impressions

Make sure the appearance of your assignments matches the quality of their content. Most instructors expect papers which employ the following:

- a standard typeface if prepared on a computer
- use of one side of the paper only
- 1-inch margins at the top, bottom, and both sides
- black or dark blue ink if handwritten
- indentation of the first word of each paragraph (one-half inch, or five spaces if typed)
- double-spacing of the text when typing or using a computer

EXERCISE C Focusing Topics

A. *The topics below are too general to be the subjects of single paragraphs. Select five from the list and, for each, write a tightly focused topic sentence that could be adequately developed in one paragraph.*

- heavy metal music
- the Olympics
- teenage marriages
- the Internet
- daily exercise

- the warming of the planet
- Social Security
- Wal-Mart stores
- late-night television
- being an only child

B. *Read each of the following professionally written paragraphs carefully. Then follow the directions after each paragraph.*

■ Although each tribe or peoples has its own unique system of spiritual beliefs and practices, there are some commonly held philosophical ideas that are generally shared by Native American people throughout the hemisphere. The natural world is the focal point of American Indian spirituality. From this foundation springs a number of understandings regarding the nature of the world and the cosmos generally, as well as the appropriate role of human beings in it. Humans are viewed as intimately linked, and morally bound, to the natural world in such a way that one's individual, family and community past are intertwined with the Old Stories that teach how things came to be as they are today, as well as right behavior for ensuring that future generations will continue to rely on a balanced relationship with the natural world. All creatures—the two-legged (humans), the four-legged, the winged ones, the green things, creatures that swim in the rivers and seas, even rocks and things that from a non-Indian philosophical perspective are considered inanimate—are part of this spirituality or sacred life force. For many Indians living today, this circle of the sacred to which we human beings are connected, ideally in balance and harmony with nature, also includes the life-giving sun, the many stars of the night sky, and Mother Earth herself. Because this perspective encompasses all time, all places, and all beings, Native Americans generally prefer the word *spirituality* of the *sacred* rather than religion.

—Lobo and Talbot, eds., *Native American Voices,* pp. 266–67

Notice that this paragraph begins with a topic sentence that signals to the reader what he or she can expect to find in the sentences that follow: "there are some commonly held philosophical ideas that are generally shared by Native American people throughout the hemisphere." The rest of the paragraph gives examples of those "commonly held philosophical ideas." Develop one of the following subjects into a topic sentence that can be adequately developed in at least six supporting sentences. Remember that a good topic sentence is narrow enough to be developed in one paragraph.

- *ocean pollution*
- *honesty*
- *careers*
- *credit cards*

- *shopping malls*
- *women's sports*
- *censorship*
- *teenage parents*

■ Oprah Winfrey—actress, talk-show host, and businesswoman—epitomizes the opportunities for America's entrepreneurs. From welfare child to multimillionaire, Ms. Winfrey—resourceful, assertive, always self-assured, and yet unpretentious—has climbed the socioeconomic ladder by turning apparent failure into opportunities and then capitalizing on them.

With no playmates, Oprah entertained herself by "playacting" with objects such as corncob dolls, chickens, and cows. Her grandmother, a harsh disciplinarian, taught Oprah to read by age 2½, and as a result of speaking at a rural church, her oratory talents began to emerge.

At age 6, Winfrey was sent to live with her mother and two half-brothers in a Milwaukee ghetto. While in Milwaukee, Winfrey, known as "the Little Speaker," was often invited to recite poetry at social gatherings, and her speaking skills continued to develop. At age 12, during a visit to her father in Nashville, she was paid $500 for a speech she gave to a church. It was then that she prophetically announced what she wanted to do for a living: "get paid to talk."

Her mother, working as a maid and drawing available welfare to make ends meet, left Oprah with little or no parental supervision and eventually sent her to live with her father in Nashville. There Oprah found the stability and discipline she so desperately needed. "My father saved my life," Winfrey reminisces. Her father—like her grandmother—a strict disciplinarian, obsessed with properly educating his daughter, forced her to memorize 20 new vocabulary words a week and turn in a weekly book report. His guidance and her hard work soon paid off, as she began to excel in school and other areas.

—Mosley, Pietri, and Megginson, *Management: Leadership in Action,* p. 555

C. *Select one of the following topics and write a paragraph of at least six sentences. Underline your topic sentence and be certain that your paragraph does not contain any sentences that do not support or develop the topic sentence.*

1. What is Oprah Winfrey's success based on? How did she turn disadvantages into opportunities and then capitalize on them?
2. Do you know of someone else—perhaps a person not as famous as Oprah Winfrey and known to only a small group—who has overcome similar handicaps and has also climbed the socioeconomic ladder? You might consider a relative or a person in your community.

Writing Tips Topic Sentences

Be sure that your paragraph contains a topic sentence that tells the reader what he or she can expect to find in the paragraph.

- Is your topic sentence too broad and general to be covered in just one paragraph? If so, narrow your topic.
- Do all of the facts and details in your paragraph follow logically to the end?
- Does any sentence wander off the topic? If so, get rid of it!

Computer Activity

Choose one of the topics from the list in Exercise C on page 40, and narrow its focus so that you can write about it in one paragraph. When you have finished with your paragraph, SAVE your document.

Exchange your electronic document with a classmate. Read your classmate's paragraph and italicize its topic sentence.

If your classmate did not recognize your topic sentence, discuss the reason. You may need to rewrite your topic sentence.

CHAPTER 3

FINDING THE SUBJECT AND THE VERB IN THE SENTENCE

CHAPTER PREVIEW

In this chapter, you will learn about:

- Finding the verb in the sentence
  Action verbs
  Linking verbs
  Words mistaken for verbs
- Finding the subject in the sentence
  Simple and complete subjects
  Compound subjects
- Subjects and verbs in compound and complex sentences
- Writing paragraphs: Making paragraphs coherent through chronological order

To improve your writing, you should master the sentence and its two main parts, the subject and the verb. This chapter will give you some useful tips for locating the subject and verb in every sentence. Once you have mastered this skill, you will be on your way to writing clear and effective sentences.

The Subject and the Verb

The **subject** of a sentence names a person, place, thing, or idea; it tells us *who* or *what* the sentence is about. The **verb** describes action or the subject's state of being; it tells us what the subject *does*, what the subject *is*, or what the subject *receives*.

        (subject)   *(verb)*
■ *Francis Scott Key wrote* the words to our national anthem.

        (subject) (verb)
■ *Baton Rouge is* the capital of Louisiana.

        (subject)   *(verb)*
■ *Gertrude Ederle was* the first woman to swim the English channel.

        (subject)   *(verb)*
■ *Martin Luther King Jr. received* the Nobel Prize for Peace in 1964.

(subject) (verb)
■ *I* rarely *eat* this much licorice.

Each of the above sentences contains a subject and a verb, and each makes a complete statement. In other words, they convey a sense of completeness. In conversations, sentences often lack stated subjects and verbs, but their contexts—the words and sentences that surround them—make clear the missing subject or verb. For example:

■ "Studying your sociology?"
■ "Yes. Big test tomorrow."
■ "Ready for it?"
■ "Hope so. Flunked the last one."

If this conversation were written in formal sentences, the missing subjects and verbs would be supplied, and the exchange might look something like this.

■ "Are you studying your sociology?"
■ "Yes. I have a big test tomorrow."
■ "Are you ready for it?"
■ "I hope so. I flunked the last one."

All sentences, then, have subjects, either stated or implied. Before proceeding further, therefore, it is important that you be able to locate the subject and the verb in a sentence. Because it is usually easier to locate, the verb is the best place to begin.

Finding the Verb

You will remember from Chapter 2 that the verb may be a single word (he *sleeps*) or a verb phrase of two, three, or even four words (he *had slept*, he *had been sleeping*, he *must have been sleeping*). Remember, too, that parts of the verb can be separated by adverbs (he *must* not *have been sleeping*).

Action Verbs

As you saw in Chapter 2, **action verbs** tell what the subject does.

■ Carbohydrates provide energy for body function and activity by supplying immediate calories. (What action takes place in this sentence? What do carbohydrates do? They *provide.* Therefore, the verb in this sentence is *provide.*)

■ Taiwan holds the record for most Little League World Series titles. (What does Taiwan do? It *holds.* The verb in this sentence is *holds.*)

■ The students boarded the plane for San Juan. (What did the students do? They *boarded.* The verb in this sentence is *boarded.*)

■ Oceans cover three-quarters of the earth's surface. (What action takes place in this sentence? What do the oceans do? They *cover.* Therefore, the verb in this sentence is *cover.*)

■ Blood returning from the body tissues enters the right atrium. (What does the blood do? It *enters.* The verb in this sentence is *enters.*)

■ Visitors to Disneyland buy souvenirs for their friends at home. (What do visitors do? They *buy* souvenirs. The verb is b*uy.*)

EXERCISE 3-1

Each of the following sentences contains one or more action verbs. Circle them.

1. When the siren of an ambulance (wails,) sound waves (vibrate) in all directions.
2. Scientists (describe) the effect as an acoustical sphere.
3. If the ambulance (moves) forward, the sound waves in front of it (compress) as new waves (pile up) behind older waves.
4. Behind the ambulance, the opposite (happens,) as individual waves (expand.)
5. The frequency of these sound waves (changes) their pitch.
6. As the ambulance (comes) toward you, the frequency of the waves (increases.)
7. This (creates) a higher pitch.
8. It (reaches) its pinnacle as the ambulance (passes) close to you.
9. After that, the pitch (declines) as the sound waves (stretch) out until they no longer (reach) your ear.
10. Scientists (call) this phenomenon the Doppler effect.

Linking Verbs

Some verbs do not show action. Instead, they express a condition or state of being. They are called **linking verbs,** and they link the subject to another word that renames or describes the subject. You will recall from Chapter 2 that most linking verbs are formed from the verb *to be* and include *am, are, is, was,* and *were.* Several other verbs often used as linking verbs are *appear, become, feel, grow, look, remain, seem, smell, sound,* and *taste.*

The verbs in the following sentences are linking verbs. They link their subjects to words that rename or describe them.

- My parents *seem* happy in their new apartment. (The linking verb *seem* connects the subject *parents* with the word that describes them: *happy.*)

- French *is* the language of the province of Quebec in Canada. (The linking verb *is* connects the subject *French* with the word that renames it: *language.*)

- The first-graders *remained* calm during the earthquake. (The verb *remained* connects the subject *first-graders* with the word that describes them: *calm.*)

- Bernie Mac *has become* an actor as well as a comedian. (The linking verb *has become* connects the subject *Bernie Mac* with the word that renames it: *actor.*)

- Lord Kelvin *was* a founder of the science of thermodynamics. (The linking verb *was* connects the subject *Lord Kelvin* with the word that renames it: *founder.*)

EXERCISE 3-2

Each of the following sentences contains a linking verb; circle it.

1. Few people realize how bad conditions (were) for the Pilgrims who came to Massachusetts on the *Mayflower* in 1620.
2. The *Mayflower* (was) a cargo ship, not designed to carry people.
3. There (was) not enough sleeping space for everyone, so eighty passengers slept on the deck, and others slept inside a rowboat stored below deck.
4. The passengers could not bathe during the sixty-six-day voyage because there (were) no bathrooms on the boat.
5. Bugs and mold (were) often in their food.
6. After standing in oak barrels for several weeks, the drinking water (tasted) bitter, so both adults and children began to drink beer.
7. Despite games and the presence of a cat and two dogs aboard the ship, the journey probably (seemed) boring for the children.
8. One of the women passengers (became) a mother during the voyage and named her son Oceanus.
9. Upon seeing land at last, the Pilgrims (grew) joyful at the lonely and wild look of the thickly forested shore.
10. While the men explored the countryside, the women (were) on the beach.

When looking for the verb in a sentence, you should remember that it sometimes consists of more than one word. In such cases, it is called a verb phrase, and **verb phrases** consist of a main verb and a **helping/auxiliary verb** (see Chapter 2). Any helping/auxiliary verbs in front of the main verb are part of the verb, as in the following examples.

- *may have* disappeared
- *should be* avoided
- *might* stay
- *did* guarantee
- *is* speaking
- *could have* objected

For a complete list of the words that serve as helping/auxiliary verbs, see page 16 in Chapter 2.

EXERCISE 3-3

Circle the verbs in the following sentences, including any helping/auxiliary verbs. Some sentences have more than one verb.

1. Cheese rolling (has been known) as one of Britain's most unusual customs for centuries.
2. Each year, Gloucestershire, England, (is invaded) by thousands of fans who (can't wait) for the contest.
3. They (are thrilled) to watch perfectly sane men and women (chase) seven-pound wheels of Gloucestershire cheese that (are rolled) down Cooper's Hill.
4. Once the spectators (see) the athletes (line up) along the crest of the hill, they (begin) chanting ("Roll) that cheese!"
5. When the master of ceremonies (has blown) the whistle, the athletes (give) their cheeses a push and (scramble) after them.
6. The hill (is) steep and lumpy, so contestants (know) that they (might get injured;) broken bones and sprains (are reported) each year.
7. Some competitors (win) only by accidentally tumbling down the hill, past their more careful peers.
8. At times, the cheese (rolls) into the crowd and (strikes) someone, but no one (is hurt) and the cheese (is kicked) back onto the course.
9. The winner (gets) a fine prize: the cheese that he or she (has chased.)
10. Cheese rolling (may have evolved) from early harvest or fertility rituals, and it (may date) back to the ancient Britons or Romans who (lived) in the area.

EXERCISE 3-4

Circle the verbs in the following sentences; be sure to include any helping/auxiliary verbs. Some sentences have more than one verb.

1. Normal red blood cells (look) round and plump, something like jelly doughnuts.
2. In about eight percent of American blacks, however, some red blood cells (are) much smaller than normal and (have) a sickle, or crescent, shape.
3. Sickling of the red blood cells (is) an inherited trait that (has been traced) to a mutation in a single gene.
4. A person who (has inherited) two sickling genes (has) sickle-cell anemia.
5. Sickle cells (carry) much less oxygen than normal cells, and such a person frequently (suffers) from insufficient oxygen.
6. In addition, the cells often (clog) blood vessels, (cause) severe pain, (damage) tissue, and even (cause) death if vessels that (supply) the brain or lungs (are blocked.)
7. People with sickle-cell anemia frequently (die) at an early age.
8. Certain African populations (contain) a high incidence of the sickling gene.
9. These populations (live) in areas with a high incidence of malaria.
10. People with the sickle-cell trait (one sickling gene and one normal gene) (have) a substantially lower incidence of malaria than the rest of the population.

Words Mistaken for the Verb

You may sometimes be confused by two forms of the verb that may be mistaken for the main verb of the sentence. These forms are the infinitive and the present participle.

The **infinitive** is the "to" form of the verb: *to leave, to write, to start,* and so on. The infinitive is the base form of the verb—in other words, it merely names the verb. It does not give us any information about its person, its tense, or its number. The infinitive by itself is never the verb of the sentence. Note how the following word groups fail to make sense because they use only the infinitive form—the "to" form—of the verb.

- Homeowners *to install* new roofs because of the damage from hail.
- My reading comprehension *to improve* by 15 percent.
- Missionaries from Spain *to arrive* in California in the 1760s.
- Ornithologists *to study* the mating habits of condors.
- Contractors *to build* cheaper and smaller homes in the future.

These word groups are not sentences because they try to make an infinitive do the work of a main verb. They can be corrected by placing a verb before the infinitive.

■ Homeowners *had* to install new roofs because of the damage from hail.

■ My reading comprehension *was* to improve by 15 percent.

■ Missionaries from Spain *began* to arrive in California in the 1760s.

■ Ornithologists *plan* to study the mating habits of condors.

■ Contractors *vow* to build cheaper and smaller homes in the future.

Of course, these word groups could also have been converted to sentences merely by changing the infinitives to main verbs: *installed, improved, arrived, study,* and *will build.*

The other form of the verb that sometimes looks as though it is the main verb is the **present participle,** the "-ing" form of the verb. It is the result of adding *-ing* to the verb, as in the following: *leaving, starting, writing,* and so on. Like the infinitive, the present participle can never stand by itself as the verb in a sentence. Notice how the following groups of words fail to make sense because they attempt to use the present participle—the "-ing" form—as their verb.

■ Homeowners *installing* new roofs because of the damage from the hail.

■ My reading comprehension *improving* by 15 percent.

■ Missionaries from Spain *arriving* in California in the 1760s.

■ Ornithologists *studying* the mating habits of condors.

■ Contractors *building* cheaper and smaller homes in the future.

These word groups can be corrected by placing a form of the verb *to be* in front of the present participle.

■ Homeowners *were* installing new roofs because of the damage from the hail.

■ My reading comprehension *has been* improving by 15 percent.

Tips for Finding the Verb

1. Find the verb by asking what action takes place.
2. Find the verb by asking what word links the subject with the rest of the sentence.
3. If a word fits in the following slot, it is a verb.

   "I (or *He* or *They*) _____."

   Examples: I *hunt* elk.
   He *swims* every morning.
   They *bring* us flowers each time they visit.

4. Remember that the verb in a sentence will never have *to* in front of it.
5. The "-ing" form (the present participle) can be a verb only if it has a helping verb in front of it.
6. The verb will never be in a prepositional phrase.

- Missionaries from Spain *were* arriving in California in the 1760s.
- Ornithologists *have been* studying the mating habits of condors.
- Contractors *will be* building cheaper and smaller homes in the future.

A *final warning:* You will never find the verb of a sentence in a prepositional phrase. The reason for this rule is simple. Prepositional phrases are made of prepositions and their objects, which are either nouns or pronouns—never verbs. Therefore, a prepositional phrase will never contain the verb of a sentence.

EXERCISE 3-5

Identify the italicized words by writing the appropriate letter in the space provided.
a. verb   b. present participle   c. infinitive

___a___   1. The Great Pyramids of Egypt *hold* mysteries and wonder for people throughout the world.

___a___   2. The Pyramid of Khufu *is* the largest of the three.

___c___   3. It was built by the Egyptian pharaoh Khufu around 2560 B.C. *to serve* as a tomb after his death.

___b___   4. *Building* the pyramid may have taken twenty years.

___b___   5. The pyramid consists of about two million stone blocks, each *weighing* more than two tons.

___a___   6. Laid end to end, the blocks *could form* a wall around France.

___c___   7. No one knows for certain how the workers were able *to lift* the blocks into place.

___a___   8. Archaeologists think that a huge ramp or series of ramps *was used* to raise the blocks to their positions.

___a___   9. Each side *is aligned* with one of the cardinal points of the compass—north, south, east, and west.

___b___ 10. *Sloping* of the walls is about fifty-one degrees.

___a___ 11. The pharaoh's tomb *is located* in the heart of the pyramid.

___a___ 12. His sarcophagus and the walls of his inner chamber *are made* of red granite.

___b___ 13. The pyramid's interior blocks fit so snugly that *slipping* a card between them is impossible.

___a___ 14. A huge and complex village formed nearby to house the workers; the world's oldest paved road *was found* here.

___b___ 15. *Standing* nearly five hundred feet, the pyramid of Khufu was the tallest structure on Earth for more than forty-three centuries.

Finding the Subject

A sentence is written about something or someone—the **subject** of the sentence. The verb, as you have learned, tells what the subject *is* or *does*. Every grammatically complete sentence has a subject. Sometimes, as in the case of commands, the subject is not directly stated but implied.

- Please return all overdue library books by next Friday. (Although the subject *you* is not stated, it is implied.)

The rule for finding the subject of a sentence is actually very clear. To find the subject of a sentence, first find the verb. Then ask, "Who?" or "What?" The answer will be the subject. Read the following sentences carefully to see how the rule works.

- The invoice was paid on February 10. (By asking "What was paid?" you can easily determine the subject of this sentence: *invoice.*)
- Luis follows a strict diet because of his high blood pressure. (As in the sentence above, you can find the subject in this sentence by locating the verb and asking "Who?" or "What?" *Luis* follows a strict diet and therefore is the subject.)
- Several cracks in the kitchen ceiling appeared after the last earthquake. (What appeared? *Cracks,* the subject.)

Subjects and Other Words in the Sentence

Do not be confused if a sentence has several nouns or pronouns in it. Only the word that answers "Who?" or "What?" before the verb can be the subject. In the following sentence notice that only *mayor* answers the question, "*Who* blamed?"

> *(subject)*
- The *mayor* blamed himself, not the city manager, the council, or the voters, for the defeat of the bond issue.

Do not mistake phrases beginning with such words as *along with, in addition to, including, rather than, together with,* and similar terms for a part of the subject of the sentence. Note the following sentences.

- The summary, as well as the chapters, contains several important terms to memorize. (Although *chapters* might appear to be the subject because it is closer to the verb, the subject is *summary* because it answers the question *"What* contains?")
- The basketball players, together with their coach, are featured in this week's sports special. (The subject is *players* because it answers the question *"Who* are featured?")

Simple and Complete Subjects

The main noun or pronoun without any of its modifiers that answers the questions "Who?" or "What?" before the verb is the **simple subject.** The **complete subject** is composed of the simple subject and its modifiers—the words and phrases that describe it.

In the sentence below, *waiter* is the simple subject; *a tall, gracious, smiling waiter* is the complete subject.

■ A tall, gracious, smiling waiter seated us at our table.

In the sentence below, what is the simple subject? What is the complete subject?

■ The woman in the green dress and high heels is my sister.

When you are asked to identify the subject of a sentence, you normally name the simple subject.

Compound Subjects

A sentence can have more than one subject, just as it can have more than one verb. Two or more subjects are called **compound subjects.**

■ *Athletes and celebrities* are frequently seen on television endorsing products.

■ *Polluted water and smog* made the city unattractive to tourists.

■ *Either hamburgers or hot dogs* will be served at the picnic.

EXERCISE 3-6

Underline all of the complete subjects in the following sentences. Some sentences have more than one subject.

1. The daring life and unexplained death of an American pilot, Amelia Earhart, have intrigued people for decades.
2. Her love affair with airplanes bloomed when Amelia attended an air show in California with her father.
3. Amelia received a parade and a medal from President Herbert Hoover in 1932 after she became the first woman to fly alone across the Atlantic Ocean.
4. Her most treasured goal, however, was to be the first pilot ever to circle the earth at the equator.
5. Amelia, along with her copilot, Fred Noon, took off from Miami in June 1937.
6. Articles and photographs for American newspapers, together with letters to her husband, were sent by Amelia throughout her journey.
7. The public followed Amelia and Fred's progress eagerly.

8. Everyone was stunned when their airplane suddenly vanished one month after their quest began.

9. The two flyers had completed 22,000 miles of the mission.

10. A final message from Amelia to a Coast Guard ship indicated that her plane was near New Guinea, in the South Pacific.

11. Neither the plane nor its pilots were ever found, though squads of Army planes and Navy ships searched thoroughly.

12. Numerous adventurers, scholars, and Earhart fans have launched their own unsuccessful searches.

13. Rumors about the pilots' disappearance continue to circulate today.

14. Some say that Earhart dove into the ocean deliberately, while others claim she was on a spy mission and was captured by the Japanese.

15. Nevertheless, many modern female pilots cite Earhart's courage and achievements among their reasons for learning to fly.

Subjects in Inverted Sentences

Most sentences follow the subject-verb pattern. In **inverted sentences,** however, the pattern is reversed: the subject generally comes *after* the verb. Read the following inverted sentences carefully.

- Across the street stood the abandoned schoolhouse. (The abandoned *schoolhouse* stood across the street; *schoolhouse* is the subject, although street is in the subject position before the verb.)

- On her desk is a new word processor. (What is the verb? What is the subject?)

Questions are usually inverted, with the subject coming after the verb.

- Was Charles Lindbergh the first man to fly across the Atlantic? (The verb *was* precedes the subject *Charles Lindbergh.*)

- Where are the keys to the car? (The subject *keys* follows the verb *are.*)

- What is the best time to call you? (The subject *time* follows the verb *is.*)

In sentences that begin with *here is, here are, there is,* or *there are,* the real subject follows the verb. To find the subject in such sentences, use the method you learned earlier. Ask "Who?" or "What?" before the verb.

- Here is a map of the subway route to the Bronx. (What is here? The subject, *map,* is here.)

- There are several reasons to explain his refusal. (What are there? Several *reasons,* the subject.)

Subjects with Verbs in Active and Passive Voice

The sentences that we have examined so far have contained subjects that performed actions indicated by action verbs, or they have contained subjects that were connected by linking verbs to words that described or renamed them. Occasionally, however, we may encounter or write sentences in which the subjects receive the action.

If the subject of the sentence performs the act, the verb is in the **active voice.**

■ Matthew repaired his tractor.

■ Burl's poodle attacked Bob.

In the **passive voice** the subject is replaced by the object.

■ The tractor was repaired by Matthew.

■ Bob was attacked by Burl's poodle.

As you can see, in the active voice the emphasis is on the *subject,* which performs the action of the verb. In the passive voice the emphasis is shifted to the *object* instead of the subject, which is "passive" or acted upon. The passive voice of a verb always consists of a form of the helping/auxiliary verb *be* (such as *is, was, has been,* and so on) plus the **past participle** of the main verb. (The past participle of a regular verb is the form that usually ends in *-ed.*)

To change a sentence from active to passive voice, we turn the sentence around and use a form of *be* as a helping/auxiliary verb.

■ **Active:**   The intruder *surprised* the hotel guests.
■ **Passive:**   The hotel guests *were surprised* by the intruder.

■ **Active:**   Gustaf *threw* the winning touchdown.
■ **Passive:**   The winning touchdown *was thrown* by Gustaf.

To change a sentence from passive to active voice, we substitute a new subject for the previous one.

■ **Passive:**   Tides *are caused* by the moon.
■ **Active:**   The moon *causes* tides.

■ **Passive:**   The soldiers *were wounded* by the snipers.
■ **Active:**   The snipers *wounded* the soldiers.

You will often be able to choose between active and passive voice when composing sentences. The active voice is usually more direct and forceful. For this reason you should use active verbs except in cases when you have good reason to use passive ones.

EXERCISE 3-7

Revise the following sentences by changing passive verbs to the active voice when possible.

1. Short stature is caused by a number of problems and diseases.

   A number of problems and diseases cause short stature.

2. The condition has been called "dwarfism" by many people, though those who live with it prefer the term "short stature."

   Many people call the condition "dwarfism," though those who live with it prefer

   the term "short stature."

3. Most often, the bones are prevented from growing normally by any one of a group of conditions called skeletal dysplasia.

   Most often, any one of a group of conditions called skeletal dysplasia prevents

   the bones from growing normally.

4. More than five hundred kinds of skeletal dysplasia have been identified by scientists, but the most common is Achondroplasia.

   Scientists have identified more than five hundred kinds of skeletal dysplasia,

   but the most common is Achondroplasia.

5. All races and both genders are struck with Achondroplasia with equal frequency.

   Achondroplasia strikes all races and both genders with equal frequency.

6. About one in every forty thousand newborns is affected by it.

   It affects about one in every forty thousand newborns.

7. A number of daily frustrations—ill-suited chairs, stairs, gas and brake pedals—are faced by Little People.

   Little People face a number of daily frustrations—ill-suited chairs, stairs,

   gas and brake pedals.

8. Use of many ATMs, gas pumps, pay phones, vending machines, and elevator buttons is made impossible by what Little People call the Six-Inch Barrier.

   What Little People call the Six-Inch Barrier makes impossible the use of many ATMs,

   gas pumps, pay phones, vending machines, and elevator buttons.

9. Thanks to the Internet, a worldwide network of socializing and support has been formed by Little People.

   Thanks to the Internet, Little People have formed a worldwide network

   of socializing and support.

10. Events, scholarships, and specially designed products are offered by hundreds of Web sites.

Hundreds of Web sites offer events, scholarships, and specially designed products.

Subjects and Prepositional Phrases

The subject of a sentence will never be in a prepositional phrase. The reason for this rule is simple. Any noun or pronoun in a prepositional phrase will be the object of the preposition, and the object of a preposition cannot also be the subject. Examine the following sentences, in which the subjects can be confused with objects of prepositions.

■ Thousands of tourists from countries throughout the world visit Chesapeake Bay in Maryland. (*Tourists, countries,* and *world* are in the subject position before the verb *visit,* but they are all objects of prepositions, and therefore cannot be the subject. By asking "Who visits?" you can determine the subject: *Thousands* visit. *Thousands* is the subject.)

■ The author of *Adam Bede* was better known as George Eliot, rather than by her real name, Mary Anne Evans. (Although *Adam Bede* is in the subject position, it is the object of a preposition and cannot therefore be the subject of this sentence. Who was better known? The *author* of *Adam Bede.* The subject is *author.*)

■ One of the Beatles continues to produce records. (*Beatles* is the object of a preposition and therefore is not the subject. Who continues to produce records? The subject is *One.*)

By placing parentheses around the prepositional phrases in a sentence, you can more easily identify the subject and verb. Examine the sentence below.

■ The warden (of a jail) (in the northern part) (of Minnesota) explained (in an interview) (on television) (during the past week) his position (on the death penalty.)

By discarding the prepositional phrases, we can easily see the subject (*warden*) and the verb (*explained*).

Tips **for Finding the Subject in a Sentence**

1.   The subject will answer the questions *Who?* or *What?* before the verb.
2.   In questions or inverted sentences, the subject will usually come after the verb.
3.   The subject of a sentence will never be *here* or *there.*
4.   The subject of the sentence will never be in a prepositional phrase.

EXERCISE 3-8

Underline the subject and circle the verb in these sentences. Some sentences have more than one subject or verb.

1. Many <u>animals</u> (are) friendly, helpful, or amusing, but <u>others</u> (possess) venom <u>that</u> (can cause) their victims pain or even death.
2. Rattlesnake <u>bites</u>, for example, (can cause) severe pain, swelling, and temporary paralysis.
3. Several old horror <u>movies</u> (feature) Gila monsters, a type of venomous lizard <u>that</u> (frequents) the southwestern United States and Mexico.
4. <u>Bites</u> from Gila monsters (can bring) horrible pain and dangerously low blood pressure.
5. Many <u>people</u> (are) allergic to bites from bees, wasps, hornets, and even ants.
6. Allergic <u>reactions</u> (can include) swelling and rashes.
7. Some <u>victims</u> (are) so allergic that <u>they</u> (may die) of shock within minutes of being bitten.
8. Though most spiders' <u>bites</u> (cause) only itching and swelling, <u>others</u> (are) much more harmful.
9. Black widow <u>spiders</u> (cause) severe pain, weakness, and convulsions, though <u>survival</u> from their bites (is) likely.
10. The brown recluse <u>spider</u> (is) often (called) a "fiddleback" because of its oblong body.

Subjects and Verbs in Compound and Complex Sentences

You have seen that sentences may have more than one subject and more than one verb.

   (subject) *(verb)*   *(verb)*
a. *Mark Twain piloted* a riverboat and later *wrote* several novels.

   (subject)   *(subject)* *(verb)*
b. *Mia Hamm* and *Julie Foudy were* two of America's most popular professional soccer players.

   (subject)   *(subject)* *(verb)*   *(verb)*
c. *Nelson Mandela* and *Vaclav Havel were* political prisoners and later *became* elected leaders of their countries.

Sentence (a) above has one subject and two verbs; sentence (b) has two subjects and one verb; sentence (c) has two subjects and two verbs. All three sentences are **simple sentences** because they each contain only one **independent clause.** An independent clause is a group of words with a subject and verb capable of standing alone. As we saw above, the subject and the verb may be compound.

We will now look briefly at two other kinds of sentences: the **compound sentence** and the **complex sentence.** Both kinds of sentences are discussed in detail in Chapter 8, "Compound and Complex Sentences." At this point we need to learn only enough to recognize their subjects and verbs.

A **compound sentence** consists of two or more independent clauses containing closely related ideas and is usually connected by a **coordinating conjunction.** In other words, it is two or more simple sentences connected by one of the following conjunctions.

Coordinating Conjunctions						
and	but	for	nor	or	so	yet

The following are simple sentences because each contains one independent clause.

■ The violin has only four strings.

■ It is difficult to play.

By combining these two simple sentences with the conjunction *but*, we can create a compound sentence.

■ The violin has only four strings, *but* it is difficult to play.

Each of the independent clauses in the preceding sentence has its own subject (*violin* and *it*) and its own verb (*has* and *is*) and is capable of standing alone. A compound sentence, therefore, has at least two subjects and two verbs. Of course, a compound sentence can have more than two independent clauses. But regardless of the number of clauses, a compound sentence remains the same: two or more independent clauses usually connected by a coordinating conjunction. (In Chapter 8 you will see that semicolons may also connect independent clauses to form compound sentences.)

Notice that the conjunction *but*, which connected the two independent clauses in the compound sentence above, was preceded by a comma. In general, a coordinating conjunction linking two independent clauses in a compound sentence should be preceded by a comma. Chapter 8 will give you greater practice in the punctuation of compound sentences.

EXERCISE 3-9

In each of the following compound sentences, underline the simple subjects and circle the verbs in each independent clause.

1. Acupuncture (is) a method of inhibiting or reducing pain impulses, but it (is) also (used) to abandon habits like smoking and nail-biting.

2. The word (comes) from two Latin words meaning "needle" and "to sting," but most acupuncture treatments (are) virtually painless.

3. Needles (are inserted) through selected areas of the skin, and then they (are twisted) gently by the acupuncturist or by a battery-operated device.

4. The location of the needle insertion (depends) on the patient's ailment, and each part of the body (corresponds) to certain illnesses.

5. Acupuncture (is used) in China as an anesthetic, and in an operation for the removal of a lung, one needle (is placed) in the forearm, midway between the wrist and the elbow.

6. To pull a tooth, the acupuncturist (inserts) a needle in the web between the thumb and the index finger, and for a tonsillectomy, one needle (is inserted) about two inches above the wrist.

7. There (is) no satisfactory explanation to account for the effects of acupuncture, but according to one theory, the twisting of the acupuncture needle (stimulates) two sets of nerves.

8. One very narrow nerve (is) the nerve for pain, and the other, a much thicker nerve, (is) the nerve for touch.

9. The impulse passing along the touch nerve (reaches) the spinal cord first, and it ("closes) the gate" to the brain, blocking the pain impulse.

10. Acupuncture still (encounters) much skepticism in the United States; nevertheless, increasing numbers of Americans, including medical doctors, (are investigating) its claims.

A **complex sentence** is a sentence containing a **dependent clause.** A dependent clause is a group of words containing a subject and verb but is not capable of standing alone as a sentence. (An independent clause, you remember, has a subject and a verb and can stand alone to form a sentence.) A dependent clause always needs to be attached to an independent clause in order to complete its meaning. Examine carefully the following sentence:

■ Because a cure for cancer does not exist, some patients resort to bizarre diets and remedies.

This sentence is made up of two clauses, each containing a subject and a verb. The first clause (*because a cure for cancer does not exist*) will not stand alone to form a sentence, and therefore it is a *dependent clause*. The second clause (*some patients resort to bizarre diets and remedies*) is capable of standing alone as a sentence, and therefore it is an *independent clause*. The entire sentence is a *complex sentence* because it contains a dependent clause.

You can recognize dependent clauses because they do not express complete thoughts. You can also spot them because they usually begin with **subordinating conjunctions.** Here are some of the most common subordinating conjunctions.

Subordinating Conjunctions					
after	although	as	because	if	since
though	unless	until	when	while	why

In Chapter 8 you will learn how to recognize and form compound and complex sentences so that your writing will have variety and will not consist only of simple sentences.

EXERCISE 3-10

Place parentheses around the dependent clause in each of the following complex sentences. Then underline all of the subjects in the sentences and circle the verbs.

1. Many Native American tribes were forced from their ancestral lands (when the Indian Removal Act was passed in 1830.)

2. President Andrew Jackson began to annex "Indian territory" (after settlers heard reports of gold deposits there.)

3. Sharing land was deemed unreasonable by the government, (even after many tribes agreed to adopt Anglo culture.)

4. (Though some tribes traded their land for tracts out West,) other tribes refused to leave their homes.

5. American soldiers used physical force (if any Native American resisted eviction.)

6. Most Native Americans left food and belongings behind (as they were marched at gunpoint from their land.)

7. Hundreds of Native Americans were buried along the westward route (because they froze or starved to death during the winter march.)

8. (Because the Native Americans suffered such deep loss and anguish,) their forced journey is known as the Trail of Tears.

9. (When the Cherokee tribe appealed to the Supreme Court for help,) the Court ruled against them.

10. (Although Andrew Jackson is regarded as an admirable president by many students of history,) others hold him responsible for the grief and humiliation of so many Native American tribes.

EDITING EXERCISES

The following paragraphs consist of a series of choppy simple sentences. By changing the structure of the sentences, revise each paragraph in order to make it flow more smoothly. For example, you might combine two simple sentences into a compound sentence or into a simple sentence with a compound subject and compound verb. Other changes could include creating complex sentences by converting simple sentences into dependent clauses and attaching them to independent clauses or changing passive verbs to the active voice.

Everyone wants to spend less money on gasoline. Take better care of your car. Then you can get better gas mileage. Mileage is affected by the cleanliness of your engine. One way to keep your engine clean is to replace the spark plugs often. Check whether the air filter and fuel filter are clean. If they're not, replace them. Invest in a new oxygen sensor. It can improve gas mileage by as much as fifteen percent. Monitoring the fullness of your tires seems minor. Tire pressure affects mileage. Keeping tires inflated properly can mean a six percent boost in mileage. Extra weight in your vehicle lowers mileage. Mileage is typically cut by one mile per gallon for every two hundred pounds of weight. Inspect your trunk, truck bed, or cargo space. Remove all unneeded items. These tips are easy. They are inexpensive and bound to reduce your gasoline expenses.

For nearly two centuries the Alamo has symbolized Texans' pride. It has also symbolized Texans' independent spirit. The Alamo was established as a Catholic mission in 1718. Mexican general Martin Perfecto de Cos converted it into a fort in 1835. He was attempting to squelch a revolt by white settlers. They had wanted to separate from Mexico. Cos's effort failed. Mexico's ruler, General Antonio Lopez de Santa Ana, sent 4,000 troops to attack the Alamo and subdue the settlers. Texas General Sam Houston ordered Colonel James Bowie to destroy the fort rather than let it suffer attack by Santa Ana's huge army. Determined to fight for Texas's independence, Bowie ignored Houston's orders. He had fewer than two hundred soldiers to help him. The famous fight for the Alamo started on February 23, 1836. It lasted thirteen days. Meanwhile, Bowie died of pneumonia. On the morning of March 6, Santa Ana's troops stormed the Alamo's north wall. They killed all of the Texan soldiers, including famed adventurer Davy Crockett. Today, visitors can explore the Alamo, including its chapel, Long Barracks, and a research library. Displays of artifacts and slain soldiers' personal items can also be seen.

WRITING SENTENCES Identifying Subjects and Verbs

This review exercise asks you to identify the subjects and verbs in sentences that you write. When writing your sentences, do not hesitate to review the appropriate pages in this chapter as needed.

1. Write two original sentences; each sentence should contain a compound subject. Circle the subjects.
2. Write two inverted sentences. Circle the subject and verb in each sentence.
3. Write a sentence in which the verb is in the active voice. Circle the verb.
4. Using the same verb used in the preceding sentence, write a sentence with the verb in the passive voice. Circle the verb.
5. Write three compound sentences. Circle the subject and the verb in each independent clause.
6. Write three complex sentences. Circle the subject and the verb in each dependent (subordinate) and independent clause.

Language Tip

Avoid repeating the subject unnecessarily in your sentences. Study the following examples.

Examples: My sister ~~she~~ is a nurse at Belleville Hospital. (*Sister* and *she* refer to the same person, and therefore *she* is unnecessary repetition.)

The class that I signed up for ~~it~~ was canceled. (*It* is unnecessary because *that* replaces *it*.)

REVIEW TEST 3-A
Finding the Subject and the Verb in the Sentence

A. *Identify the italicized word or words by writing the appropriate letter in the space before each sentence.*

   a. action verb   b. linking verb   c. helping/auxiliary verb   d. none of the above

___a___ 1. The Liberty Bell *cracked* while tolling for the death of Chief Justice John Marshall, in 1835.

___b___ 2. Hinduism *is* the primary religion of India, practiced by eighty percent of its population.

___c___ 3. The longest time anyone *has* spent in a hot air balloon is about 477 hours.

___a___ 4. Idaho and Utah still *use* firing squads for capital punishment.

___d___ 5. The Pura Belpre Awards honor Latino *writers* and book illustrators.

___a___ 6. More than fifteen hundred people died when the Titanic *sank* in 1912.

___c___ 7. The Hubble telescope *was* named for the American astronomer Edwin P. Hubble.

___c___ 8. The United States *has* been divided into eight time zones.

___b___ 9. North Dakota *is* the most rural of our fifty states.

___a___ 10. A Norwegian *invented* the aerosol can in 1926.

B. *In the space before each sentence, write the letter that corresponds to the simple subject of the sentence.*

___a___ 11. Americans eat 140 pounds of potatoes each year.
        a. Americans   b. pounds   c. potatoes   d. year

___c___ 12. Followed by Spain and Italy, France is the world's top tourist destination.
        a. Spain   b. Italy   c. France   d. tourist

___c___ 13. A blue metal, lead can cause kidney problems and learning disabilities in children.
        a. blue   b. metal   c. lead   d. cause

___b___ 14. The Civil War battlefield at Antietam, Maryland, is the nation's largest.
        a. Civil War   b. battlefield   c. Antietam, Maryland   d. nation's

___d___ 15. In Los Angeles, California, the average driver spends more than 130 hours per year in traffic delays.
        a. Los Angeles   b. California   c. average   d. driver

_____a_____ 16. Cars are much more dangerous than buses, trains, and airplanes.
  a. cars   b. dangerous   c. buses   d. trains

_____a_____ 17. Sport utility vehicles continue to rank among the world's most polluting vehicles.
  a. vehicles   b. rank   c. world's   d. polluting

_____b_____ 18. As a worker, you are eligible to start receiving Social Security benefits in your sixties.
  a. worker   b. you   c. Social Security   d. benefits

_____b_____ 19. Though criticized by some people for its labor practices, Wal-Mart is one of the nation's largest and most profitable companies.
  a. people   b. Wal-Mart   c. one   d. companies

_____a_____ 20. Vatican City is the world's smallest country.
  a. Vatican City   b. City   c. world's   d. country

_____d_____ 21. Although a beautiful and richly historic country, Sudan has suffered civil war for decades.
  a. beautiful   b. richly   c. country   d. Sudan

_____c_____ 22. After constructing six nuclear bombs, South Africa voluntarily disabled them.
  a. constructing   b. bombs   c. South Africa   d. them

_____b_____ 23. At approximately four percent, Mexico has one of the world's lowest tax burdens.
  a. four percent   b. Mexico   c. one   d. burdens

_____a_____ 24. Spanish is the official language of the people of Argentina.
  a. Spanish   b. official   c. language   d. Argentina

_____b_____ 25. Many people enjoy canoeing in the summertime.
  a. many   b. people   c. canoeing   d. summertime

Name _____ Date _____

REVIEW TEST 3-B
Finding the Subject and the Verb in the Sentence

A. *Identify the italicized word or words by writing the appropriate letter in the space before each sentence.*

   a. action verb   b. linking verb   c. helping/auxiliary verb   d. none of the above

___d___   1. Instead of *playing* jazz, the band decided to feature show tunes.

___b___   2. The charges against his client *were* false, according to his attorney.

___b___   3. *Is* there anything to be gained by leaving now, rather than later?

___a___   4. The dark clouds *obscured* the sun, suggesting an approaching storm.

___a___   5. After DeShondra *joined* the YWCA, she learned to swim.

___c___   6. Learning to play the piano *has* helped Hoang learn to type.

___d___   7. By *purchasing* a reliable car, you will avoid repair bills later.

___a___   8. The ringing of the doorbell *announced* Farouk's arrival.

___b___   9. What *is* the difference between longitude and latitude?

___c___ 10. Many immigrants from Southwest Asia *have* settled in California.

B. *In the space before each sentence, write the letter that corresponds to the simple subject of the sentence.*

___b___ 11. Despite his tendency to exaggerate, Andre's story about the fish was true.
            a. tendency   b. story   c. exaggerate   d. fish

___b___ 12. Here are my reasons for my decision to leave early tomorrow.
            a. here   b. reasons   c. decision   d. tomorrow

___a___ 13. Neither of the twins could be identified by their teachers.
            a. neither   b. twins   c. identified   d. teachers

___b___ 14. For her birthday Maximina was given a subscription to her favorite magazine.
            a. birthday   b. Maximina   c. subscription   d. magazine

___d___ 15. Beyond the bright façade of the building was concealed its decay.
            a. beyond   b. façade   c. building   d. decay

___a___ 16. One of the most popular radio programs in our city is about car repair.
            a. one   b. programs   c. city   d. car

___a___ 17. The insurance company, as well as the restaurant, was sued by a diner.
            a. insurance company   b. restaurant   c. sued   d. diner

   c   18. Many years ago there were flowers and trees on this site.
                a. many   b. years.   c. flowers and trees   d. site

   a   19. The convertible, not the van, was fully insured by its owner.
                a. convertible   b. van   c. insured   d. owner

   c   20. Because of his high blood pressure, Chris no longer skis in Colorado.
                a. because   b. blood pressure   c. Chris   d. Colorado

   c   21. Declaring his love for Muriel, Don asked her to marry him and move to Iowa.
                a. love   b. Muriel   c. Don   d. Iowa

   a   22. The walls of the cave, as well as the floor, are painted red.
                a. walls   b. cave   c. floor   d. red

   c   23. Among the survivors of the massacre was a nun from Detroit.
                a. survivors   b. massacre   c. nun   d. Detroit

   c   24. A pitcher of iced tea on his desk, Mitchell began to work on his taxes.
                a. pitcher   b. desk   c. Mitchell   d. taxes

   a   25. Doesn't your car have a CD player or a radio?
                a. car   b. CD   c. player   d. radio

Go to www.ablongman.com/yarber to complete Review Test 3-C.

Writing Paragraphs

Coherence in the Paragraph Through Chronological Order

Coherence means "sticking together," and in a *coherent* paragraph, all the ideas stick together. You have seen that when a paragraph is unified, all the other sentences support or develop the topic sentence. If sentences are placed in the right order with the right connecting words so that the reader is never confused, the writer's train of thought is easy to follow from sentence to sentence and from paragraph to paragraph.

Good writers make their paragraphs coherent in two ways: they arrange their ideas in an *order* that best fits their subject, and they use *linking words or phrases* between their sentences to help the reader understand how the ideas are related.

To tell a story, give directions, explain a process, summarize historical events, or report on the steps or actions taken by an individual, paragraphs are usually arranged in *chronological order*—they present their ideas in the order in which they happened.

In the following paragraph notice that all of the details are presented in the order in which they happened.

■ After his arrival in Illinois at the age of twenty-one, Abraham Lincoln tried his hand at a variety of occupations. In 1830 he worked as a flatboatman, making a voyage down the Mississippi River to New Orleans. On his return he worked as a storekeeper, postmaster, and surveyor. With the coming of the Black Hawk War in 1832, he enlisted as a volunteer. After a brief military career he was elected to the state assembly. In 1836, having passed the bar examination after private study, he began to practice law. The next year he moved to Springfield and began a successful career. By the time he started to become prominent in national politics in 1856, he had made himself one of the most distinguished lawyers in Illinois.

When you use chronological order to organize your paragraphs, it is important that you relate the events in the order in which they occurred. The paragraph above would have been confusing to readers if the writer had started with Lincoln's career in national politics, then detailed his early days as a storekeeper, then jumped ahead to his practice of law, and so on. You can avoid confusion by including all points or incidents as they happened.

Chronological order can also be used in personal narrative writing. A personal narrative is simply a story taken from your life. Your life is organized chronologically—that is, it moves along in time from one event to another as they happen. Whenever writers want to tell what happened, they rely on narration, sometimes in combination with description and other kinds of writing.

A personal narrative is easy to write because you are an authority on its subject: yourself. A personal narrative has a beginning, a middle, and an end. If it is brief, it should be about one main point or incident. By arranging the details and incidents chronologically, you can help your reader see and feel the experience as he or she reads about it.

Select one of the topics from (a) or (b) below and develop it into a paragraph in which the ideas are arranged chronologically. Underline your topic sentence. Before writing your final copy, make certain that you have asked yourself the following questions.

1. Are all of my ideas and details in the right order or sequence?
2. Have I stayed with the main idea as stated in my topic sentence, or have I included sentences that wander off the topic?
3. Did I read my paragraph carefully, looking for any errors in spelling, punctuation, or usage?

   a. • meeting my boyfriend's or girlfriend's parents
      • a childhood memory
      • getting lost in a strange city
      • how a friend took advantage of my trust
      • my first attempt to play a musical instrument

   b. • changing the oil in an automobile
      • downloading a software program
      • selecting the right dress or suit for a formal affair
      • preparing a favorite dish
      • planning a hiking trip

EXERCISE B Chronological Development

The paragraphs below are developed in chronological order. Read both paragraphs carefully and then follow the directions in either (a) or (b).

■ Sometimes at the flea market, Afghan acquaintances made remarks about Baba's weight loss. At first, they were complimentary. They even asked the secret to his diet. But the queries and compliments stopped when the weight loss didn't. When the pounds kept shedding. And shedding. When his cheeks hollowed. And his temples melted. And his eyes receded in their sockets.

—Khaled Hosseini, *The Kite Runner,* p. 158

■ Although the Donner party was not the first group of European emigrants to cross the Sierra Nevada westward, it is surely the most famous. Brothers Jacob and George Donner and their friend James Reed formed the party of adventurous families in April 1846. Soon the wagon caravan of ninety people left Illinois for California. When they reached the South Pass, the party's leaders made a fatal error: to try a haphazard shortcut through Utah into Nevada. But soon they became lost. When early winter storms began in October, the travelers were still battling the trail. Humans and ani-

Writing Tips **Timely Transitions . . .**

Paragraphs arranged chronologically should include words that signal the order in which events happen. Words like *first, second, next, then, before, after, during, finally,* and *while* help the reader follow the ideas in a paragraph. Be sure to include them in your chronologically arranged writing.

mals grew weak or ill. Then, personal grudges blossomed; one member stabbed another and was banished from the party. Most of the group members were too frail to cross the mountains in the blizzard. Eventually, the party broke into several smaller groups, depending on how fast each was able to travel. Some, stranded at a makeshift campsite near modern day Reno, Nevada, resorted to cannibalism in order to survive. By winter's end, about half of the emigrants had died of illness or starvation. Today, descendents of the Donner party hold an annual summertime reunion in Nebraska, far from the fateful trail that is now named Donner Pass.

a. *Narrate in chronological order an event that occurred in a short time span—perhaps even a matter of seconds. Remember that brief narratives can be enriched with the use of descriptions based on the five senses (sight, sound, touch, taste, and smell). Some possible topics:*

- *a practical joke*
- *receipt of good or bad news*
- *a family gathering*

- *an awards ceremony*
- *a frightening experience*
- *a memorable date*

b. *Presenting your ideas in chronological order, write a paragraph of at least 150 words on an event that unfolded over several days, months, or years. Use an event from world history, current news, or your own life. Some possible topics are*

- *the origins of a war*
- *a natural disaster*
- *an unforgettable vacation*

Computer Activity

Using your computer can make an easy task of correcting errors in paragraphs written in chronological order. Choose a topic from (a) or (b) on page 68 and write a paragraph in which the chronology or sequence is important.

Exchange your paragraph with a writing partner.

Use the SAVE, CUT, and PASTE commands to move any sentences that are out of chronological order in your classmate's paragraph. Ask a classmate to do the same for your paragraph.

CHAPTER 4

MAKING THE SUBJECT AND VERB AGREE

CHAPTER PREVIEW

In this chapter, you will learn about:

- Subject-verb agreement
  In number
  In person
- Writing paragraphs: Coherence in the paragraph
  through spatial order

Mistakes in subject-verb agreement are among the most common writing and speaking errors, and they are particularly irritating to readers. Luckily, mistakes in subject-verb agreement are easy to repair if we keep one simple rule in mind: The subject and the verb in a sentence must agree in number and in person. This chapter will explain what *number* and *person* mean, as well as give you dozens of examples to illustrate the rule.

■ The subject and the verb must agree in number and in person.

Subject-Verb Agreement

Agreement in **number** means that a singular subject takes a singular verb and a plural subject takes a plural verb. The singular form of all verbs except *be* and *have* is formed by adding *-s* or *-es*: *goes, takes, writes, fishes, brings, drives.* The singular forms of *be* and *have* are *is* and *has.* The singular form of the verb is used when the subject is *he, she, it,* a singular indefinite pronoun (such as *anyone* or *somebody*), or a singular noun. Plural verbs do not have these endings, and they are used when the subject is *I, you, we, they,* or a plural noun.

A singular subject with a singular verb:

■ Celia's *father makes* delicious empanadas.

A plural subject with a plural verb:

■ Celia's *parents maintain* their Salvadoran customs.

Notice that adding an *-s* or *-es* to a noun makes the noun **plural** but adding *-s* or *-es* to a verb in the present tense makes the verb *singular*.

Agreement in *person* means that a subject and its verb must both be in the same person (*first*, *second*, or *third*). The following sentences illustrate this rule.

First person (I, we):

■ I *work* (not *works*) during the summer to pay for the courses that I *take* (not *takes*) in the fall.

■ We *stay* (not *stays*) with my brother-in-law in San Jose when we *take* (not *takes*) a trip to northern California.

Second person (you):

■ You *are* (not *be* or *is*) required to pass a stringent physical examination when applying for a job with the fire department.

■ You *receive* (not *receives*) one day of vacation for each month you *work* (not *works*).

Third person (he, she, it, and they):

■ The Colonial Parkway *connects* (not *connect*) the towns of Jamestown, Williamsburg, and Yorktown.

■ Jazz and the blues *are* (not *is*) American contributions to music, and they *appeal* (not *appeals*) to listeners of all ages and races.

EXERCISE 4-1

Circle the verbs that can be used with the following subjects. There may be more than one verb.

Example: She   bring, (walks,) study, (plays)

1. She   (knows,) sing, (skates,) treat
2. The beaver   run, sit, bite, (sleeps)
3. They   (join,) tries, (flee,) (travel)
4. You   says, (leap,) (count,) watches

5. We (shudder,) listens, laughs, (sigh)
6. He go, say, (takes,) (bows)
7. My sons (ski,) climbs, (squint,) (tell)
8. Cher dance, (acts,) ask, sing
9. It remain, (wants,) (proves,) mean
10. The teachers meets, (explain,) (protest,) (shout)
11. The rain soak, (streaks,) (chills,) (inconveniences)
12. I asks, (say,) (remind,) plants
13. You hums, (exercise,) lifts, (yawn)
14. The reader (thinks,) question, (groans,) respond
15. Movies (frighten,) entertains, (educate,) (record)

If the rule given above is so simple, why are there so many errors in subject-verb agreement? Probably because of the writer's or speaker's uncertainty about the identity of the real subject of the sentence and confusion about whether the subject and verb are singular or plural.

Here are three steps to ensure subject-verb agreement. *First*, find the subject of the sentence. (You may want to review Chapter 3.) *Second*, determine whether the subject is singular or plural. *Third*, select the appropriate singular or plural form of the verb to agree with the subject. The suggestions below will help you follow these steps.

1. Remember that a verb must agree with its subject, not with any words that follow the subject but are not part of it. These include terms such as *as well as, including, such as, along with, accompanied by,* and *rather than.* If the subject is singular, use a singular verb; if the subject is plural, use a plural verb.

   ■ A tape-recorded confession by the suspects, as well as statements by eye-witnesses, *has* (not *have*) been read to the jury.

   ■ Stuffed grape leaves, often accompanied by strong Turkish coffee, *are* (not *is*) featured in many Armenian restaurants.

   ■ The ambassadors from the West African countries, accompanied by a translator, *intend* (not *intends*) to meet with the president this afternoon.

   ■ The plan for the new convention center, together with proposals for raising tax revenues, *is* (not *are*) to be debated by the city council members today.

2. Do not confuse the subject with words that rename it in the sentence.

   ■ The referee's only reward *was* (not *were*) taunts and threats.

   ■ Transcripts of the senator's remarks *are* (not *is*) the basis of the article.

   ■ Automobile accidents *are* (not *is*) the chief cause of death on New Year's Eve.

3. Do not be confused by sentences that are not in the usual subject-verb pattern.

   ■ Where *is* (not *are*) the box of paper clips that was on my desk?

   ■ *Are* (not *is*) cumulus clouds a sign of rain?

   ■ Under the sofa *were* (not *was*) the missing cuff links. **But:** Under the sofa *was* (not *were*) the set of missing cuff links.

   ■ There *are* (not *is*) many reasons for her success.

   ■ There *is* (not *are*) one particular reason for her success.

EXERCISE 4-2

Draw a line under the simple or compound subject. Then choose the correct verb and write the appropriate letter in the space provided.

__a__ 1. The <u>subject</u> of the lecture (a. was b. were) Israel, as well as its neighbors.

__a__ 2. <u>Goalies</u>, rather than defensive players, often (a. receive b. receives) most of the publicity.

__b__ 3. In the newspaper (a. was b. were) several <u>stories</u> about the famine in Africa.

__b__ 4. On the curb (a. was b. were) sitting several young <u>men</u>.

__b__ 5. (a. Has b. Have) the <u>results</u> of the election been announced yet?

__a__ 6. A <u>problem</u> facing the area (a. was b. were) killer bees.

__a__ 7. Car <u>alarms</u> (a. are b. is) a source of irritation for many.

__b__ 8. Around the bend (a. was b. were) seen the <u>outlaws</u> on their horses.

__b__ 9. The <u>expectations</u> of the people (a. has b. have) caused disappointment.

__b__ 10. There (a. are b. is) a good <u>reason</u> for the many divorces that occur among young people today.

4. Subjects connected by *and* or by *both . . . and* usually require a plural verb.

   ■ Following the proper diet *and* getting enough exercise *are* important for maintaining one's health.

   ■ *Both* Al Unser *and* his son *have* raced in the Indianapolis 500.

Exception: Use a singular verb when a compound subject refers to the same person or thing.

   ■ Vinegar and oil *is* my favorite salad dressing.

   ■ The best hunter and fisherman in town *is* Joe Patterson.

Exception: Use a singular verb when a compound subject is preceded by *each, every, many a,* or *many an.*

- *Each* owner and tenant *has* been given a copy of the new zoning regulations.
- *Every* cable and pulley *receives* a monthly inspection.

Exception: Use a plural verb when a compound subject is followed by *each.*

- The tenor and the soprano *each wear* different costumes in the final act.

5. If the subject consists of two or more words connected by *or, either . . . or, neither . . . nor,* or *not only . . . but also,* the verb agrees with the subject that is closer to it.

- *Either* the frost *or* the aphids *have* killed my roses. (The plural noun *aphids* is closer to the verb, and therefore the verb is plural.)

This rule presents few problems when both subjects are plural or singular.

- *Neither* the politicians *nor* the voters *show* much interest in this year's election. (Both subjects are plural, and therefore the verb is plural.)
- *Not only* the car *but also* the greenhouse *was* damaged by the tornado. (Both subjects are singular, and therefore the verb is singular.)

Sentences with singular and plural subjects usually sound better with plural verbs. Notice the difference between the following sentences.

- Neither the players nor the coach *doubts* they will win the Stanley Cup. (Although technically correct, this sentence would sound less awkward if the subjects were reversed and a plural verb used.)
- Neither the coach nor the players *doubt* they will win the Stanley Cup. (This version is less awkward and has not sacrificed the meaning of the sentence.)

Remember . . .

1. Adding an *-s* or *-es* to a *noun* makes the noun *plural.* Adding an *-s* or *-es* to a *verb* makes the verb *singular.*
2. If the subject is singular, the verb must be singular; if the subject is plural, the verb must be plural.
3. The verb must agree with its *subject,* not with any other words in the sentence. Do not be confused by sentences not in the usual subject-verb pattern.

EXERCISE 4-3

Write the letter of the correct verb in the space before each sentence.

___a___ 1. Mars (a. is   b. are) Earth's closest neighbor.

___a___ 2. The tallest of Mars's volcanoes (a. stands   b. stand) taller than Mt. Everest.

___b___ 3. Scientists say that dried riverbeds, gullies, salt deposits, and a large quantity of ice (a. means   b. mean) that water was once present on Mars.

___b___ 4. Varying rocks and sediments, found in a huge basin, (a. shows   b. show) that Mars once experienced floods more torrential than any recorded on Earth.

___a___ 5. None of Earth's canyons, including the Grand Canyon, (a. is   b. are) as large or deep as Mars's most notable canyon.

___b___ 6. The sizes of polar caps on Mars (a. changes   b. change) with the seasons.

___b___ 7. The desert sands of Mars (a. appears   b. appear) red because of their iodized iron.

___b___ 8. Mars's days (a. is   b. are) 37 minutes longer than Earth's.

___a___ 9. The thin atmosphere of Mars (a. has   b. have) been determined to contain mostly carbon dioxide.

___b___ 10. Therefore, humans (a. is   b. are) unable to breathe on Mars unless specially equipped.

6. Indefinite pronouns that are singular take singular verbs, and indefinite pronouns that are plural take plural verbs. Some pronouns may be either singular or plural in meaning, depending on the noun or pronoun to which they refer. An **indefinite pronoun** is one that does not refer to a specific thing or person.

When used as subjects or as adjectives modifying subjects, the following indefinite pronouns are always singular and take singular verbs.

Singular Indefinite Pronouns			
another	each one	everything	nothing
anybody	either	much	one
anyone	every	neither	somebody
anything	everybody	nobody	something
each	every one	no one	someone

■ Everybody *is* eligible for the drawing tonight.

■ Much of the work on the engine *has* been done.

■ Something *tells* me that I am wrong.

■ Each dismissed worker *receives* two weeks' pay.

When used as subjects or as adjectives modifying subjects, the following indefinite pronouns are always plural and take plural verbs.

Plural Indefinite Pronouns				
both	several	others	few	many

■ *Few* of the passengers on the tragic cruise of the *Titanic are* living today.

■ *Many* of the parts in an American car *are* manufactured in other countries; *several come* from Japan.

When used as subjects or as adjectives modifying subjects, the following indefinite pronouns may be singular or plural, depending on the nouns or pronouns to which they refer.

Pronouns That May Be Singular or Plural					
all	any	more	most	none	some

■ Unfortunately, *all* of the rumors *were* true.

■ *All* of the snow *has* melted.

■ *Most* of the food *tastes* too spicy for me.

■ *Most* of my freckles *have* disappeared.

Note: *None* is considered a singular pronoun in formal usage. According to informal usage, however, it may be singular or plural, depending on the noun to which it refers. Note the difference in the following sentences.

■ **Formal usage:**   None of the babies *has* learned to speak yet.

■ **Informal usage:**   None of the babies *have* learned to speak yet.

EXERCISE 4-4

In the space before each sentence, write the letter corresponding to the correct verb.

___a___ 1. No motorcycle (a. has   b. have) enjoyed more fame or mystique than the Harley-Davidson.

___b___ 2. The motorcycle company's history of innovations and achievements (a. span   b. spans) nearly a century.

___a___ 3. The main goal of founders William Harley and Arthur Davidson (a. was b. were) "to take the work out of bicycling."

___a___ 4. A total of three motorcycles (a. was   b. were) produced in 1903, Harley-Davidson's first year of manufacturing.

___a___ 5. One of the company's many unique features, the V-Twin engine, (a. was b. were) introduced in 1909.

___a___ 6. Sixty miles per hour (a. was   b. were) the 1909 model's top speed, a pace considered amazing at the time.

___b___ 7. More than a hundred thousand Harleys (a. has   b. have) been used in American military efforts, including World Wars I and II.

___b___ 8. Even border skirmishes with Pancho Villa, the Mexican revolutionary, (a. was   b. were) won on Harley-Davidson motorcycles.

___a___ 9. One of Harley-Davidson's 1921 models (a. was   b. were) the first bike ever to win a race at speeds averaging one hundred miles an hour.

___a___ 10. Over the next few years, a spate of innovations, including the Teardrop gas tank and front brake, (a. was   b. were) boosting Harley-Davidson's appeal even more.

___a___ 11. Harley-Davidson's 1980 Tour Glide, with its five-speed transmission, hidden rear chain, and vibration-isolated engine, (a. was   b. were) nick-named "King of the Highway."

___a___ 12. Today's touring bikes (a. are   b. is) derived from the Tour Glide.

___a___ 13. The Harley Owners Group (a. has   b. have) organized local and even cross-country rides, often to raise money against diseases such as breast cancer and muscular dystrophy.

___b___ 14. Many unofficial riding clubs, consisting of friends or residents from a specific region, (a. has   b. have) blossomed throughout the country.

___a___ 15. Though some people think that the typical Harley-Davidson owner is an outlaw, the majority (a. are   b. is) quiet citizens who may wear business suits and drive family vans when they are not enjoying their motorcycles.

> ## Remember . . .
> Some indefinite pronouns always take *singular* verbs; some always take *plural* verbs; and still other indefinite pronouns may be singular or plural, depending on the nouns or pronouns to which they refer. Look over the lists on pages 75–76 if you are not sure.

7. If the subject is *who, which,* or *that,* be careful: all of these pronouns can be singular or plural, depending on their antecedents. When one of them is the subject, its verb must agree with its antecedent in number.

    ■ Sergei is one of those musicians *who are* able to play music at first sight. (*Who* refers to *musicians;* several musicians are able to play music at first sight, and Sergei is one of them.)

    ■ Hoang is the only one of the musicians *who has* forgotten his music. (*Who* refers to *one.* Among the musicians, only one, Hoang, has forgotten his music.)

    ■ I ordered one of the word processors *that were* on sale. (*That* refers to *word processors* and therefore takes a plural verb.)

    ■ I also bought a desk *that was* reduced 40 percent. (*That* refers to *desk* and therefore takes a singular verb.)

EXERCISE 4-5

In the space before each sentence, write the letter corresponding to the correct verb.

____b____ 1. Before 1940, African Americans (a. was   b. were) not allowed to fly aircraft for the U.S. military.

____b____ 2. Blacks only (a. receives   b. received) assignments in kitchen duty, construction, and other menial categories.

____a____ 3. As World War II progressed, however, there (a. was   b. were) pressure from civil rights leaders and the black press to integrate the pilot ranks.

____b____ 4. The Army Air Corps officials (a. opens   b. opened) Moton Field, a few miles from the Tuskegee School.

____b____ 5. The Tuskegee program and its graduates (a. has   b. have) become famous as the first experiment in training black combat pilots.

____a____ 6. President Roosevelt's wife, Eleanor, visited the program and (a. was   b. were) photographed in the back of an African-American pilot's plane.

____a____ 7. The photograph, which appeared in many magazines, (a. shows   b. show) Mrs. Roosevelt smiling broadly; her enthusiasm helped persuade her husband to order the integration of the armed forces.

___a___   8. The pilots (a. had   b. have) trained for eight to ten months before joining some of World War II's most crucial air battles.

___b___   9. By the end of the war, 992 pilots (a. has   b. had) trained at Tuskegee.

___b___   10. These men (a. is   b. are) credited with flying almost sixteen hundred combat missions, destroying 260 enemy planes, and sinking a German ship.

___b___   11. They never (a. lose   b. lost) a single plane in more than 200 escort flights.

___b___   12. Ninety-five Distinguished Flying Crosses, eight Purple Hearts, and a Distinguished Unit Citation (a. was   b. were) earned by the Tuskegee Airmen.

___a___   13. Thirty-two of the airmen (a. became   b. become) prisoners of war, and about 150 died in combat or training.

___a___   14. Decades later, President Clinton (a. signed   b. signs) a bill to build the Tuskegee Airmen National Historic Site.

___a___   15. The site (a. features   b. feature) the original buildings and tower, photographs, pilot gear, and aircraft.

8. Collective nouns take singular verbs when the group is regarded as a unit, and plural verbs when the individuals of the group are regarded separately. A **collective noun** is a word that is singular in form but refers to a group of people or things. Some common collective nouns are *army, assembly, committee, company, couple, crowd, faculty, family, flock, group, herd, jury, pair, squad,* and *team.*

When the group is thought of as acting as one unit, the verb should be singular.

■ The faculty *is* happy that so many students are volunteering for community service.

■ The committee *has* published the list of finalists.

■ The couple *was* married last week.

If the members of the group are thought of as acting separately, the verb should be plural.

■ The faculty *have* been assigned their offices and parking spaces.

■ The committee *are* unable to agree on the finalists.

■ The couple constantly *argue* over their jobs and their children.

9. Some nouns appear plural in form but are usually singular in meaning and therefore require singular verbs. The following nouns are used this way: *athletics, economics, electronics, measles, mathematics, mumps, news, physics, politics,* and *statistics.*

■ Mathematics *frightens* many students.

■ The news from the doctor *is* encouraging.

■ Politics *is* the art of the possible.

■ Electronics *is* an intriguing field offering relative job security.

When the items they refer to are plural in meaning, these words are plural.

■ The economics of the your plan *sound* reasonable.

■ My measles *are* spreading.

■ The statistics *indicate* that little progress has been made.

10. Subjects plural in form that indicate a quantity or number take a singular verb if the subject is considered a unit, but a plural verb if the individual parts of the subject are regarded separately. Such expressions include *one-half of* (and other fractions), *a part of*, *a majority of*, and *a percentage of*.

If a singular noun follows *of* or is implied, use a singular verb.

■ Two-thirds of her fortune *consists* of stock in computer companies.

■ Part of our intelligence, according to geneticists, *depends* on our genes.

■ A majority of the herd of sick cattle *has* to be destroyed.

If a plural noun follows *of* or is implied, use a plural verb.

■ Three-fourths of the students in the third grade *speak* a foreign language.

■ A large percentage of the film actors *live* in either Los Angeles or New York.

■ A majority of the lawyers *want* to make the law exam more difficult.

11. Words that refer to distance, amounts, and measurements require singular verbs when they represent a total amount. When they refer to a number of individual items, they require plural verbs.

■ More than six hundred dollars *was* spent on my dental work.

■ Many thousands of dollars *were* collected for Thanksgiving meals for the poor.

■ Two miles *is* the maximum range of his new rifle.

■ The last two miles *were* paved last week.

■ Six months *is* a long time to wait for an answer to my complaint.

■ Six months *have* passed since we last heard from you.

12. When *the number* is used as the subject, it requires a singular verb. *A number* is always plural.

■ The number of students who work part-time *is* increasing.

■ A number of students *receive* financial support from government loans.

Remember . . .

Collective nouns take singular verbs if you consider the group as a unit; they take plural verbs if you regard the individuals in the group separately.

Example: *A number* are, but *the number* is.

13. Some words taken from foreign languages, especially Greek and Latin, keep their foreign plural forms, but others have acquired English plural forms. As a result, it is not always obvious when to use the singular or the plural form of the verb. For example, "Data *are* available" is preferred to "Data *is* available." If you are not sure about a word's plural form, consult your dictionary. Here are some of the more common words from Greek and Latin and their plural forms.

Plural Form of Words from Greek and Latin	
singular	**plural**
alumna	alumnae
alumnus	alumni
criterion	criteria
crisis	crises
medium	media
memorandum	memoranda
parenthesis	parentheses
phenomenon	phenomena
stimulus	stimuli
thesis	theses

EXERCISE 4-6

In the space before each sentence, write the letter corresponding to the correct verb.

___b___   1. The couple (a. was   b. were) awarded prizes for their costumes.

___b___   2. Every year the board of education in most school districts (a. recognize b. recognizes) the outstanding high school graduates.

___a___   3. Four miles (a. was   b. were) the distance that he ran every week last year.

__b__ 4. Approximately $1,200 (a. remain   b. remains) in my bank account to pay my expenses next semester.

__b__ 5. About half of the drivers on the road (a. has   b. have) no liability insurance.

__a__ 6. The cab driver decided that fifteen minutes (a. was   b. were) long enough to wait for his fare.

__b__ 7. Statistics (a. are   b. is) a required course for psychology majors.

__b__ 8. Approximately two-thirds of last semester's graduates (a. has   b. have) been unable to find jobs.

__a__ 9. Statistics (a. reveal   b. reveals) that women are still paid less than men for doing the same work.

__b__ 10. The last two miles of the marathon (a. was   b. were) the most difficult.

EDITING EXERCISES

The paragraphs below contain a series of errors in subject-verb agreement. Improve each paragraph by correcting the errors. Revise the sentences when necessary.

A cartoonist from Argentina who go by just one name, Maitena, is winning fans throughout Latin America and the world. Her cartoons were first published in Argentine magazines when she were just seventeen. Legions of women sees her as a friend and source of support. Maitena's cartoons, originally published in Spanish, focuses on solitude, loss, falling in love, fear of failure, raising of children, and striving for success. Her fans enjoy and appreciates the way that Maitena tackle issues with humanity, honesty, and compassion. Many men also reads Maitena's work for a glimpse into the "female mind." Her popular cartoon strip "Women on the Edge" or "Mujeres Alteradas" have been compiled into five volumes in many languages, which includes English, Italian, Greek, Dutch, and French. Her latest work, titled "Dangerous Curves," appear in a number of languages. At one time, Maitena worked as a graphic artist; she illustrated a number of textbooks and even a booklet about a new Argentinean constitution.

Shark! Even the word referring to the terror of the ocean waters are enough to send chills down the average swimmer's back. Stories of shark attacks resulting in injury or death appears frequently in the media. Sharks have been sighted in shallow water near the beach as well as in deep ocean trenches. But sharks, despite their fearsome reputation, are not all man-eaters. In fact, the majority of sharks is not interested in devouring human swimmers. They are also different in their appearance, depending on their species. The hammerhead, for example, is named for its hammer-shaped head which bear an eye and nostril at each end. The thresher is recognized by its extremely long tail. Differences in shark behavior is equally obvious. Some species swim in schools, while others swim alone. Because they are slaughtered in such large numbers each year, the shark population are in danger of becoming an endangered species.

WRITING SENTENCES Subject and Verb Agreement

In this exercise you are asked to write original sentences in which the subject and verb agree in number and person. Refer to the appropriate section of the chapter as needed.

1. Write an original sentence with two subjects connected by *both . . . and* and requiring a plural verb.
2. Write a sentence in which the subject consists of two or more words connected by *either . . . or, neither . . . nor,* or *not only . . . but also.*
3. Write two sentences that use an indefinite pronoun as a singular subject. Circle the pronoun and the verb in each sentence.
4. Write two sentences that use an indefinite pronoun as a plural subject. Circle the pronoun and the verb in each sentence.
5. Select two of the following pronouns and use them as subjects of two sentences: *all, any, more, most, none, some.*
6. Write a sentence in which you use a collective noun as a singular subject. Circle the noun and its verb.
7. Write a sentence in which you use a collective noun as a plural subject. Circle the noun and its verb.

Language Tip

Don't forget that verbs used with third person singular nouns and pronouns (*he, she,* and *it*) end with *-s.*

Examples: The college bookstore *close* at nine o'clock tonight. (nonstandard)
The college bookstore *closes* at nine o'clock tonight. (standard)
Linda usually *wear* a hat to church. (nonstandard)
Linda usually *wears* a hat to church. (standard)
He *study* two hours every night with his chemistry lab partner. (nonstandard)
He *studies* two hours every night with his chemistry lab partner. (standard)

REVIEW TEST 4-A
Making the Subject and Verb Agree

Identify the correct verb by using the appropriate letter.

___a___ 1. Just after the United States (a. was b. were) established, the president's annual salary was $25,000.

___b___ 2. The worst soccer disaster occurred at a game between Peru and Argentina in 1964, when more than 300 fans (a. was b. were) killed in a protest against a referee's ruling.

___a___ 3. *The Young and the Restless* consistently (a. wins b. win) awards for being the best daytime soap opera.

___a___ 4. The real name of Judy Garland, star of *The Wizard of Oz* and many Broadway shows, (a. is b. are) Frances Gumm.

___b___ 5. Indonesia, Pakistan, and India (a. has b. have) the largest Muslim populations.

___a___ 6. The Congressional Medal of Honor, given to men and women in the armed forces, (a. recognizes b. recognize) uncommon valor.

___a___ 7. The last veteran of the American Revolution died in 1869, which (a. means b. mean) that he lived to see the War of 1812, the Spanish-American War, and the Civil War.

___b___ 8. Sirius is the brightest of all the stars that (a. shines b. shine) in our galaxy.

___b___ 9. Not many people (a. knows b. know) that there is a $100,000 bill or that it holds President Woodrow Wilson's portrait; it is used only in transactions between government offices.

___a___ 10. Spanish, the official language of two dozen countries, (a. is b. are) the foreign language most often studied by U.S. college students.

___a___ 11. An outbreak of Spanish influenza, which killed half a million people, (a. ranks b. rank) as our nation's worst single epidemic.

___a___ 12. The St. Lawrence Seaway, between the United States and Canada, (a. hosts b. host) the world's longest ship canal.

___a___ 13. 43,560 square feet (a. makes b. make) an acre.

___a___ 14. 212 degrees (a. is b. are) the boiling point of water.

_a_ 15. The duration of trademark registrations (a. is   b. are) ten years, though they can be renewed at the end of each term.

_a_ 16. Afghanistan, along with Ethiopia, Haiti, Nepal, and Samoa, (a. is b. are) one of the world's poorest countries.

_b_ 17. A number of diverse and beautiful vacation spots, including Antigua, Canada, Scotland, and Australia, (a. is b. are) under the British monarch's rule.

_b_ 18. Snowfields, glaciers, and a large section of the snowy Alps (a. covers b. cover) much of Austria.

_a_ 19. The Atacama Desert, the driest of all Earth's deserts, (a. lies   b. lie) in the north of Chile.

_a_ 20. Olympic gymnastics (a. is   b. are) divided into two categories: artistic and rhythmic.

_b_ 21. The records for all-time scoring and all-time receiving both (a. belongs b. belong) to one man: Jerry Rice.

_a_ 22. The Stanley Cup, recognizing the world's best hockey teams, (a. has b. have) been awarded since 1893.

_a_ 23. The United Nations' General Assembly (a. discusses   b. discuss) world events and makes recommendations, but it does not enforce any.

_b_ 24. The Urdu words "pak," meaning pure, and "stan," meaning nation, (a. forms   b. form) the name Pakistan.

_a_ 25. Norway, located near Sweden and Denmark, (a. extends   b. extend) farther north than any other European country, and about seventy per cent of it is uninhabitable.

REVIEW TEST 4-B
Making the Subject and Verb Agree

Identify the correct verb by using the appropriate letter.

___a___ 1. Ms. Gupta is one of those instructors who (a. are   b. is) easy to speak to outside the classroom.

___a___ 2. One of the ladders (a. has   b. have) a broken rung.

___b___ 3. Justin is the only one of the players who consistently (a. practice   b. practices) every day.

___b___ 4. The chief disadvantage of her new job (a. are   b. is) the long hours.

___b___ 5. The president, not the cabinet officers, (a. believe   b. believes) that the treaty should be signed.

___b___ 6. Emil insisted that it is Jennifer's personality, not her riches, that (a. fascinate   b. fascinates) him.

___a___ 7. Janet Jackson, along with her brothers and sisters, (a. has   b. have) become wealthy because of musical fame.

___a___ 8. There (a. remain   b. remains) two additional problems to solve.

___b___ 9. Here (a. are   b. is) the site of the earliest settlers in the area.

___a___ 10. When practicing golf, there (a. are   b. is) several things to remember.

___b___ 11. A hobby such as chess or checkers (a. require   b. requires) hours of one's time.

___a___ 12. Doctor Cisneros is one of those people who (a. possess   b. possesses) a photographic memory.

___b___ 13. One of the benefits of the new computers (a. are   b. is) their reduced price.

___b___ 14. Anyone who studies bees and wasps soon (a. learn   b. learns) how to handle them without fear.

___b___ 15. Here is a photograph of the only surviving member of the team who (a. live   b. lives) in the United States.

___b___ 16. A number of bomb threats (a. has   b. have) caused panic among the crowd.

___a___ 17. The frequency of his absences from meetings of the city council (a. has   b. have) triggered rumors that he will resign.

___a___ 18. Members of the band (a. travel b. travels) together in a large bus.

___b___ 19. Politics often (a. attract b. attracts) those who merely seek fame.

___a___ 20. Rita is one of those drivers who (a. take b. takes) unnecessary chances.

___b___ 21. Across the river (a. was b. were) three hunting dogs that were stranded.

___a___ 22. Every tile and shingle (a. was b. were) blown loose by the storm.

___a___ 23. On the last page of the manuscript (a. was b. were) the signature of the author.

___a___ 24. Everyone who volunteered (a. has b. have) experience at the job.

___a___ 25. Sales on the Internet (a. are b. is) subject to taxes in some states.

Go to www.ablongman.com/yarber to complete Review Test 3-C.

WRITING PARAGRAPHS

COHERENCE IN THE PARAGRAPH THROUGH SPATIAL ORDER

If the purpose of your paragraph is to tell how something looks, the most effective organization pattern is usually *spatial*. Spatial order presents a visual effect: through your careful attention to detail, word choice, and organization, you can draw a mental picture for your readers. This means that in order for your readers to see your subject, you have to select details that make the subject clear and you have to present those details in a pattern that your reader can follow. The arrangement often used in this kind of paragraph follows the sequence in which you would look at a scene or an object: from top to bottom, side to side, front to back, or near to far.

The following paragraph, written by a student, describes a museum containing a replica of a street scene from the early 1930s. Notice that she begins her paragraph with a topic sentence that presents the main idea. Notice, too, that she supplies details in a spatial order to support that topic sentence.

■ As you open the doors of the museum, you will think that you have stumbled onto the main street of a small Western town as it was in the early 1930s. Hitched to a wagon immediately in front of you are four huge black mules, standing fetlock-deep in gray mud. The wagon is piled high with suitcases, children's toys, and mattresses. Through the open doors of a drugstore on your left come the big-band sounds of a Nickelodeon and the chatter of young people clustered around the soda fountain. On the right a couple stands hand in hand gazing at a poster featuring a movie starring Myrna Loy and Gary Cooper. In the muddy street a Model A Ford clugs patiently, unable to move, its wheels stuck in the ooze. Suddenly the sky darkens, and lightning cracks the gathering clouds. Everyone stops and looks up, expecting another downpour that will turn the street into a river of mud.

Spatial order presents a *visual effect*. Notice how the use of specific details helps to make clear the image of the newborn baby.

■ Babies right after birth are not beautiful. The trip through the birth canal compresses the unfused bones of the skull, and many babies' heads are temporarily cone-shaped. The pressure also pastes back their ears. Newborns are covered with vernix, a white protective skin coating that looks like cheese, and are splotched with their mothers' blood. Some have virtually no hair on their heads, and some are born with a coat of fine hair (lanugo) all over their bodies. Even after they're cleaned up, most have mottled red skin from their arduous passage to birth. The struggle to be born is so exhausting that most newborn babies fall asleep within a couple of hours and stay fast asleep for many hours afterward.

After you've revised your paragraph the best you can, let a friend or classmate read it to make sure it conveys exactly the points you intend. Ask him or her to consider the following questions:

- What is the point of the paragraph?
- Do you accept the writer's argument or point of view? Why or why not?
- Could any ideas be expanded? Omitted?
- Are some sentences unclear?
- Are there any grammatical or spelling errors?
- What is the paragraph's strongest quality?
- Does the paragraph stick to its topic?
- Does the author avoid slang, vagueness, repetition, and careless word choice?

EXERCISE A Spatial Order

Arranging your ideas in spatial order, write a paragraph of at least one hundred words on one of the following topics. Underline your topic sentence.

- *my roommate's closet*
- *my grandparent*
- *the ugliest building in town*
- *my city from the air*
- *a favorite restaurant*
- *a favorite painting*

After you write your first draft, answer the following questions.

1. Does my paragraph concentrate on describing one thing, scene, person, or object, or does it try to describe too much?
2. Have I given my reader specific details so that he or she can see what I am describing, or is my paragraph just a series of general and vague statements?
3. Does my paragraph have a plan, or does it jump around, confusing my reader?
4. Does my paragraph reflect the care I put into it, or is it filled with careless spelling mistakes or other errors?

These paragraphs, the first written by a well-known American writer of the nineteenth century, and the second written by a modern American novelist, are both based on spatial order. Read each paragraph carefully and then write a response.

■ The most foreign and picturesque structures on the Cape, to an inlander, not excepting the salt-works, are the wind-mills,—gray-looking octagonal towers, with long timbers slanting to the ground in the rear, and there resting on a cart-wheel, by which their fans are turned round to face the wind. These appeared also to serve in some measure for props against its force. A great circular rut was worn around the building by the wheel. The neighbors who assemble to turn the mill to the wind are likely to know which way it blows, without a weathercock. They looked loose and slightly locomotive, like huge wounded birds, trailing a wing or a leg, and reminded one of pictures of the Netherlands. Being on elevated ground, and high in themselves, they serve as landmarks,—for there are no tall trees, or other objects commonly, which can be seen at a distance in the horizon; though the outline of the land itself is so firm and distinct that an insignificant cone, or even precipice of sand, is visible at a great distance from over the sea. Sailors making the land commonly steer either by the wind-mills or the meeting-houses.

—Henry David Thoreau, *Cape Cod*, p. 39

■ Sighing, she raised her eyes and gazed out at Paris's dazzling landscape. On her left, across the Seine, the illuminated Eiffel Tower. Straight ahead, the Arc de Triomphe. And to the right, high atop the sloping rise of Montmartre, the graceful arabesque dome of Sacre-Coeur, its polished stone glowing white like a resplendent sanctuary. Here at the westernmost tip of the Denon Wing, the north-south thoroughfare of Place du Carrousel ran almost flush with the building with only a narrow sidewalk separating it from the Louvre's outer wall. Far below, the usual caravan of the city's nighttime delivery trucks sat idling . . . .

—Dan Brown, *The Da Vinci Code*, p. 78

EXERCISE B Spatial Order

Presenting your ideas in spatial order, write a paragraph of at least 150 words on one of the following:

- *a campus hangout*
- *your best friend's appearance*
- *a popular vacation spot*
- *your neighborhood*

- *your favorite room in your house*
- *a cherished possession*
- *a favorite article of clothing*
- *an offbeat place*

Writing Tips Now Hear This!

One of the best ways to revise your paragraph is to hear it. Seeing your writing is usually not enough. As you read it silently, you unconsciously fill in missing punctuation marks, letters, and even words. You might even miss rough sentences or clumsy expressions. When you read it aloud, however, you use different cognitive and critical skills that will expose the errors that might escape a silent reading.

Computer Activity

Follow the directions for writing a paragraph in Exercise A or B. Use SAVE, COPY, and PASTE commands to make a second copy.

Exchange your file with a classmate.

Italicize words or phrases that refer to spatial order such as *to the left* (or *right*), *behind, in front of, to one side, under, beyond,* or *next to.*

Ask your classmate to do the same for your paragraph.

CHAPTER 5

COMMON ERRORS
INVOLVING VERBS

CHAPTER PREVIEW

In this chapter, you will learn about:

- Regular and irregular verbs: The four principal parts
- Using the correct tense
- Four irregular verbs: *Lie, lay, sit,* and *set*
- Writing paragraphs: Coherence in the paragraph through order of importance

One reason why so many mistakes are made in verb usage is that most sentences contain more than one verb, and consequently there are more chances to go wrong. Furthermore, the verbs most often used in the English language are irregular, which means that they change in a variety of ways. Therefore, they must be memorized. To make matters even worse, verbs change their forms and appearance more often than any other part of speech. As a result, they force us to pick our way through them carefully and deliberately.

Is the case hopeless, then? Is it impossible to learn to use verbs correctly and confidently? Not at all; despite the difficulties mentioned above, problems with verbs fall into a few manageable categories. A common problem, for instance, is not knowing the correct form of the verb needed to express when a particular action is taking place. Another difficulty is not knowing the correct form of an irregular verb. This chapter will present solutions to these and other common problems that many writers and speakers have in using verbs.

Before we begin, however, look at the following sentences to see whether you have been using the correct verb form. Each sentence contains a verb that is often used incorrectly. The incorrect verb is in parentheses.

Place near the body.

- Lila was thrilled that we *came* (not *come*) to see her at the hospital.

- Although we *saw* (not *seen*) Paris Hilton at the restaurant, we were too shy to ask for an autograph.

- I slept in and then learned that my friends had *gone* (not *went*) for coffee without me.

- Brandon *sneaked* (not *snuck*) out of the play before intermission.

- Senator Berger's popularity rating *sank* (not *sunk*) when she broke her promise not to raise taxes.

If you discovered that you have been using any of these verbs incorrectly, this chapter will give you some practical tips for their correct use. We will begin by examining the principal parts of regular and irregular verbs and will move next to the most common problems connected with the use of verbs, including shifts in tense and troublesome pairs like *lie* and *lay* and *sit* and *set*.

All verbs have four principal parts (or forms): the present, the past, the past participle, and the present participle. By learning these four parts, you can build all of the verb tenses. By the way, the word *tense* comes from a Latin word meaning "time." When we talk about the **tense** of a verb, therefore, we mean the *time* expressed by the verb; for example, the *present* tense (or time), the *past* tense, and the *future* tense.

Regular Verbs

Regular verbs form the **past** and **past participle** by adding *-ed* or *-d* to their present forms (*watch*, *watched*, and *watched*). The past participle is the form used with the helping verbs *have*, *has*, or *had* or with a form of *be* (*have been watched* and *were watched*). The **present participle** is formed by adding *-ing* to the **present** form, and it is used with a form of *to be* to form the other tenses (*am studying*, *was studying*, *have been studying*, and so on).

Here are the four principal parts of some common regular verbs.

Four Principal Parts of Common Regular Verbs			
Present	**Past**	**Past Participle**	**Present Participle**
shop	shopped	shopped	shopping
dance	danced	danced	dancing
wash	washed	washed	washing
love	loved	loved	loving
help	helped	helped	helping

Notice that the past (*shopped, danced, washed,* and so on) and the past participle are identical and are formed by adding *-ed* or *-d* to the present. Remember, too, that the past participle is used with helping verbs to form past tenses: *I have talked, I had talked,* and *she has talked; I was helped, we were helped,* and *they had been helped;* and so on.

Irregular Verbs

Irregular verbs are irregular in the way their past and past participle forms are made. Instead of adding *-ed* or *-d* for their past and past participle forms, irregular verbs change in ways that cannot be predicted. This means that you will have to memorize their past and past participle forms. Fortunately, irregular verbs form their present participles in the same way as regular verbs: by adding *-ing* to the present form.

To understand why it is difficult to make any generalization about irregular verbs, let us examine the verbs *sing* and *bring*. From our familiarity with the English language, we know that *sing* is the present ("I *sing* in church every Sunday"), *sang* is the past ("I *sang* last Sunday"), and *sung* is the past participle ("I have *sung* every Sunday this month"). Imagine the confusion of someone learning English who, having mastered *sing,* applies the same changes by analogy to the verb *bring*. He or she logically concludes that the past of *bring* is *brang* ("I *brang* my lunch yesterday") and that the past participle is *brung* ("I have *brung* my lunch"). To native speakers of English these forms are humorous; to others who have not mastered the inconsistencies of our verbs, there is nothing within the verb *bring* to suggest that the past and past participle are *brought* ("I *brought* my lunch yesterday" and "I *have brought* my lunch").

The English language contains over two hundred irregular verbs, and irregular verbs are the verbs most often used. Consult your dictionary if you are not sure about the past and past participle forms of irregular verbs. Don't trust your ear; what "sounds right" may only be the result of having repeatedly heard, said, and written the incorrect form. The "piano" you have been playing all these years may be out of tune.

On pages 96–97 is a list of some common irregular verbs, as well as a few regular verbs that often present problems. Practice their correct forms by putting *I* in front of the present and past forms, *I have* in front of the past participle form, and *I am* in front of the present participle form (*I begin, I began, I have begun,* and *I am beginning*). Practice saying them correctly until they sound correct and natural.

Suggestions for Using Irregular Verbs

1. Resist the temptation to add *-ed* to an irregular verb: do not write or say "catch*ed*," "burst*ed*," "know*ed*," and so on.
2. Use *have, has,* and *had* with the past participle (the forms in the third column of the chart that begins on page 96) to form past tenses.

   ■ She *has done* several music videos for her newest CD.

   ■ We *had begun* to eat dessert before the guest of honor finally arrived.

   ■ I *have flown* on an airplane and *ridden* on a train.

Common Irregular Verbs and Problem Regular Verbs

Present	Past	Past Participle	Present Participle
[I] arise	[I] arose	[I have] arisen	[I am] arising
awake	awoke or awaked	awaked, awoken	awaking
bear (carry)	bore	borne	bearing
begin	began	begun	beginning
blow	blew	blown	blowing
break	broke	broken	breaking
bring	brought	brought	bringing
burst	burst	burst	bursting
catch	caught	caught	catching
choose	chose	chosen	choosing
come	came	come	coming
dig	dug	dug	digging
dive	dived or dove	dived	diving
do	did	done	doing
drag	dragged	dragged	dragging
draw	drew	drawn	drawing
drink	drank	drunk	drinking
drive	drove	driven	driving
drown	drowned	drowned	drowning
eat	ate	eaten	eating
fly	flew	flown	flying
freeze	froze	frozen	freezing
give	gave	given	giving
go	went	gone	going
grow	grew	grown	growing
hang	hung	hung	hanging
hang (execute)	hanged	hanged	hanging
hide	hid	hidden	hiding
know	knew	known	knowing

(Continued on next page)

Common Irregular Verbs and Problem Regular Verbs			
Present	**Past**	**Past Participle**	**Present Participle**
[I] lay	[I] laid	[I have] laid	[I am] laying
lead	led	led	leading
leave	left	left	leaving
lie	lay	lain	lying
light	lighted or lit	lighted or lit	lighting
ride	rode	ridden	riding
ring	rang	rung	ringing
rise	rose	risen	rising
run	ran	run	running
see	saw	seen	seeing
set	set	set	setting
shake	shook	shaken	shaking
shine (glow)	shone	shone	shining
shine (polish)	shined	shined	shining
shrink	shrank, shrunk	shrunk or shrunken	shrinking
sing	sang	sung	singing
sink	sank	sunk	sinking
sit	sat	sat	sitting
sleep	slept	slept	sleeping
sneak	sneaked	sneaked	sneaking
speed	sped	sped	speeding
spring	sprang	sprung	springing
strike	struck	struck	striking
swim	swam	swum	swimming
swing	swung	swung	swinging
take	took	taken	taking
tear	tore	torn	tearing
throw	threw	thrown	throwing
wake	woke or waked	waked or woken	waking
wear	wore	worn	wearing
write	wrote	written	writing

Tips **on Forming the Past Tense, Past Participle, and Present Participle Forms**

1.   To form the past and past participle forms of a regular verb, add -ed or -d to the present form. To form the present participle, add -ing to the present form.
2.   Irregular verbs change their spelling and therefore have to be memorized. Study the list on pages 95–97 for the correct past and past participle forms of irregular verbs.

---

3.   Use *am, are, is, was, were, has been,* and other forms of *be* with the past participle forms to form all verbs in the passive voice.

   ■ Vanya *was given* a varsity letter for managing the softball team.

   ■ The dogs *were caught* before they could attack anyone.

   ■ The sketch *had been drawn* especially for my father and *was hung* over his fireplace.

4.   Use forms of *be* before the present participle (the forms in the fourth column of the chart that begins on page 96) to form tenses where the action continues to happen.

   ■ Chemistry *is beginning* to make more sense to me.

   ■ They *have been winning* more of their matches this season.

   ■ The soda cans *were bursting* from being put in the freezer by accident.

EXERCISE 5-1

Fill in the blank in each sentence with the past tense form of the verb in parentheses.

1.   A new theory about the dinosaurs' extinction _____**arose**_____ (arise) recently.

2.   Some scientists now believe that a giant comet _____**struck**_____ (strike) the earth some 65 million years ago.

3.   The comet _____**dived/dove**_____ (dive) twenty-five miles deep into the earth's crust.

4.   The comet _____**dug**_____ (dig) a giant crater when it landed at the tip of the Yucatan Peninsula.

5.   A giant fireball soon _____**burst**_____ (burst) into the air.

6. The fireball _____ **bore** _____ (bear) small particles which blocked the sun's light.

7. Eventually, the earth _____ **grew** _____ (grow) too dark and cold for animals or plants to survive.

8. As a result, dinosaurs and some other animal species _____ **became** _____ (become) extinct.

9. Scientists _____ **gave** _____ (give) the press some interesting evidence for their theory.

10. However, the debate over this theory, which _____ **began** _____ (begin) in the early 1980s, still continues today.

EXERCISE 5-2

Fill in the blank in each sentence with the past participle form of the verb in parentheses.

1. Did you know that the last active submarine of World War II was _____ **sunk** _____ (sink) off the Long Island coast?

2. In April of 1945, the German U-boat had _____ **reached** _____ (reach) its attack post a few miles from Rhode Island and Long Island.

3. The sub, a U-853 body type, was _____ **nicknamed** _____ (nickname) Der Seiltaenzer, or The Tightrope Walker, because of her stealth and mobility.

4. Meanwhile, an American freighter had _____ **begun** _____ (begin) a routine delivery of coal from Virginia to Massachusetts.

5. With one blast from the U-boat, the freighter had _____ **capsized** _____ (capsize) and become the last U.S. ship sunk by a German foe.

6. For the next hour, three U.S. Navy and Coast Guard ships were _____ **engaged** _____ (engage) in a cat-and-mouse game with the German sub.

7. After an assault with depth charges, some debris, including a pillow and the German captain's hat, was _____ **observed** _____ (observe) on the water, but it was a trick by the Germans.

8. Soon, a pair of blimps was _____ **flown** _____ (fly) to the area to look for oil slicks or air bubbles that would indicate the sub's location and condition.

9. The Navy's sonar had _____ **detected** _____ (detect) the U-boat's eastward movement, and a full assault had begun.

10. Ten hours later, the U-boat was _____ **destroyed** _____ (destroy) and its sixty crew members drowned.

11. The sad irony of the story is that, one day before the U-boat sank the freighter, the German leader who had replaced Adolf Hitler had _____ordered_____ (order) all U-boats to "cease hostilities" and return home immediately.

12. No one knows what might have _____kept_____ (keep) the Tightrope Walker from obeying the order.

13. Some say that weather and distance could have _____blocked_____ (block) the U-boat from receiving the crucial message on its radios.

14. In the decades since its sinking, the U-boat, which sits upright in just 130 feet of water, has _____become_____ (become) a favorite destination for experienced divers.

15. The sub's hull has _____retained_____ (retain) numerous artifacts, including china, bottles, and gold rings.

Using the Correct Tense

You have noticed in your study of verbs that they can indicate different tenses or times by the ending -ed or -d, by a change in spelling, and by the helping verbs that go with them. The forms of the verb change according to the time expressed—when the action or state of being occurs. Each tense has a specific purpose, and careful speakers and writers select the appropriate tense according to that purpose.

Here is a list of the six common tenses in English and their uses.

The Six Common Tenses

Present:	I jog, or I am jogging.
Past:	I jogged, or I was jogging.
Future:	I will* jog, or I will be jogging.
Present Perfect:	I have jogged, or I have been jogging.
Past Perfect:	I had jogged, or I had been jogging.
Future Perfect:	I will* have jogged, or I will have been jogging.

*Shall is often substituted for will in the future and future perfect tenses.

The accompanying list shows the six common tenses of take. Showing all of the tenses of a verb in this way is called **conjugating a verb.**

Conjugation of *Take*

Present Tense

Singular	Plural
I take	we take
you take	you take
he, she, or it takes	they take

Present Perfect Tense

Singular	Plural
I have taken	we have taken
you have taken	you have taken
he, she, or it has taken	they have taken

Past Tense

Singular	Plural
I took	we took
you took	you took
he, she, or it took	they took

Past Perfect Tense

Singular	Plural
I had taken	we had taken
you had taken	you had taken
he, she, or it had taken	they had taken

Future Tense

Singular	Plural
I will (shall) take	we will (shall) take
you will take	you will take
he, she, or it will take	they will take

Future Perfect Tense

Singular	Plural
I will (shall) have taken	we will (shall) have taken
you will have taken	you will have taken
he, she, or it will have taken	they will have taken

Each of the six tenses has an additional form called the **progressive form,** which expresses action that continues to happen. The progressive form is not a separate tense but an additional form of each of the six tenses in the conjugation. It consists of a form of the verb *be* plus the present participle of the verb.

Progressive Forms

Present Progressive:	am, are, is taking
Past Progressive:	was, were taking
Future Progressive:	will (shall) be taking
Present Perfect Progressive:	has, have been taking
Past Perfect Progressive:	had been taking
Future Perfect Progressive:	will (shall) have been taking

The *present tense* is used in the following situations:

To express a condition or an action that exists or is going on now.

- Her car *is* fast.
- But she *is driving* under the speed limit.

To express an action that is habitual or is always true.

- He *competes* in calf-roping events every summer.
- He always *beats* his opponents.
- There *is* no game like baseball.
- Cincinnati *is* the home of the Reds baseball team.

The *past tense* expresses an action or a condition completed in the past.

- The Coalition forces *attacked* the terrorists in their caves.
- Sheldon *visited* his mother last night.
- The Security Council charged that several nations *were participating* in illegal arms shipments.

The *future tense* expresses an action that will take place in the future.

- Javier *will race* his bicycle in the next Olympics.
- Uncle Jim *will be* fifty years old next August.
- Fourteen Americans *will be participating* in the freestyle swimming competition next Wednesday.

The *present perfect tense* is used for an action that began in the past and continues into the present.

- *I have gone* to many freshwater fishing tournaments. (And I still go.)
- *I have lived* in Atlanta since 1997. (And I still live in Atlanta.)
- Our neighbor's dog *has barked* for two days now. (And he's still barking.)
- Crystal *has been taking* Spanish lessons in preparation for her trip to Madrid. (And she is still taking lessons.)

The *present perfect tense* can also be used for an action that started in the past and has been completed at some indefinite time.

- The fire in the warehouse *has been extinguished.*
- My grandfather *has been* to a doctor only once in his lifetime.

■ Chen-Li *has taken* French lessons in preparation for his trip to Paris. (He has finished taking lessons.)

The *past perfect tense* is used for an action that began and ended in the past. Additionally, it conveys that the action was completed before something else happened.

■ I *had lived* in Mobile before I moved to Atlanta. (**Not:** I *lived* in Mobile before I moved to Atlanta.)

■ Everyone knew that Clark's father *had been* a member of President Clinton's cabinet. (**Not:** Everyone knew that Clark's father *was* a member of President Clinton's cabinet.)

■ Monica asked us if we *had watched* the Rose Bowl Parade on television. (**Not:** Monica asked us if we *watched* the Rose Bowl Parade on television.)

■ Renee *had been rehearsing* her part as an understudy for only three days when she was suddenly asked to replace the star of the play. (**Not:** Renee *rehearsed* her part as an understudy for only three days when she was suddenly asked to replace the star of the play.)

The *future perfect tense* is used for an action that will end in the future before a particular time.

■ Her parents *will have been married* forty years next Thanksgiving.

■ I *will have used up* all of my vacation time by the time your visit ends next week.

■ Fatima *will have been dieting* for six months this Thursday.

A Few Suggestions for Using the Correct Tense

1. Do not use the past tense of a verb when it should be in the present tense.

■ Naomi took a course in anthropology last year. She said that it was an interesting subject that studied cultures and societies throughout the world. (Incorrect. *Was* and *studied* imply that anthropology no longer is interesting and no longer studies other societies and cultures. The correct verbs are *is* and *studies.*)

Reminders **About Tenses**

1. Use the past tense only if the action referred to took place at a specific time in the past.
2. Use the past perfect tense (*had* plus the past participle) only when you want to place a completed action before another action in the past.

2. Use the present infinitive (*to write, to invent, to leap,* and so on) unless the action referred to was completed before the time expressed in the governing verb.

    ■ Annika and Sanjay planned *to stay* (not *to have stayed*) awake for *Saturday Night Live.*

    ■ I am fortunate *to have had* (not *to have*) my life jacket during the stormy boat trip.

3. When a narrative in the past tense is interrupted by a reference to a preceding event, use the past perfect tense.

    ■ No one could believe that I *had known* him before he became a movie star.

    ■ The film's ending made no sense to me because I *had missed* the beginning.

EXERCISE 5-3

In the space before each sentence, identify the tense of the italicized verb by writing past, present, future, present perfect, past perfect, or future perfect.

present perfect	1.	Scientists *have begun* to study one of nature's strangest creations, the corpse flower.
past	2.	This flower *earned* its name from the overwhelmingly putrid odor that it occasionally emits.
present	3.	The corpse flower *stands* as tall as a man, but some specimens have grown to nine feet.
future	4.	Every two to four years, a huge bucket-shaped bloom *will sprout* from the giant stalk.
future perfect	5.	Within a day or two of blooming, the flower *will have died.*
past	6.	A corpse flower at a California university, nicknamed Ted, *bloomed* for a record four days.
past perfect	7.	In the past, scientists *had seen* corpse flowers only in Indonesia.
present	8.	Now, however, specimens *grow* around the world.
future	9.	Scientists have just begun to analyze the flower's chemical make-up, but they suspect that tests *will show* the presence of sulphur (which makes rotten eggs smell) and two chemicals that cause dead flesh to smell.
future perfect	10.	Believe it or not, thousands of tourists *will have visited* these flowers during their next brief—but overpowering—bloom, including a sturdy plant in a public garden next to the U.S. Capitol.

EXERCISE 5-4

In the space before each sentence, write the verb shown in parentheses in the tense indicated.

are 1. There (*be*—present) some simple steps you can take to prepare your mind and body for an exam.

have slept 2. First, you should (*sleep*—present perfect) at least eight hours the night before the test.

ate 3. The best students always (*eat*—past) a healthy breakfast before taking their exams.

have drunk 4. I (*drink*—present perfect) orange juice for an energy boost before tests this semester.

grew 5. Some students said their concentration (*grow*—past) stronger after they had drunk a cup of coffee.

have sat 6. Once you (*sit*—present perfect) down at your desk, relax your body and mind.

Draw 7. (*Draw*—present) in a deep breath, hold it for a few seconds, and then release it.

left 8. My brother reported that his tension (*leave*—past) his body when he tried this breathing technique.

lay 9. Make sure you (*lay*—present) your pencils, calculators, and other needed supplies on the desk ahead of time.

has given 10. Most important, read all of the instructions that the instructor (*give*—present perfect) you before the exam begins.

Shifts in Tense

Having learned the use of the six common tenses, you should use them consistently, avoiding unnecessary shifts from one tense to another. If, for example, you begin a paragraph using the past tense to describe events in the past, do not suddenly leap to the present tense to describe those same events. Similarly, don't abruptly shift to the past tense if you are narrating an incident in the present tense. This does not mean that you can't use more than one tense in a piece of writing. It does mean, however, that you must use the same tense when referring to the same period of time.

In the paragraph below, the writer uses verbs in the past tense to describe events that occurred in the past and then shifts correctly to the present tense to describe events occurring in the present.

■ I learned to respect fine craftsmen when I was a young girl helping my father build the house that I lived in until I married. My father had an exact, precise air about him that could make sloppy people like me somewhat nervous. When he laid out the dimensions of the house or the opening of a door he did it with an exactness and precision that would not allow for the careless kind of measurements that I would settle for. When he measured a board and told me to cut it, I knew that it would have to be cut in an unwavering line and that it would fit exactly in the place assigned to it. Doors that he installed still fit tightly, drawers slide snugly, and joints in cabinets and mortices can scarcely be detected. Today, when I measure a piece of new screenwire to replace the old or a fence to put around the rosebushes, I can still hear the efficient clicking of his 6-foot rule as he checks my calculations.

This passage is correct in its use of tenses. The events of the past are recalled by the author and narrated in the past tense (*I learned, my father had, he laid out,* and so on). When she shifts to the present, she changes her tense accordingly (*when I measure, I can still hear,* and so on). The paragraph below, on the other hand, is confusing because of its inconsistent use of tenses, shifting from the past to the present tense to refer to the same time.

■ Flamenco is the traditional song and dance of the Andalucian people in southern Spain. Developed over several centuries, flamenco has roots in Romani, Moorish, Indian, and other types of music. Some songs were intense and profoundly sad. Others are moderately serious, and still other songs will be light tunes of joy and romance. The men's dance features speedy toe- and heel-clicking steps. The women's dance featured graceful hand and body movements. Guitarists usually accompany the dancers. Onlookers participated, too, by clapping their hands or snapping their fingers in rhythm with the dancers.

You probably noticed that the first and second sentences are in the present tense (*flamenco is* and *flamenco has roots*), signaling the reader that the paragraph will be related in the present tense. Therefore, we are not prepared for the shift to the past tense in the third sentence (*some songs were*), the return to the present in the fourth sentence (*others are*), the subsequent jump to the future tense (*other songs will be*), and so on. The jumble of tenses jerks the reader from present to past to present to future without warning.

To avoid such confusion, ensure that the tense forms you are using correspond to the time in which the action takes place.

EXERCISE 5-5

Some of the following sentences contain confusing tense shifts. Revise the sentences so that the tenses are consistent. If a sentence is correct, mark "C" in front of it.
[Student responses will vary.]

1. Most people know that cigarettes were bad for their health, but many don't know exactly how cigarettes affect their bodies.
2. First, the nicotine speeds up the heartbeat and the blood pressure rose.
3. The tar found in cigarettes is even more harmful because it bore ingredients that cause cancer.

> ## Tips **for Using *Lie* and *Lay* and *Sit* and *Set***
>
> 1. *To lie* means "to be at rest"; you don't "lie" anything down. The forms are *lie, lay, lain,* and *lying.*
> 2. *To lay* means "to place or put somewhere"; an object must always follow this verb. The forms are *lay, laid, laid,* and *laying.*
> 3. *To sit* means "to occupy a seat"; you don't "sit" anything down. The forms are *sit, sat, sat,* and *sitting.*
> 4. *To set* means "to put in place," and except for idioms like "The hen sets" and "The sun sets," it is always followed by an object. The forms do not change in the present, the past, or the past participle: *set, set,* and *set.* The present participle is *setting.*

To set resembles *to lay* in meaning. *To set* means "to put in place." Like *to lay,* it is a transitive verb and is followed by another word (a direct object) to complete its meaning.[1] Its principal parts remain the same in all forms: *set* (the present tense,) *set* (the past tense), *set* (the past participle), and *setting* (the present participle). Study the following sentences carefully.

Forms of *Set*	
Present:	Jin-Sun always *sets* the compact disc player for "continuous play."
Past:	Last night I *set* the volume control too high and almost blew the speakers.
Past participle:	I have *set* your 50 Cent disc back on the shelf.
Present participle:	*Setting* his old records near the heater was careless.
	As we watched the *setting* sun on the western horizon, we could hear the distant sounds of campers unpacking their gear.

As in the case of *lie* and *lay,* the most effective way of mastering *sit* and *set* is to memorize their forms: *sit, sat, sat,* and *sitting; set, set, set,* and *setting.*

---

[1]In a few idioms such as "The hen *sets* on her nest" and "The sun is *setting,*" set does not require a direct object. In most other cases, however, it is followed by a direct object.

EXERCISE 5-6

Use the correct form of "lie" and "lay" in the following sentences.

1. Yesterday afternoon I _____lay_____ at the beach.
2. It is my favorite stretch of sand, and I have _____lain_____ there every summer since childhood.
3. Because the sky was overcast, not many people were _____lying_____ on the beach.
4. My radio _____lay_____ by my head and played my favorite tunes.
5. I had _____laid_____ my pink volleyball in the sand beside me.
6. After I _____lay_____ in the sun for a few minutes, I fell asleep.
7. When I woke up, the ball was not where I had _____laid_____ it.
8. This was no time to _____lie_____ around in the sand; I had to find it.
9. After I _____laid_____ the radio and towel next to my ice cooler, I began searching for the ball.
10. I asked everyone who had _____lain_____ on the beach if they had seen the ball.
11. After looking everywhere on the beach, I _____lay_____ down by the pier and became despondent.
12. It was all my fault because I had _____laid_____ the ball near me, but I had not kept my eye on it.
13. Soon a big but friendly dog _____lay_____ down next to me.
14. I caught a glimpse of something pink _____lying_____ in the sand by his head.
15. There _____lay_____ my prized volleyball—with a few teeth marks but still good as new.

EXERCISE 5-7

Use the correct form of "sit" and "set" in the following sentences.

1. Everything was finally _____set_____ for our Super Bowl party.
2. Trenton and I had _____sat_____ in the kitchen for hours last night, deciding which refreshments to serve.
3. We worried whether there would be room for all of our friends to _____sit_____ on the couch in front of the television set.

4. We _____ **set** _____ out some extra folding chairs to make certain that everyone had a seat.

5. "Some of them will _____ **sit** _____ on the floor," Trenton said.

6. I had already _____ **set** _____ a tray of cups and plates on the coffee table.

7. I asked him to _____ **set** _____ our new vase in the other room so that it would not be broken.

8. Everyone _____ **sat** _____ down as soon as they arrived.

9. The children were _____ **sitting** _____ in front so that they could see the television.

10. Trenton _____ **sat** _____ down and soon the ball game began.

11. We didn't notice that our cat had _____ **sat** _____ down by my cousin Rita.

12. Rita began sneezing violently and overturned a bowl of popcorn that _____ **sat** _____ nearby.

13. I _____ **set** _____ a box of tissues near her, and she recovered from her attack.

14. The cat, meanwhile, was now _____ **sitting** _____ on the television and had somehow become entangled in the antenna.

15. Although several people had _____ **sat** _____ by the television set trying to repair the antenna, the picture disappeared, and so did our party.

EDITING EXERCISES

The paragraph below describes the custom of sending flowers to express various feelings or emotions. The subsequent paragraph describes how to avoid a dog attack. As you read each paragraph, you will notice several errors in verb usage. Improve the paragraphs by correcting the errors and revising the sentences when necessary.

The use of sending flowers to express deep feelings begun in early Roman times. One of the most famous were the white lily, which frequently laid in the hands of the Virgin Mary in numerous paintings; it symbolizes purity and chastity. Many other early artists use flowers not only for their beauty but for the subtle meanings they add. The Elizabethans and Victorians had gave meanings to nearly every flower that growed in Britain. By the end of the nineteenth century, however, the language of flowers was largely forgot. Today, most people do not know the meanings that had been associated with many common flowers. Although nearly everyone knows that a red rose means true love, for example, many people do not know that other flowers can convey similar feelings. The red tulip and little blue forget-me-not are declarations of love, and the sturdy ivy, whether growing on a wall or in a porcelain vase setting on a table, promises fidelity. Honeysuckle, which can be growed in most parts of this country, shows love for friends and relatives. Although many people send a bouquet to someone in mourning, few choose flowers specifically for meaning, such as marigolds for grief or red poppies for consolation. After you have chose a flower for its specific meaning, you should attach a note that explains that meaning to its recipient.

Each year, thousands of people is injured or killed in dog attacks. With a few simple tips, you can avoid this kind of trouble. When you seen a leashed dog approaching, keep a safe distance from it. Don't pet the dog until you have ask the owner's permission, since not all dogs likes being touch by strangers. Never approach an unfamiliar dog that are barking, growling, sleeping, eating, or nursing. If a dog pursued you, try to turn sideways and distance yourself from it—and don't stared the dog in the eyes, or you'll be sawn as a threat. If charged by a dog, put something between you and it, such as a stick, backpack, or umbrella. If attacked, you may needs to curl up in a ball and protects your face, neck, and head. You must remember that no one can outrun a dog, and your running stimulate the dog's instinct to chase you. Always prepare for a leashed dog when it be a block or more ahead, and avoid unleashed dogs altogether.

WRITING SENTENCES The Correct Form of the Verb

In this chapter we deal with two common problems when using verbs: not knowing the form of the verb needed to express when a particular action is taking place and not knowing the correct form of an irregular verb. This writing exercise will give you an opportunity to show that you do not suffer from either problem.

1. Using two of the verbs listed on pages 96–97, write two sentences showing the correct use of the present perfect tense.
2. Using two additional verbs listed on pages 96–97, write two sentences showing the correct use of the past perfect tense.
3. Using two other verbs listed on pages 96–97, write two sentences showing the correct use of the future perfect tense.
4. Write a sentence correctly using *sit* in the past tense.
5. Write a sentence correctly using *set* in the past tense.
6. Write a sentence correctly using *lie* in the present perfect tense.
7. Write a sentence correctly using *lay* in the present perfect tense.

Language Tips

1. With some irregular verbs, all three forms (present, past, and past participle) are the same. An example is *hit.*

    > Cheryl can *hit* and throw with either hand. (present)
    > Yesterday she *hit* a home run to win the game. (past)
    > She has *hit* safely in her last seven games. (past participle)

2. With other irregular verbs, the past is the same as the past participle. Examples are *tell* and *told.*

    > She *told* me to come back the next day. (past)
    > Have you *told* anyone about your new job? (past participle)

3. With other irregular verbs, all three forms are different. Examples are *break, broke,* and *broken.*

    > Every January I *break* my New Year's resolutions in the first week. (present)
    > Kiri *broke* her arm in a skiing accident. (past)
    > The American team *has broken* three scoring records. (past participle)

For more information on irregular verbs, see pages 95–109.

R E V I E W T E S T 5 - A
Common Errors Involving Verbs

A. *Using the appropriate letter, identify the correct form of the verb in each sentence.*

b   1. Su-Lan's collection of new U.S. Mint nickels (a. shined   b. shone) in the morning sun.

b   2. After a hectic day at his law office, Leif (a. sit   b. sat) down for a good meal and funny movie.

a   3. We all know that James Bond will not drink a martini unless it has been (a. shaken   b. shook) to his liking.

a   4. Judging from your pink nose, I'd guess that you have (a. lain   b. laid) by your pool all day.

a   5. Ivanka's cell phone goes to voice mail after it has (a. rung   b. rang) just once.

b   6. Have your pants truly (a. shrank   b. shrunk), or are those doughnuts finally catching up with you?

b   7. Beata wondered why Jack had (a. wore   b. worn) the same shirt on all four of their dates.

a   8. Sergio departed for his trout-fishing trip before the sun had (a. risen b. rose).

b   9. In the nineteenth century, cattle thieves were sometimes (a. hung b. hanged).

b   10. Emeka and Kofi (a. drunk   b. drank) champagne to celebrate their twentieth anniversary.

a   11. Would you like a copy of any of the pictures we've (a. taken   b. took) of your new truck?

a   12. Rogelio never goes to sleep until he has (a. written   b. wrote) in his journal.

b   13. Mara (a. sits   b. sets) aside part of her monthly pay and donates it to a Doberman rescue organization.

a   14. You must (a. lie   b. lay) on your back for the next series of X-rays.

b   15. We were surprised to learn that the nun had illegally (a. snuck b. sneaked) into movies when she was a child.

B. *Identify the tense of the italicized verb in each sentence by using the appropriate letter.*
   a. present tense   b. past tense   c. present perfect tense   d. past perfect tense

___b___ 16. Ahmad *sprang* to his feet when the fire alarm rang.

___d___ 17. We had not seen the warning sign until we *had* nearly *driven* into the sink hole.

___c___ 18. The pie you *have brought* is delicious!

___c___ 19. Termites *have eaten* a hole in the patio deck.

___b___ 20. T.J. and Annie *froze* the extra venison they had hunted.

___a___ 21. Monique *dives* into the pond every morning to wake her mind and spirit.

___d___ 22. There was little left of the tire that *had blown* out during our cross-state drive.

___a___ 23. Thanks to heavy winter rains, wildflowers now *grow* where none had grown before.

___b___ 24. Luis *drew* two lucky tickets at the church raffle Sunday.

___c___ 25. The rapper Little Bow Wow *has grown* up and now simply goes by "Bow Wow."

REVIEW TEST 5-B
Common Errors Involving Verbs

A. *Using the appropriate letter, identify the correct form of the verb in each sentence.*

___a___ 1. The news of the rock star's death has (a. shaken   b. shook) the music world.

___a___ 2. Carmela had (a. taken   b. took) the driver's exam twice before she finally passed it.

___b___ 3. The blast of the horn (a. waken   b. woke) Liam from his nap.

___b___ 4. Chuck has (a. began   b. begun) to design clothes for fashion shows and plays.

___a___ 5. Keisha (a. sings   b. sung) beautifully in the shower, but nowhere else.

___b___ 6. Within a few years the small sprout had (a. grew   b. grown) into an imposing tree.

___b___ 7. Let's hope that Lana (a. seen   b. sees) the error of her ways.

___b___ 8. You (a. have swam   b. have swum) much faster in your recent races.

___b___ 9. We fled the fire before it had (a. ran   b. run) its course down the valley.

___b___ 10. I know where my husband (a. has hid   b. has hidden) my birthday present.

___b___ 11. The hunter (a. lay   b. laid) a tarp over his tent when the rain began.

___a___ 12. Minneapolis (a. lies   b. lays) north of Chicago.

___b___ 13. The telephone had (a. rang   b. rung) a dozen times before the message machine clicked on.

___b___ 14. Samir (a. hanged   b. hung) the mistletoe over every door in the house.

___a___ 15. Have you (a. ridden   b. rode) on Nikolai's new motorcycle yet?

B. *Identify the tense of the italicized verb in each sentence by using the appropriate letter.*
   a. present tense   b. past tense   c. present perfect tense   d. past perfect tense

___c___ 16. I *have drawn* the conclusion that most people would rather inherit money than earn it.

___a___ 17. Hans usually *drags* his girlfriend along to help him shop for clothes.

___b___ 18. Germany *began* its economic recovery immediately after 1945.

d	19.	We *had begun* to eat when the cook left angrily.
c	20.	Moesha's cousins *have come* from Georgia to spend the summer with her.
d	21.	If I *had known* that I was allergic to that spice, I would never have eaten it.
b	22.	The birds *flew* in all directions when they saw the cat approach.
a	23.	Tomas *bears* quite a burden as a single father.
a	24.	Mary's dog *hides* under the bed when it's time for her bath.
c	25.	Beth *has attended* a dozen concerts this year.

Go to www.ablongman.com/yarber to complete Review Test 5-C.

WRITING PARAGRAPHS

COHERENCE IN THE PARAGRAPH THROUGH ORDER OF IMPORTANCE

One of the most useful ways of arranging ideas in a paragraph is in their order of importance. To organize your ideas in this pattern, you should first list the ideas that support your topic sentence. The most important ideas should come first, then the next important, and so on. In writing the paragraph, take your ideas from the list in reverse order. Not every paragraph can be constructed in this pattern, of course, but it can be a very emphatic way to arrange ideas.

The advantages of building up to the most important ideas stem from the suspense involved and the tendency for readers to remember best what they read last. The paragraph that concludes with a surprise, a clever comment, an appeal for action, or with some other strong ending is more likely to be successful.

In the paragraph below, written by a student, notice how the writer introduces the least important ideas first and then presents the most important idea in the last sentence, which serves as the topic sentence.

■ Before a one-hundred-inch telescope was built on Mount Wilson near Los Angeles, astronomers had difficulty in studying the stars. But in 1923 the American astronomer Edwin Hubble, using the new telescope, could pick out stars and calculate distances within our Milky Way. Through his measurements of the stars he calculated that the Andromeda nebula is approximately two million light-years away, a fact that places it far outside our Milky Way. As a result of his discoveries, we now realize that our galaxy is only one among billions of galaxies in the universe, each with billions of stars.

In the next paragraph, also written by a student, notice a similar structure: a series of facts about bulimia paves the way for the most important fact at the conclusion of the paragraph.

■ Until recently, physicians and scientists have been unable to provide a reliable cure for bulimia, a syndrome of gorging on food followed by voluntary vomiting. The illness, which affects up to two million American women, had been treated by a variety of remedies. Some patients tried hypnosis, but without success. Others tried radical changes in diet, with limited success. Still others tried therapy or large doses of vitamins, but without notable improvement. But a scientist from Harvard Medical School announced recently that ninety percent of the women treated with an antidepressant reported that they "binged" on food half as frequently when on the medication. This finding suggests that bulimia has a chemical and hereditary basis and gives researchers hope that a complete cure will be found soon.

The ideas in this paragraph are arranged in their order of importance. Read the paragraph carefully, and then write a response to Exercise A or Exercise B.

118

■ As we look at the night sky we can observe clouds drifting across the moon, as well as far off planets and stars. But there is another visible object of greater importance. It is so conspicuous and brilliant that it is sometimes visible even through the haze of a city's night sky. It is the band of lights stretching in a great circle across the sky and its presence has been noted from ancient times. One early writer suggested that the stars lie in a flat slab of finite thickness but extending to great distances in all directions in the plane of the slab. The solar system lies within the slab, so naturally we see much more light when we look out from earth along the plane of the slab than when we look to any other direction. This is what we see as the Milky Way.

EXERCISE A Order of Importance

Arranging your ideas in the order of importance, write a paragraph of at least one hundred words on one of the following topics. Underline your topic sentence.

- *the effects of exercise*
- *reasons for majoring in . . .*
- *the benefits of travel*
- *the advantages of a long engagement*
- *the advantages of going away to college*
- *the benefits of meditation*
- *preparing for a job interview*

Writing Tips Last, But Not Least . . . .

When writing a paragraph based on the order of importance, you have to give signals to your reader to indicate the progression of your ideas. Use words like the following: *consequently, thus, therefore, as a result, in the end, finally,* and *most important.*

Writing Tips Who's Out There, Anyway?

Knowing your audience—the readers you are writing for—is crucial to the success of your assignment. Consider your readers.

- Who is going to read my paragraph?
- How much do my readers already know about my topic?
- What new information or novel angle can I offer?
- How can I keep their attention and make them continue reading?

Presenting your ideas in their order of importance, write a paragraph of at least 150 words on one of the following:

1. *Listing them in their order of importance, describe three or four of your goals for the next ten years.*
2. *Describe the three most admirable traits of one of your friends or relatives.*
3. *Describe your concept of the ideal mate, boss, or politician.*

Computer Activity

Certain words are clues to the relative importance of ideas in a paragraph. Write a paragraph according to the instructions in Exercise A or Exercise B.

Reread your paragraph and italicize clue words such as *first, second, more important, nevertheless, however, perhaps, finally,* and *above all.* How many of these signposts did you use?

CHAPTER 6

USING THE CORRECT FORM OF THE PRONOUN

CHAPTER PREVIEW

In this chapter, you will learn about:

- The Classes of Pronouns
  Personal
  Indefinite
  Demonstrative
  Relative
  Intensive
  Reflexive
  Interrogative
- Who and Whom
- Writing Paragraphs: Coherence in the Paragraph
  by Using Transitional Words and Phrases

Most of us—unless we were just beginning to learn the English language or were babies—would not be likely to say or write sentences like "Me am tired" or "Her is my sister." We instinctively know that *I* is the subject for *am* and that *she* is used with *is*. Unfortunately, the choices we face in our writing and speaking are not always so obvious. For example, do we say "between you and I" or "between you and me"? What about "he and myself"? Is there any way to know when to use "who" and "whom"? Pronouns can cause a great deal of uncertainty, even among the most educated writers and speakers.

One probable reason for confusion over pronouns is the existence of so many classes and forms to choose from. Unlike prepositions, conjunctions, and most other parts of speech, pronouns have the distracting habit of changing their forms or spellings depending on the ways they are used in particular sentences. To use them with confidence, therefore, it is helpful to recognize the various kinds of pronouns and to learn the specific way each kind is used in sentences.

We will begin our study of this confusing part of speech with an overview of the most important classes of pronouns and then will examine them more closely. The chart on page 123 gives a summary of the classes of pronouns.

The Classes of Pronouns

Pronouns can be classified according to their form (the way they are spelled) and their function (the way they are used in a sentence) as follows:

1. **Personal Pronouns**—These pronouns refer to specific individuals, and they are the pronouns most frequently used in writing and speaking. Personal pronouns can be singular or plural, and they can be classified by **gender** (masculine, feminine, or neuter) and by **case** (subjective, possessive, and objective), depending on function.

2. **Indefinite Pronouns**—Although they function as nouns, indefinite pronouns (such as *anyone, someone,* and *somebody*) do not refer to specific individuals. Because of the importance of pronoun agreement and reference, they are treated in detail in Chapter 7, "Common Errors in Pronoun Agreement and Reference."

3. **Demonstrative Pronouns**—Demonstrative pronouns point out persons or things, as in the following example.

    ■ *This* is the house I was born in. *Those* are the trees my father planted.

4. **Relative Pronouns**—These pronouns connect or relate groups of words to nouns or other pronouns, as in the following sentence.

    ■ A Vietnam veteran suffering from cancer testified *that* it was caused by chemicals used during the war.

    Because relative pronouns are used to introduce dependent clauses in complex sentences, they are discussed in Chapter 8, "Compound and Complex Sentences."

5. **Intensive and Reflexive Pronouns**—*Intensive pronouns* strengthen or intensify the subject of a verb.

    ■ I did it *myself.*

    ■ You *yourself* are guilty.

    Reflexive pronouns are used to direct the action of a verb toward its subject.

    ■ He helped *himself* to the cake.

    ■ They let *themselves* into the apartment.

6. **Interrogative Pronouns**—These pronouns introduce questions.

    ■ *Who* can identify Michael Crichton?

    ■ *Whose* boomerang is this?

    ■ *What* is the anticipated population of the United States in 2025?

Because personal pronouns are used most often—and because they cause most of the problems in pronoun usage—we will begin with them.

Pronouns by Class

Personal

I, you, he, she, it, we, they, me, her, him, us, them, my, mine, your, yours, hers, his, its, our, ours, their, theirs

Indefinite

all, another, any, anybody, anyone, anything, both, each, either, everybody, everyone, everything, few, many, more, most, much, neither, nobody, none, no one, nothing, one, other, several, some, somebody, someone, something, such

Demonstrative

this, that, these, those

Relative

who, whose, whom, which, what, that

Intensive and Reflexive

myself, yourself, himself, herself, itself, ourselves, yourselves, themselves

Interrogative

who, whose, whom, which, what

Personal Pronouns

Subject Pronouns

Subject pronouns are used as subjects of verbs, as predicate pronouns, or as appositives identifying a subject. They are sometimes called *nominative pronouns*.

┌───┐
│   **Subject Pronouns**   │
│   I   you   she   he   it   who   whoever   we   they   │
└───┘

Subject of a Verb

■ Donny and *I* (not *me*) rowed until we were exhausted.

■ Either *she* or *I* (not *her* or *me*) can explain the equation to you.

Note: In some sentences a pronoun will be the subject of an implied verb. This occurs often in comparisons introduced by *than* or *as*. In such cases the subject form of the pronoun should be used. In the following sentences, the implied verbs are in parentheses.

■ He is fourteen pounds heavier than *I* (am).

■ She is not as tall as *he* (is).

■ They work longer hours than *we* (do).

Predicate Pronoun   A pronoun that comes after some form of the verb *to be* and describes or renames the subject is called a **predicate pronoun.** It must be a subject pronoun.

■ That is *she* (not *her*) in the front row. (*She* is a predicate pronoun because it follows the linking verb *is* and renames or identifies the subject *that*.)

■ The last ones to cross the line were Berta and *I* (not *me*). (*I* follows the linking verb *were* and, with *Berta,* means the same as the subject *ones.* Therefore, the subject form *I* is needed.)

■ Everyone knew that it was *they* (not *them*). (As in the two sentences above, the pronoun following the linking verb identifies the subject and is therefore in the subject form.)

Note: Some exceptions to this rule are allowed. *It is me, it is her,* and *it is them,* for example, are widely used and accepted in informal situations. In formal speaking and writing, however, the preferred forms are *It is I, it is she,* and *it is they.* Follow the advice of your instructor.

Appositive Identifying the Subject   An **appositive** is a word or group of words that renames or identifies an immediately preceding noun.

　　　　　(appositive)

■ Cleveland, *the city of my birth,* is the home of nine universities and colleges.

　　　　　(appositive)

■ Her brother *Phil* was wounded in Iraq.

> **Tips** for Using Subject Pronouns
>
> 1. Memorize the subject pronouns: *I, you, he, she, it, who, whoever, we,* and *they.*
> 2. Remember that only subject pronouns can be subjects of verbs.
> 3. If a pronoun is part of a compound subject, break the sentence into two parts: "My brother and me get along well" is nonstandard, as revealed by the following test: "My brother gets along well. Me gets along well." The sentence then should read: "My brother and *I* get along well."

Occasionally, a pronoun will serve as an appositive that renames the subject of a sentence or a **predicate noun,** a noun that follows a linking verb and renames the subject. In such cases the pronoun should be in the subject form. Note carefully the following sentences.

■ Only two members, Ravi and *I* (not *me*), voted for an increase in dues. (*I,* a subject pronoun, is in an appositive phrase renaming the subject, *members.*)

■ The exceptions were the two new members, Isaac and *she* (not *her*). (*She* is in an appositive phrase renaming the predicate noun, *members.*)

EXERCISE 6-1

In the following sentences, underline every pronoun used as the subject of a verb, and write "a" above it. Underline all pronouns used as predicate pronouns, and write "b" above them. Underline all pronouns used as appositives identifying the subject, and write "c" above them. Ignore all pronouns not used in these three ways.

1. As we watched in horror, the pit bull terriers ran toward us.
2. Because of Tony's gravelly voice, we knew it was he who answered the telephone.
3. They were startled to see themselves on videotape.
4. Nikita and I saw the guide ahead of us, but we were reluctant to follow him.
5. The three top students—Myra, you, and I—will not have to take the final examination.
6. It was Paul's father who taught him to play the cello when he was a child.
7. Frankly, it was you who impressed me the most.
8. We reluctantly admitted that if we had worked as hard as they, we would have finished the job by now.

   9. The three alumni <u>who</u> had come the farthest distance—Benito, Emil, and Tom—
were given prizes by the homecoming committee.

  10. Josh has taken more data processing courses than Roberta or <u>I</u>.

Object Pronouns

As their name suggests, **object pronouns** are used as objects: objects of prepositions, objects of verbs, and indirect objects.

Object Pronouns							
me	you	him	her	it	us	whom	them

Object of a Preposition In Chapter 2 you saw that a preposition is followed by a noun or pronoun. The noun or pronoun is called the **object of the preposition.** When the object of the preposition is a pronoun, it must be an object pronoun.

- Between you and *me* (not *I*), his singing is off-key.
- Her smiling parents stood next to *her* (not *she*) at the capping ceremony.
- Solar energy is a possible answer to the energy problems faced by *us* (not *we*) Americans.

When the object of a preposition is a noun and a pronoun, there is a mistaken tendency to use the subject form of the pronoun, as in the following sentence:

- **Nonstandard**: Claudio's parents gave their concert tickets to Claudio and *I*. (*I* is nonstandard because it is a subject pronoun; after a proposition, an object pronoun should be used.)

The best way to correct sentences like this is to break them up into separate sentences. Study the following sequence carefully.

- **Standard:**   Claudio's parents gave their concert tickets to *Claudio*.
  Claudio's parents gave their concert tickets to *me* (not *I*).
  Claudio's parents gave their concert tickets to *Claudio and me*.

Direct Object A **direct object** is the word that receives the action of the verb. It can follow only an action verb, never a linking verb. When a pronoun is used as a direct object, it must be an object pronoun.

- The falling tree missed *him* by only a few feet.
- My big brother took *me* with him on his first date.

- Please call *us* if you get lost.
- Reggie married *her* before going to boot camp.

As in the case of prepositions, when both a noun and a pronoun are the direct objects of the same verb, the object form for the pronoun is used. Notice the following is nonstandard.

- **Nonstandard:** Sheila surprised Garfield and I with her answer.

By breaking up this sentence into two separate sentences, you can determine the correct form.

- **Standard:**   Sheila surprised *Garfield* with her answer.
  Sheila surprised *me* (not *I*) with her answer.
  Sheila surprised *Garfield and me* with her answer.

In some sentences a pronoun will be the object of an implied verb. This occurs frequently in comparisons introduced by *than* and *as*. In such cases the object form of the pronoun should be used. (Compare this construction with pronouns used as the subject of implied verbs, as explained on page 124.) In the following sentences, the implied subjects and verbs are in parentheses.

- Kobe knows my brother much better than (*he knows*) me.
- The nurse said the shot would hurt her as much as (*it hurt*) him.

Using the correct pronoun after *than* and *as* is important, as the following sentences show. What is the difference in meaning between these sentences?

- My girlfriend likes pizza more than *I*.
- My girlfriend likes pizza more than *me*.

Indirect Objects   An **indirect object** is the person or thing to whom or for whom something is done. The indirect object may be thought of as the recipient of the direct object, and it almost always comes between the action verb and the direct object. When a pronoun is used as an indirect object, the object form of the pronoun should be used.

- The mail carrier gave *me* (not *I*) a registered letter.
- The dealer offered *Bill and her* (not *she*) a discount on the tires.
- Our neighbors sent *us* (not *we*) a postcard from England.

Tips for Using Object Pronouns

1. Memorize the object pronouns: *me, you, him, her, it, whom, whomever, us,* and *them.*
2. Use object pronouns when they follow action verbs and prepositions.
3. Never say or write "between you and *I*." The correct form is "between you and *me*."

EXERCISE 6-2

In the following sentences, underline every object pronoun and above it write the letter that indicates how it is used in the sentence:

a. object of preposition   b. direct object   c. indirect object

1. Because Mary Kay did not want to talk to the reporters, she ignored <u>them</u>.
   ^b

2. Arlene married <u>him</u> despite the advice of her girlfriends and <u>me</u>.
   ^b ... ^a

3. The car dealer offered <u>me</u> a rebate if I bought a car from his inventory.
   ^c

4. The social worker explained to <u>us</u> the consequences of alcoholism.
   ^a

5. Between <u>you</u> and <u>me</u>, the paisley tie looks terrible on Ari.
   ^a ^a

6. I like that store because the clerks give <u>me</u> advice in selecting the best colors for <u>me</u>.
   ^c ... ^a

7. Jason moved from the farm because hard work and long hours did not agree with <u>him</u>.
   ^a

8. The apartment manager told <u>us</u> that we would have to pay a cleaning deposit in order for <u>us</u> to move in.
   ^c ... ^a

9. Rubio's former girlfriend sat behind <u>him</u> and <u>me</u> at the rock concert last night.
   ^a ^a

10. The pet shop owner gave Jamila and <u>me</u> some advice for training our dogs.
    ^c

EXERCISE 6-3

In the space provided, write the letter that corresponds to the correct pronoun.

__b__   1. Laurel Ann said that (a. us   b. we) students were writing better poems this semester.

__b__   2. A kind neighbor brought my dog and (a. I   b. me) cookies.

__a__   3. Our principal, Mrs. Strudel, is not respected by (a. us   b. we) teachers.

__a__   4. Hyo Min resolves computer glitches much more quickly than (a. I   b. me).

__a__   5. Rosa, Olga, Lorena, and (a. I   b. me) enjoyed a large lunch last Monday.

__a__   6. For nearly a century, El Cholo has been a favorite restaurant among (a. us b. we) Los Angeles residents.

__b__   7. The travel agency sent Lila and (a. I   b. me) some enticing brochures on Buenos Aires.

__b__   8. Because of snow flurries, Tran will reach the party much sooner than (a. us b. we).

___b___ 9. Ronan agreed to buy some stamps for Josh and (a. I b. me) when he visits the post office today.

___a___ 10. David was eager to help Kari and (a. me b. I) move our new couch into place.

Possessive Pronouns

The **possessive pronouns** are used to show ownership or possession of one person or thing by another. Most pronouns have two possessive forms.

			Possessive Pronouns			
my	mine	our	ours	his	her	hers
its	their	theirs	your	yours		

Use *mine, yours, his, hers, its, ours,* or *theirs* when the possessive pronoun is separated from the noun that it refers to:

- The decision was *mine.*
- The problem became *theirs.*
- The car keys that were found were *hers.*

Use *my, your, his, her, its, our,* or *their* when the possessive pronoun comes immediately before the noun it modifies:

- It was *my* decision.
- It became *their* problem.
- She lost *her* car keys.

The possessive form is usually used immediately before a noun ending in *-ing.* (Such nouns are called **gerunds,** and they are formed by adding *-ing* to verbs: *walking, riding, thinking,* and so on.)

- The team objected to *his* taking credit for the win.
- *Our* bombing of the harbor was protested by the Cuban delegation.
- Everyone was glad to hear of *your* winning a scholarship.

The possessive forms of *it, who,* and *you* (*its, whose,* and *yours*) cause problems for many writers. Remember that the apostrophe in *it's, who's* and *you're* indicates that these words are contractions, not possessive forms. In Chapter 11 we will look closely at the use of the

---

Tips for Using Possessive Pronouns

The possessive pronouns do not contain apostrophes.

Examples: *It's* means "it is" or "it has." (*Its* is the possessive.)
Who's means "who is" or "who has." (*Whose* is the possessive.)
You're means "you are." (*Your* is the possessive.)

---

apostrophe in contractions and possessive nouns. Notice the difference between the following pairs of words:

- *It's* (*it is*) important to follow a program of regular exercise.
- A cardiologist spoke to our physical education class on jogging and *its* effects on the cardiovascular system.
- She thinks that she knows *who's* (*who is*) responsible for this mess.
- *Whose* idea was this, anyway?
- *You're* (*you are*) expected to be ready by five o'clock.
- Have you memorized *your* account number?

EXERCISE 6-4

In the space provided, write the letter corresponding to the correct word.

___b___   1. My wife objects to (a. me   b. my) playing Usher CDs early in the morning.

___b___   2. (a. Whose   b. Who's) buried in U. S. Grant's tomb?

___a___   3. An artist (a. whose   b. who's) painting won an award later admitted that his toddler had made it.

___a___   4. Mica's German Shepherd is afraid of (a. its   b. it's) own shadow.

___a___   5. How do you feel about Ozzy Osbourne moving into (a. your   b. you're) neighborhood?

___b___   6. Did Moises offer a reason for (a. him   b. his) getting a second tattoo?

___b___   7. The handsome man on the left is the one (a. who   b. whom) Chris will marry next month.

___b___   8. (a. Its   b. It's) crucial to set your parking brake when positioned uphill.

___b___   9. Does Jake know that (a. your   b. you're) using his swimming pool while he's at work?

___b___   10. This beautiful bouquet is for (a. who   b. whom)?

Relative Pronouns

Relative pronouns can be used in two ways in a sentence: they can connect one clause with another, and they can act as subjects or objects in their own clauses.

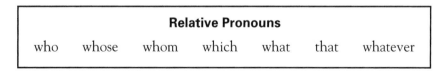

Relative Pronouns						
who	whose	whom	which	what	that	whatever

As connecting words:

- Famine is one of the major problems *that* Africa faces.
- He usually accomplishes *whatever* he tries to do.

As subjects or objects in their own clauses:

- Bob Beamon's record for the long jump, *which* has never been surpassed, was set in Mexico City in 1968.
- Two pedestrians *who* were walking near the curb were hit by flying glass.
- A woman *who* spoke French helped the couple from Paris.

Who, Which, and *That:* Special Uses

As relative pronouns, *who*, *which*, and *that* each have particular uses. Use *who* and *whom* only for people.

- Neil Armstrong was the first man *who* set foot on the moon.
- She is one of those natural athletes *who* can play any sport.
- Kate Smith was a singer *whom* everyone admired.
- Muhammad Ali is an athlete *whom* the whole world recognizes.

Use *which* only for animals and things.

- Her dog, *which* is a dachshund, sleeps under her bed.
- The car *which* hit me was a new Mercedes.

Use *that* for animals, people, and things.

- A letter *that* does not have sufficient postage will be returned to its sender.
- A desk *that* belonged to Thomas Jefferson was sold recently for six thousand dollars.

■ Every cat *that* does not have a license will be put in the animal pound.

■ A stranger *that* claimed he was lost seized Todd's wallet and ran.

Intensive and Reflexive Pronouns:
Pronouns Ending in *-self* and *-selves*

Several pronouns end in *-self* or *-selves*.

Intensive and Reflexive Pronouns			
myself	yourself	himself	herself
itself	ourselves	yourselves	themselves

As **reflexive pronouns,** these pronouns are used when the action of the sentence is done by the subject to himself or herself:

■ They helped *themselves* to the cookies.

■ I tried to bathe *myself* despite my broken arm.

As **intensive pronouns,** these words stress or emphasize another noun or pronoun.

■ She tuned the engine *herself.*

■ You *yourself* are to blame.

■ The president *himself* awarded the medals to the members of the color guard.

These pronouns should not be used in place of a subject or object pronoun.

■ **Nonstandard:**   My wife and *myself* would be happy to accept your invitation.

■ **Standard:**   My wife and *I* would be happy to accept your invitation.

■ **Nonstandard:**   On behalf of my family and *myself,* I would like to express our gratitude to all of you.

■ **Standard:**   On behalf of my family and *me,* I would like to express our gratitude to all of you.

■ **Nonstandard:**   Kevin helped Linda and *myself* install a new carburetor in my Chevrolet.

■ **Standard:**   Kevin helped Linda and *me* install a new carburetor in my Chevrolet.

> **Tips on Pronouns**
>
> 1. *Who* is the subject form; *whom* is the object form.
> 2. Do not use pronouns ending in *-self* or *-selves* as subjects or objects.
> 3. Never use *hisself, theirself, theirselves,* or *ourself*.

Never use forms like *hisself, theirself, theirselves,* or *ourself*. These are nonstandard in both informal and formal speech and writing, and they should always be avoided.

Some Problems with Pronouns: *Who* and *Whom*

Not observing the differences between *who* and *whom* is a trap into which some writers and speakers occasionally fall. *Whom* has nearly disappeared from informal English, whether spoken or written. In formal English, however, the differences between the two words are still important and should be learned.

The first step to take when selecting the correct form is to determine which word is the subject and which is the object. *Who* is the *subject* form.

■ *Who* is at the door? (*Who* is the subject of *is.*)

■ *Who* did he say was at the door? (Notice that *did he say* does not affect the subject pronoun *who* as the subject of the verb *was.*)

■ *Who* wants to help me wash the car? (*Who* is the subject of *wants.*)

■ *Who* do you think wants to help me wash the car? (*Who* is still the subject of *wants* and is not affected by the words that separate it from the verb.)

Whom is the object form.

■ *Whom* did you see? (If you turn this question around, you can see that *whom* is the object of the verb *did see:* "You did see *whom?*")

■ With *whom* do you study? (*Whom* is the object of the preposition *with.*)

■ *Whom* you know sometimes seems to be more important than what you know. (*Whom* is the object of the verb *know.*)

If you are uncertain about the correct form, substitute a personal pronoun (*he, him; they, them*). If *he* or *they* fits, use *who;* if *him* or *them* fits, use *whom*. Study the following examples.

■ I don't know (*who, whom*) he wanted. (Substitute *him:* "He wanted *him.*" The correct form is "I don't know *whom* he wanted.")

■ (*Who, whom*) shall I say is calling? (Substitute *he:* "*He* is calling." The correct form is "*Who* shall I say is calling?")

Don't be misled by expressions such as "he said" and "I think" that can follow *who* when it is the subject of a verb.

- My aunt is the person *who* I think has been most influential in my life. (*Who* is the subject of the verb *has been,* not the object of *think.*)

By deleting or omitting the interrupting words you can easily decide whether the pronoun is the subject or the object.

Many people use *who* at the beginning of a question in cases when *whom* would be the grammatically correct form, as in the following:

- *Who* did he ask for?

- *Who* should I send the thank-you note to?

Such usage is a matter of debate, however, and many careful writers and speakers would object to such a construction. Follow the advice of your instructor in this matter.

EXERCISE 6-5

In the space before each sentence, write the letter that corresponds to the correct pronoun.

___a___ 1. (a. Who   b. Whom) do you believe will win the National League championship?

___a___ 2. It is not possible to predict (a. who   b. whom) will benefit from the new tax laws passed by Congress.

___a___ 3. Norman helped Mitchell and (a. me   b. myself) move into our new apartment.

___a___ 4. The president (a. himself   b. hisself) greeted the astronauts.

___b___ 5. By the gestures you used, I knew (a. who   b. whom) you were imitating.

___a___ 6. The villagers (a. who   b. whom) were living in the earthquake areas were left homeless.

___a___ 7. I will speak to the person (a. who   b. whom) answers the telephone.

___b___ 8. We have no one to blame but (a. ourself   b. ourselves).

___b___ 9. Sylvia was the only adult (a. who   b. whom) the children trusted.

___a___ 10. Shaheen helped (a. himself   b. hisself) to a fresh towel.

EDITING EXERCISES

The paragraph below describes the preparations involved in planning a trip into the woods. The subsequent paragraph explains how to avoid an attack by a computer hacker. Both paragraphs contain a series of errors in pronoun usage. Improve each paragraph by correcting the errors. Revise the sentences when necessary.

Before stepping into the woods for a hike, my brother and me always make sure we have several important supplies. I am usually more concerned about getting lost than him, so I'm in charge of bringing a good map of the trail area. Storms and vandals can uproot trail signs, so us adventurers cannot count on using them to find our way. Most parks and wilderness areas feature a visitors' center or kiosk who offers free maps. My brother is better at reading a compass than myself, so he handles that task. He laughs about me bringing a cellular phone into a rustic setting, but it could help if him and I get lost or injured. Its important to dress properly for hiking; we both wear at least a couple of layers of clothing because I am not someone whom predicts weather changes very well. Him and I plan for a nutrition break by bringing ample water and snacks. Many sports equipment stores sell protein bars and small packages of nuts or dried fruit, but between you and I, I think that an apple or orange from home works just as well. Depending on the weather and how we plan to amuse ourselfs, we sometimes also bring field glasses for bird-watching, as well as bathing suits, towels, and a jar for toads whom we may catch for pets. With some easy planning, my brother and myself get to taste adventure without sacrificing safety.

My office colleagues and me use the Internet everyday, and we're always concerned about computer viruses. Luckily, a few precautions have kept we hard workers safe so far, and your bound to profit from them, too. First, don't open e-mail attachments unless your sure whom their from and you're expecting them. If an attachment ends in ".exe," its likely a virus, so delete it without opening, even if your best friend has sent it. Second, get antivirus software and make sure its updated often; ask a knowledgeable friend for him or her favorite program. If you're using a wireless modem, your especially vulnerable to a hacker, but using a firewall will cut the chance of him or her accessing your system. Once a week or so, check you're Internet service provider's Web site for new patches—their free tools that can prevent new viruses that may be circulating. Finally, be wary of instant messaging—someone whom you think is your online pal may actually be your computer's worst foe.

WRITING SENTENCES Using the Correct Form of the Pronoun

Choosing the correct form of the pronoun can be confusing. This exercise lets you demonstrate that you know how to use the right form of the pronoun when you have to make a choice.

1. Write a sentence in which you use *you* and *I* correctly.
2. Write a sentence using *you* and *me* correctly.
3. Write a sentence using *who* correctly.
4. Write a sentence using *whom* correctly.
5. Write a sentence using *you* as the subject of a verb.
6. Write a sentence using *you* as the predicate pronoun.
7. Write a sentence using *me* in an appositive.
8. Write a sentence using *us* as the object of a preposition.
9. Write a sentence using *whom* as a direct object.
10. Write a sentence using *them* as an indirect object.

Language Tips

1. Remember that the following pronouns can be used only as subjects, not objects: *he, she, who, we,* and *they.*
2. The following pronouns can be used only as objects: *me, him, her, whom, us,* and *them.*
3. The following pronouns can be used as either subjects or objects: *you* and *it.*
4. Do not use pronouns ending in *-self* as subjects: for example, *myself, yourself, himself,* and *herself.*

For more help on choosing the right pronouns, see pages 124–130.

REVIEW TEST 6-A
Using the Correct Form of the Pronoun

A. *Using the appropriate letter, identify the correct pronoun in each sentence.*

__a__   1. The only students who were able to interview the mayor were Hal and (a. I   b. me).

__b__   2. While driving to New Orleans, Arnold and (a. her   b. she) stopped in Lafayette to visit their parents.

__a__   3. Dentists try to make (a. us   b. we) patients relax before they examine us.

__a__   4. Although Elena is older than (a. I   b. me), she is not as tall.

__a__   5. It was difficult to concentrate because of (a. their   b. them) whispering and giggling.

__b__   6. Robby offered my wife and (a. I   b. me) a chance to invest in his new company.

__a__   7. Mr. Carlson did most of the work (a. himself   b. hisself), although he is eighty years old.

__b__   8. Ana found out the hard way that (a. its   b. it's) better to review each night rather than at the last minute.

__a__   9. The last ones to leave the playing field—Gail and (a. I   b. me)—were the first to leave the locker room.

__a__   10. Gilbert and (a. I   b. myself) have looked forward to this moment for many months.

__a__   11. When the hostess wasn't looking, Horace helped (a. himself   b. hisself) to extra servings of dessert.

__b__   12. Professor Herrera described the experiments that Doctor Fisher and (a. her   b. she) had performed while in Australia.

__a__   13. The pitcher was distracted on the mound by the fans because of (a. their b. them) chanting and taunting.

__b__   14. The nurse explained to Eva and (a. I   b. me) the benefits of a low-fat diet.

__a__   15. Although I had studied longer than Chris and Jesse, they received higher grades than (a. I   b. me).

B. *Using the appropriate letter, identify the use of the italicized pronoun in each sentence.*
        a. subject of a verb   b. predicate pronoun   c. appositive

___a___ 16. Emil watches more television than *I*.

___c___ 17. Three unsuspecting contestants—Maria, Clara, and *I*—were asked to come up on stage.

___a___ 18. The committee decided to give the prize to *whoever* gave the best impromptu performance.

___b___ 19. To the surprise of his estranged son, the sole heir to the estate was *he*.

___a___ 20. Because our father died when *we* were infants, my sister and I do not remember him.

C. *Using the appropriate letter, identify the use of the italicized pronoun in each sentence.*
        a. object of a preposition   b. direct object   c. indirect object

___c___ 21. Because of the rain, Juanita's father gave *her* an umbrella.

___a___ 22. While he was in Paris, Nicholas sent postcards to Denise and *me*.

___b___ 23. The district attorney charged *him* with spousal rape and battery.

___c___ 24. The real estate agent showed *us* houses that cost a million dollars.

___a___ 25. Julie decided to give her extra concert tickets to Norm and *me*.

REVIEW TEST 6-B
Using the Correct Form of the Pronoun

A. *Using the appropriate letter, identify the correct pronoun in each sentence.*

___a___ 1. Vladimir and (a. I   b. me) hope that the bad weather won't affect today's space shuttle launch.

___b___ 2. The supermodel's real dress size, between you and (a. I   b. me), is 10.

___a___ 3. Raj blamed (a. himself b. hisself) for sleeping through two final exams.

___b___ 4. Would you please let Alfredo and (a. I   b. me) know when you're coming to town?

___b___ 5. Without the right tools, (a. its   b. it's) impossible to pull the door from its hinges.

___a___ 6. I decided that Joon and (a. I   b. myself) would vacation in Oaxaca this year.

___a___ 7. Jamil is one of those students (a. whose   b. who's) grades make other students envious.

___a___ 8. Anne and Ivan bought (a. themselves   b. theirselves) a new PlayStation, and we haven't seen them since.

___b___ 9. (a. Whose   b. Who's) interested in sharing a ride across the country with my nine cats and me?

___b___ 10. The salesman offered Janna and (a. I   b. me) a hefty discount, but we weren't interested in buying a tractor.

___a___ 11. What would a dog do if it finally caught (a. its   b. it's) tail?

___a___ 12. Would you care for a few cookies with (a. your   b. you're) coffee?

___b___ 13. Steve will house-sit for Corinne and (a. she   b. her) next weekend.

___a___ 14. The children are now old enough to get (a. themselves   b. theirselves) ready for bed.

___a___ 15. Hollywood's most popular ice cream parlor is one (a. whose   b. who's) most famous flavor is rosewater.

B. *Using the appropriate letter, identify the use of the italicized pronoun in each sentence.*
    a. subject of a verb   b. predicate pronoun   c. appositive

___b___ 16. The best middlebacks on the soccer team are Claudia and *she*.

    <u> a </u>   17. *Whoever* wants a movie ticket should get in the line to my left.

    <u> b </u>   18. Our history teacher was the *one* voted Outstanding Teacher.

    <u> a </u>   19. My own son is now taller than *I*.

    <u> c </u>   20. Three students—Julia, Lena, and *you*—will star in the spring musical.

C. *Using the appropriate letter, identify the use of the italicized pronoun in each sentence.*
         a. object of a prepostion   b. direct object   c. indirect object

    <u> a </u>   21. Henrik says he is too advanced to play tennis with Jim or *me*.

    <u> b </u>   22. The policeman caught Michael, Brandon, and *me* driving over the speed limit.

    <u> c </u>   23. Our English instructor should give *us* students a break and not assign homework tonight.

    <u> c </u>   24. Ricardo can't figure out which of his beautiful classmates sent *him* the love note.

    <u> a </u>   25. There is no reason to honk so angrily at *us*!

Go to www.ablongman.com/yarber to complete Review Test 6-C.

Writing Paragraphs

Coherence in the Paragraph by Using Transitional Words and Phrases

In the preceding chapters you learned to arrange your ideas in paragraphs in a logical order. Now you will learn that you can make your paragraphs coherent by linking one sentence to the next by using *transitional words and phrases*. They signal the direction of thought as you read through the paragraph. With them, the reader is prepared for each new idea and can relate each new statement to the last. Without them, a paragraph can sound like a list of unrelated ideas.

Notice how each sentence in the following paragraph stands isolated from the next, making it sound wooden and stiff.

■ Speaking and writing are different in many ways. Speech depends on sounds. Writing uses written symbols. Speech developed about 500,000 years ago. Written language is a recent development. It was invented only about six thousand years ago. Speech is usually informal. The word choice of writing is often relatively formal. Pronunciation and accent often tell where the speaker is from. Pronunciation and accent are ignored in writing. A standard diction and spelling system prevails in the written language of most countries. Speech relies on gesture, loudness, and the rise and fall of the voice. Writing lacks gesture, loudness, and the rise and fall of the voice. Careful speakers and writers are aware of the differences.

Notice how much smoother this paragraph becomes when transitional words and phrases and other linking devices are used. They make the paragraph more coherent and the thought much easier to follow.

■ Speaking and writing are different in many ways. Speech depends on sounds; writing, *on the other hand,* uses written symbols. Speech was developed about 500,000 years ago, *but* written language is a recent development, invented only about six thousand years ago. Speech is usually informal, *while* the word choice of writing, *by contrast,* is often relatively formal. *Although* pronunciation and accent often tell where the speaker is from, they are ignored in writing because a standard diction and spelling system prevails in the written language of most countries. Speech relies on gesture, loudness, and the rise and fall of the voice, *but* writing lacks these features. Careful speakers and writers are aware of the differences.

Transitional words and phrases show the relationship between sentences. In some ways they are like traffic signs. They tell the reader what is ahead, warning of a turn, advising when to slow down, and so on.

Examine the following sentences for their use of transitions.

- The shortstop took an extra hour of batting practice. *As a result,* she hit two home runs in the game. (*As a result* shows how the second sentence is the effect or consequence of the first.)

- Many older people look forward to retirement. *However,* some want to continue to work beyond the maximum age limit. (*However* alerts the reader to a contrasting idea ahead.)

Here is a list of some of the most common transitional words that connect sentences, making them more coherent.

Common Transitional Words

also	however	on the contrary
although	in addition	on the other hand
and	in conclusion	second
as a result	in fact	similarly
besides	later	still
but	likewise	that is
consequently	meanwhile	therefore
finally	moreover	though
for example	nevertheless	whereas
furthermore	next	yet

EXERCISE A Using Transitions

Here are ten sentences. Supply the missing transition that seems most fitting for each. Reword the sentences as necessary, but try to avoid using the same transition more than once.

1. _____**Although, Though**_____ Lance is an excellent surfer, we urged him to avoid the beach during the storm.

2. Noelli is a gifted dancer; _**thus, therefore, consequently, as a result**_ no one was surprised when she was asked to audition for a leading role in *Swan Lake*.

3. We were careful in spending our money, _____**but, yet**_____ we still didn't save enough for our ideal vacation.

4. Rudolfo is smart, witty, and handsome; _**also, in addition, moreover, likewise, furthermore**_, he is honest and generous.

5. Sitta has climbed Mt. McKinley and K2; <u>next, finally, later, therefore</u> she'll attempt Mt. Everest.

6. The children slathered themselves with bug lotion; <u>still, however, nevertheless</u>, they were bitten by a swarm of mosquitoes. in fact, as a result,

7. Ana is a sensational tennis player; <u>for example, consequently</u>, she has won our league's trophy four times.

8. I enjoy a good martini; <u>however, on the other hand</u>, Joseph prefers an icy lemonade.
besides, moreover,

9. I don't need a new car; <u>furthermore, in addition</u>, I can't afford one right now.

10. She is a model employee; <u>that is, for example</u>, she's capable, friendly, and punctual.

Writing Tips   Using Traffic Signs in Paragraphs

Transitions give the reader directions, just as a traffic sign gives a driver directions. Here are some common transitions arranged according to their purpose.

Common Transitions

Purpose	Transitions
Addition (developing with ideas and details)	and, also, too, furthermore, in addition, then
Time (stating when)	before, after, earlier, since, later, now, meanwhile, until
Space (stating where)	here, there, above, below, behind, on this side, on the other side, to the right, to the left
Qualification (stating exceptions or modifying)	but, however, though, nevertheless
Repetition (restating for emphasis and clarity)	in other words, in particular, in summary
Exemplification (illustration)	for example, that is
Cause and Effect (showing consequences)	as a result, consequently, therefore
Comparison and Contrast (showing similarities and differences)	similarly, by comparison, likewise, by contrast, on the other hand, on the contrary
Summary (restating chief ideas)	in brief, in conclusion, in summary, finally

Writing Tips He Said, She Said . . .

Plagiarism is presenting someone's ideas or words as your own without giving proper credit. It is stealing, and many colleges and universities discuss it in their catalogs or student codes. Most of the time, students plagiarize without meaning to; they simply don't know which material requires an attribution. Here are some ways to avoid the quicksand of plagiarism.

- Enclose all quoted passages within quotation marks and state their source immediately before or after the passage
- Even if you paraphrase (restate or summarize) someone else's ideas, give credit to the source.
- If a fact or statistic is not generally known, provide your reader with the source where you found it.

EXERCISE B Fixing Choppy Sentences

The paragraph below is filled with choppy and disconnected sentences. Rewrite the paragraph, inserting the appropriate transitions and connecting words and phrases. Reword the paragraph as necessary.

■ Humanity's first walk on the moon occurred on the evening of July 16, 1969. American astronauts Neil Armstrong, Mike Collins, and Ed Aldrin lifted off in *Apollo II*. Thirty-four hours passed in flight. They began a live color broadcast of their activities. They traveled about 250,000 miles by the third day. They went into an elliptical orbit around the moon. Their landing craft gradually approached the surface of the moon. With advice from Houston headquarters, they brought the ship down toward the surface above a rocky crater. Armstrong changed his mind and decided to aim for another landing site. They touched down. The astronauts remained in their cabin for six hours. They opened the hatch and slowly went down the ladder. Armstrong reached the second rung. He let down a television camera. His foot landed on the surface. He stopped to say his now-famous words: "That's one small step for man, one giant leap for mankind."

EXERCISE C Using Transitions

The following paragraph describes the steps necessary when judging the taste of a wine. Note the use of transitions (first, next, then, and finally). Read the paragraph carefully and then respond to (a) or (b) in the accompanying directions.

■ Anyone can learn to judge the taste of a wine by following a series of steps. First, pour the wine into a glass, noting its color, hue, and clarity. These traits reveal the age of a wine and the strength of its flavor. The lighter the color, the younger and lighter-bodied the wine will be. Next, take a long sniff of the poured wine. Swirl the glass in slow, even circles, and then sniff it again. The aroma of the wine, called the nose, may be any combination of smells such as fruity, spicy, floral, or woody. Then take a small sip along with a bit of air. Whirl the wine around in your mouth. Notice how the wine changes, becoming more varied as it swirls and strikes your palate. Finally, note the aftertaste. The more intense and complex the aftertaste, the more hearty the wine.

a. *In a paragraph of at least six sentences, summarize a memorable episode in a book, movie, or television program. Place transitional words or phrases where needed.*

b. *In a paragraph of at least six sentences, summarize the steps needed when doing your least-favorite task or chore. Place transitional words or phrases where needed.*

Computer Activity

Choose a writing suggestion from (a) or (b) in Exercise C on pages 144–145.

When you have finished your paragraph, exchange your file with a classmate who has completed the same exercise.

Use boldface to emphasize the transitional words or phrases that you find in your classmate's paragraph. Ask him or her to do the same for your paragraph.

CHAPTER 7

COMMON ERRORS IN PRONOUN AGREEMENT AND REFERENCE

CHAPTER PREVIEW

In this chapter, you will learn about:

- Making pronouns agree in number and person
- Avoiding vagueness and ambiguity by clear pronoun reference
- Avoiding sexism in pronoun usage
- Writing paragraphs: Developing a paragraph by using examples

In the last chapter we noted that even the most educated speakers and writers are occasionally uncertain about the correct forms of pronouns to use. Another area of usage that causes confusion is pronoun agreement and reference.

Pronouns should agree with the words to which they refer. In other words, if a pronoun refers to a plural antecedent, the pronoun should be plural; if the antecedent is singular, the pronoun should also be singular; and if the antecedent is a pronoun in the third person, the pronoun should also be in the third person. (An **antecedent** is the word or term referred to by the pronoun.)

The rules for pronoun agreement and reference are usually easy to follow. However, there are a few situations in which the choice of a pronoun is not clear or when the antecedent is not obvious. Such cases can result in confusion or ambiguity on the part of the reader, as well as the writer. Because pronoun agreement and reference are necessary if your writing is to be logical and effective, this chapter will examine the situations when they are most critical.

Agreement in Number

A pronoun must be in **agreement** in **number** with its antecedent. If the antecedent is singular, the pronoun is singular. If the antecedent is plural, the pronoun is plural. This rule poses no problems in sentences in which the pronouns and their antecedents are close, as in the following examples.

- *Elizabeth* wanted to buy a used *car,* but *she* did not want to pay more than nine thousand dollars for *it.* (This sentence has two singular pronouns, each matched with its singular antecedent: *she* (*Elizabeth*) and *it* (*car*).)

- Her *parents* told Elizabeth that *they* would be willing to lend her an additional two thousand dollars. (The plural pronoun *they* matches its plural antecedent *parents.* Do you see another pronoun in this sentence? What is its antecedent?)

- *Anton* purchased *his* tickets yesterday for the Janet Jackson concert. (The singular pronoun *his* matches its singular antecedent, *Anton.*)

Problems in pronoun agreement occur when the writer loses sight of the antecedent or confuses it with other nouns in the sentence, as in the following sentence.

- **Nonstandard:**   The faculty committee presented *their* recommendations for new graduation requirements to the deans of the college.

This sentence is nonstandard because the plural pronoun *their* does not agree with its singular antecedent, *committee.* How many committees were there? Only one. Therefore, the pronoun referring to it should be singular: *its.* The writer of this sentence may have been thinking of the individuals on the committee or of the recommendations that were submitted, or even of the deans, and therefore wrongly selected *their,* a plural pronoun.

Here, then, is the standard version.

- **Standard:**   The faculty committee presented *its* recommendations for new graduation requirements to the deans of the college.

The following rules will help you to use pronouns in your sentences that will agree with their antecedents in number:

1. In general, use a singular pronoun when the antecedent is an **indefinite pronoun,** a pronoun that does not refer to a specific person or thing. (For a review of indefinite pronouns, see Chapter 6.) Some indefinite pronouns present exceptions to this general rule—they are always plural, or they can be singular or plural depending on the kind of noun they represent.

   a. The following indefinite pronouns are always *singular,* which means that the other pronouns referring to them should be singular: *another, anybody, anyone, anything, each, each one, either, every, everybody, everyone, everything, many a, much, neither, nobody, no one, nothing, one, other, somebody, someone,* and *something.*

Notice that in the following sentences the indefinite pronouns are accompanied by singular pronouns.

- *Anyone* planning a trip to Russia should apply for a visa before *he* leaves this country.
- *Each* of the girls told me *her* name.
- When I returned, *everything* was in *its* place.
- *Many a* son belatedly wishes *he* had listened to *his* father's advice.
- *Everyone* was asked to contribute as much as *he* could.
- *Everyone* is responsible for making *his* own bed.
- *Neither* of the girls wanted *her* picture taken.

You probably noticed the use of masculine pronouns (*he* and *his*) in the first, fifth, and sixth examples. Many writers and readers object to the exclusive use of masculine pronouns with indefinite pronouns such as *anybody, everyone, someone,* and *everybody.* Note carefully the following sentence.

- Everyone took *his* seat.

This is traditional usage, with *his* used to refer to humanity in general. To avoid the sole use of masculine pronouns, some writers would word the sentence like this.

- Everyone took *his or her* seat.

Because this form can be awkward, some writers prefer the following method to avoid only masculine pronouns.

- Everyone took *their* seats.

While avoiding the exclusive use of the masculine pronoun, this sentence combines a plural pronoun (*their*) with a singular antecedent (*everyone*). Those who prefer this version should be aware that it is not yet accepted in formal written English.

What is the answer to this dilemma? An increasingly popular solution is to reword the sentence, making the subject plural.

- The *members* of the audience took *their* seats.

Note: For additional suggestions for avoiding sexism in pronoun usage, see pages 156–157.

b. The following indefinite pronouns are always *plural*: *both, few, many, others,* and *several.*

When they are used as antecedents, pronouns referring to them are always plural. Note their use in the following sentences.

■ *Many* of his customers transferred *their* accounts to another company.

■ *A few* of the students admitted *they* had not studied.

■ *Several* of the golfers said *they* wanted to bring their own caddies.

■ *Both* of the cars had *their* mufflers replaced.

c. The following indefinite pronouns can be either *singular* or *plural*: *all, any, more, most, none,* and *some.*

Antecedents referring to them will be either singular or plural, depending on their meaning and the noun they represent:

■ **Plural:**   *Most* fast-food customers want less fat in *their* hamburgers.

■ **Singular:** *Most* of the hamburger has less fat in *it.*

■ **Plural:**   *All* of the leaks have been traced to *their* sources.

■ **Singular:** *All* of the water has leaked from *its* container.

■ **Plural:**   *Some* of the customers want *their* money refunded.

■ **Singular:** *Some* of the money was found in *its* hiding place.

EXERCISE 7-1

In the space provided, write the letter that corresponds to the correct pronoun.

___a___   1. Before the concert, each musician tuned (a. his or her   b. their) instrument.

___a___   2. Someone who buys a puppy must realize that (a. he or she   b. they) may see damaged rugs and furniture.

___b___   3. Some of the tools in my father's garage look like (a. it's   b. they're) from the Stone Age.

___a___   4. Each of the women returned (a. her   b. their) books to the library.

___b___   5. Many of the students earned As for (a. his or her   b. their) art projects.

___a___   6. The staff at my dentist's office (a. is   b. are) accustomed to hearing shrieks from the examination rooms.

___a___   7. Each local painter and sculptor saw at least one of (a. his or her   b. their) pieces displayed in the museum.

___a___   8. Anyone who wants (a. his or her   b. their) car washed should pull into the lot right now.

___b___   9. Both the gardenia and the hibiscus need an organic pesticide to protect (a. its   b. their) leaves.

___a___   10. Neither of the movies lived up to (a. its   b. their) promise of suspense and romance.

2. Antecedents joined by *and* usually take plural pronouns.

   ■ *Prince Charles and Prince Edward of England* are more famous for *their* private lives than for *their* political views.

   ■ *West Germany and East Germany* voted to unite *their* peoples in 1990.

When the antecedents are joined by *and* but refer to a single person or thing, the pronoun may be singular.

   ■ The *physicist and Nobel Prize winner* was able to present *her* ideas in terms that the students could understand.

   ■ The *largest tree and oldest living thing* on earth, the *Sequoiadendron giganteum,* is better known by *its* familiar name, the Giant Sequoia.

When the compound antecedent is preceded by *each* or *every*, a singular pronoun should be used.

   ■ *Each* team player and substitute received a certificate recognizing *her* participation.

   ■ *Every* father and son was assigned to *his* table.

3. **Collective nouns,** nouns that name a group of people or things (see Chapter 4), usually take singular pronouns if the group is regarded as a unit.

   ■ The *couple* was honored for *its* contribution to the church.

   ■ The *faculty* was renowned for *its* research and scholarship.

If the members of the group are acting separately, a plural pronoun should be used.

   ■ The *couple* disagreed over the amount of money *they* should pay for a new car.

   ■ The *faculty* were paid various amounts, depending on *their* education, experience, and publications.

4. When two or more antecedents are joined by *or* or *nor*, the pronouns should agree with the nearer antecedent.

   ■ Neither the defendant *nor* the witnesses changed *their* testimony.

   ■ Either the roofers *or* the carpenters left *their* radio in our driveway.

   When the antecedent closer to the pronoun is singular, the result can sometimes be awkward.

   ■ Neither the sopranos *nor* the tenor could sing his part without looking at *his* music. (Though technically correct, this sentence is confusing.)

   Such a sentence should be revised.

   ■ Neither the tenor nor the sopranos could sing *their* parts without looking at *their* music.

5. **Demonstrative pronouns,** pronouns that are used as *adjectives* (*this, that, these, those*) must agree in number with the nouns they modify. Do not say or write "these kind," "these sort," "those kind," "those type," and so on. The correct forms are "these kinds," "these sorts," "this kind," "this sort," "that kind," "those kinds," and so on. The following sentences illustrate the use of pronouns as demonstrative adjectives.

   ■ **Nonstandard:** These kind of trees are common throughout the South.
   ■ **Standard:** This kind of tree is common throughout the South.
     (**Or:** These kinds of trees are common throughout the South.)

   ■ **Nonstandard:** These type of ball bearings never need lubrication.
   ■ **Standard:** This type of ball bearings never needs lubrication.
     (**Or:** These types of ball bearings never need lubrication.)

Tips **on Pronoun Agreement**

Pronouns should agree in number with the nouns for which they stand.

1. Determine which noun is the real antecedent.
2. Determine whether the antecedent is singular or plural in meaning.
3. Remember that singular pronouns must refer to singular antecedents and that plural pronouns must refer to plural antecedents.

EXERCISE 7-2

In the space provided, write the letter that corresponds to the correct pronoun.

___a___   1. The Olympic medalist and American hero was greeted by (a. his   b. their) coach and wife.

___a___   2. Senator Calderon told the panel that (a. that   b. those) kind of change in the law would raise taxes.

___a___   3. Neither Lois nor Arlene shares (a. her   b. their) recipes with anyone.

___b___   4. Both Scott and Efrain have completed (a. his   b. their) requirements for obtaining a real estate license.

___b___   5. (a. That   b. Those) kinds of puzzles are difficult to solve.

___b___   6. The Popov family received (a. its   b. their) passports from the American Embassy.

___a___   7. Neither the witness nor the policeman would change (a. his   b. their) testimony concerning the color of the car.

___a___   8. The family was forced to sell (a. its   b. their) share of the company.

___a___   9. Each of the major religions and (a. its   b. their) beliefs was discussed in the seminar.

___a___ 10. Neither of the twin daughters looked like (a. her   b. their) mother.

Agreement in Person

You have seen that pronouns agree in number with their antecedents. If the agreement breaks down, the reader is distracted and confused. Agreement in person is equally important. **Person** refers to the differences among the person speaking (first person), the person spoken to (second person), and the person or thing spoken about (third person).

Pronouns by Person

First person pronouns:	I, me, my, mine, we, us, our, ours
Second person pronouns:	you, your, yours
Third person pronouns:	he, him, his, she, her, hers, it, its, they, them, theirs

---

When you make a mistaken shift in person, you have shown that you have lost your way in your own sentence—that you have forgotten what you were writing about. Here are some examples of confusing shifts in person.

■ **Shift:**   Swimmers in the ocean should be very careful because *you* can get caught in rip currents. (This sentence shifts from third person *swimmers* to second person *you.*)

■ **Revised:**   Swimmers in the ocean should be very careful because *they* can get caught in rip currents.

■ **Shift:**   When you fly to St. Louis, *passengers* can see the arch on the bank of the Mississippi River from miles away. (This sentence shifts from second person *you* to third person *passengers.*)

■ **Revised:**   When you fly to St. Louis, *you* can see the arch on the bank of the Mississippi River from miles away.

■ **Shift:**   When I entered the room, *you* could smell the fresh paint.

■ **Revised:**   When I entered the room, *I* could smell the fresh paint.

The best way to avoid such shifts is to decide in advance whom you are talking about—and stick with that point of view.

EXERCISE 7-3

Correct any errors involving needless shift of person in the following sentences. If a sentence is correct, write "C" in front of it.

1. Before you visit a foreign country for the first time, **you** ~~one~~ should learn a few phrases in that nation's language in case you face an emergency.

2. Drivers who use seatbelts are less likely to suffer injuries if **they** ~~you~~ have an accident.

3. Jangling your car keys or constantly looking at your watch can be signs that **you are** ~~one is~~ impatient.

4. **C** The first time an American drives a car in England, he may become confused by the movement of traffic.

5. Beginning reporters on a newspaper are assigned important stories after **they** ~~you~~ demonstrate **their** ~~your~~ ability.

6. Heidi was stunned to learn that **she** ~~you~~ must take a course in calculus for her degree in engineering.

7. People with fair skin should not stay in the sun for long periods of time because **they** ~~you~~ may suffer later from skin cancer.

8. When we left the hotel to go shopping, you^(we) had to turn in your^(our) room key to the clerk.

9. **C** Chen complained that if he wanted to do something right, he had to do it himself.

10. Once you have heard her distinctive voice, the^(you) listener will never forget it.

Pronoun Reference

Pronouns depend on other words—their antecedents—for their meaning. If **pronoun reference,** the relationship of pronouns to their antecedents, is unclear, their meaning or identity will be confusing. For this reason, you should make certain that every pronoun in your writing (except for indefinite pronouns like *anyone* and *somebody* and for idioms like "*It* is two o'clock") refers specifically to something previously named—its antecedent. In doing so, you will avoid the two most common kinds of problems in pronoun reference: *vagueness* because the writer did not furnish a specific antecedent, and *ambiguity* because the writer supplied too many antecedents.

Here is an example of each kind of error.

- **Vague:**   Several minor political parties nominate presidential candidates every four years. This is one of the characteristics of the American political system. (*What* is one of the characteristics of the American political system?)

- **Ambiguous:**   Gore Vidal wrote a biography of Abraham Lincoln that demonstrates his knowledge and sensitivity. (*Who* demonstrates his knowledge and sensitivity: Gore Vidal or Abraham Lincoln?)

By following the accompanying suggestions, you can make clear the relationship between pronouns and their antecedents.

1. The antecedent of a pronoun should be specific rather than implied. Avoid using *that, this, which,* and *it* to refer to implied ideas unless the reference is absolutely clear.

   - **Vague:**   Juana was so impressed by the lecture given by the astronomer that she decided to major in it. (Major in what? *It* has no antecedent in this sentence.)

   - **Revision:**   Juana was so impressed by the lecture given by the astronomer that she decided to major in astronomy.

   - **Vague:**   Brad consumes huge quantities of potatoes, spaghetti, and ice cream every day, and it is beginning to be noticeable. (What is beginning to be noticeable?)

- **Revision:** Brad consumes huge quantities of potatoes, spaghetti, and ice cream every day, and the increase in his weight is beginning to be noticeable.

- **Vague:** Athena enjoys singing with music groups at school, and she would like to be a professional one someday. (A professional what?)

- **Revision:** Athena enjoys singing with music groups at school, and she would like to be a professional singer someday.

Such vague sentences are corrected by supplying the missing antecedent.

2. Some sentences, however, are confusing because they have more than one possible antecedent, and the result is ambiguity. To avoid ambiguity, place pronouns as close as possible to their antecedents. Revise sentences in which there are two possible antecedents for a pronoun.

- **Confusing:** Jake's new car has leather seats, a sunroof, a digital dash with graphic readouts, a vocal warning system, power windows, and an eight-speaker stereo. It is power-driven. (What does *it* refer to? What is power-driven?)

- **Revision:** Jake's new car has leather seats, a sunroof that is power-driven, a digital dash with graphic readouts, a vocal warning system, power windows, and an eight-speaker stereo.

- **Confusing:** Spanish cooking and Mexican cooking should not be confused; it is not as spicy. (What is not as spicy?)

- **Revision:** Spanish cooking is not as spicy as Mexican cooking.

- **Confusing:** The vase has been in our family for one hundred years that you dropped.

- **Revision:** The vase that you dropped has been in our family for one hundred years.

Tips on Pronoun Reference

1. Don't shift pronouns unnecessarily from one person to another.
2. Learn the pronouns for first, second, and third person.
3. Make sure that every *that, this, which,* and *it* in your sentences has a clear antecedent.
4. Place pronouns as close as possible to their antecedents.

EXERCISE 7-4

Rewrite the following sentences to make clear any vague or ambiguous pronoun references. Add, omit, or change words as you deem necessary.   **Student responses will vary.**

1. The reason that Consuela is so knowledgeable about buying and selling stocks and bonds is that she had once been one.
2. Jamal has been transferred to the hospital's night unit, which disappoints his wife and children.
3. Norm bought a baseball bat and hockey stick and then returned it.
4. Shamika's skill in solving difficult physics problems is partly due to the influence of her mother, who is one.
5. Although Kevin has never been there, he likes Chilean food.
6. Elaine plays the piano very well, but she keeps it hidden.
7. Ray's secret ambition is to be a chef, but he has never studied it.
8. At registration time they check your record and transcript.
9. As Leo and Martin talked, his voice began to rise in anger.
10. Luciano Pavarotti is a great tenor who claims that he has practiced it every day since he was a child.

Avoiding Sexism in Pronoun Usage

One of the healthy trends taking place in our society is the recognition that American English has a masculine bias, particularly in its use of pronouns. Because English lacks a singular pronoun that refers to both sexes, *he, his,* and *him* have traditionally been used to refer to men and women when the gender of the antecedent is composed of both males and females or is unknown.

When we constantly use masculine pronouns to personify "the professor," "the lawyer," and "the supervisor," we are subtly rejecting the notion of a female professor, lawyer, and supervisor. Using *he, his,* and *him* as generic terms misleads your audience because these pronouns do not accurately represent the people behind them.

■ **Traditional:** A writer can often get ideas when he is listening to music.

Fortunately, there are several ways to make our language gender-fair to avoid exclusion of women.

1. Reword the sentence.

    ■ A writer can often get ideas when listening to music.

2. Change the sentence to the plural.

   ■ Writers often get ideas when they are listening to music.

3. Substitute another pronoun for the masculine pronoun.

   ■ A writer can often get ideas when she is listening to music.

   ■ A writer can often get ideas when he or she is listening to music.

   ■ When writing, one can often get ideas while listening to music.

The exclusive use of masculine pronouns (*he*, *his*, and *him*) with indefinite pronouns such as *anybody*, *everyone*, *someone*, and *everybody* is another example of usage that is not gender-fair.

■ **Traditional**: Everyone took *his* seat.

The use of *his* in this example to refer to humanity in general is still widespread. To avoid the sole use of masculine pronouns, four possibilities are available.

1. Substitute *his or her* for *his*.

   ■ Everyone took his or her seat.

Because this form can be awkward, many writers and readers prefer other solutions to this problem.

2. Reword the sentence.

   ■ The members of the audience took their seats.

3. Some writers prefer the following method to avoid only masculine pronouns.

   ■ Everyone took their seats.

While avoiding the exclusive use of the masculine pronoun, this sentence combines a plural pronoun (*their*) with a singular antecedent (*everyone*). Those who prefer this version should be aware that it is not yet accepted in formal written English.

4. In essays and articles, you can balance references to males and females between paragraphs or between examples in a series. Try to avoid shifting pronoun gender within individual sentences.

EDITING EXERCISES

The paragraph below describes the contributions of Frank Lloyd Wright to American architecture. The subsequent paragraph describes the job of a professional "nose," a perfume designer. Both paragraphs contain several errors in pronoun agreement and reference. Improve each paragraph by correcting the errors, revising the sentences when necessary.

Ask anyone who knows about architecture, and they will be aware of the importance of Frank Lloyd Wright. No other architect has influenced modern American design more than he. One of Wright's best-known principles is that buildings must stand as unobtrusively as possible against its natural settings. As a child, Wright spent many summers on his mother's family farm in Wisconsin where you couldn't help but develop a keen love of the land. He decided that buildings, like plants, should emerge from the soil and be a part of them. Therefore, building materials should be natural and simple, such as wood, stone, and brick. They should be presented in their natural colors, shapes, and textures; even its flaws should show. Wright simplified the components, shapes, and decor of buildings to make it more natural and less synthetic. He built low, horizontally straight ceilings so that the building would seem nestled in their setting, not tower above it. Windows became huge "light screens" rather than squares cut into walls. They looked out to dense foliage, a waterfall, or other natural features. He even omitted garages and basements from homes in warm regions, arguing that you do not need them in a warm, dry climate. Toward the end of his career Wright developed house plans that used inexpensive, prefabricated materials to help the average American afford themselves a good home.

Because a perfume inventor uses his nose to create and test a new scent, they're nicknamed "the Nose." The Nose uses raw scents and a set of scales to create their new fragrances. Able to recognize up to 3,000 smells, you sit in a lab, mix ingredients, and sample it yourself on small paper dipsticks. Although Noses increasingly rely on synthetic chemicals, you sometimes still use real flowers.

Chanel No. 5, the world's best-selling perfume, for example, lists among their main ingredients rose, jasmine, and a man-made musk. It may take months or even years before a Nose achieves a scent that they're satisfied with. There are about a thousand Noses in the world, but only about fifty are powerful enough to get his way in designing and marketing a new scent for a company.

WRITING SENTENCES Avoiding Common Errors In Pronoun Usage

As you saw in this chapter, readers can be confused if pronouns do not agree with the words to which they refer. In this exercise you will be writing sentences demonstrating the correct use of pronoun agreement and reference.

1. Write two sentences, each using a collective noun as the subject requiring a singular pronoun as its antecedent.
2. Use the collective nouns from the preceding sentences as the subjects of two new sentences, each requiring a plural pronoun as its antecedent.
3. Write two sentences that contain mistaken shifts in person. Then revise each sentence to make it correct.
4. Write two sentences that contain unclear pronoun references. Then revise each sentence to make it correct.
5. Write two sentences in which you illustrate your solution to the exclusive use of masculine pronouns with indefinite pronouns.

Language Tips

1. The following indefinite pronouns are always *singular,* which means that verbs used with them are always singular.

   another, anybody, anyone, anything, each, each one, either, every, everybody, everyone, everything, many a, much, neither, nobody, no one, nothing, one, other, somebody, someone, *and* something

2. The following indefinite pronouns are always *plural,* which means that verbs used with them are always plural.

   both, few, many, others, *and* several

3. The following indefinite pronouns can be either *singular* or *plural,* depending on their meaning and the noun they represent.

   all, any, more, most, none, *and* some

Name _____ Date _____

REVIEW TEST 7-A
Common Errors in Pronoun Agreement and Reference

A. *In the space provided, write the letter corresponding to the correct pronoun.*

___a___ 1. The cast of the play was praised by the director for (a. its   b. their) performance on opening night.

___a___ 2. Senator Benson told the panel that (a. that   b. those) kind of proposed federal regulation would discourage individual savings.

___a___ 3. Mrs. Alvarez said that each of us was responsible for preparing (a. his or her   b. our) own meals.

___b___ 4. When you visit a foreign country for the first time, (a. Americans   b. you) should prepare by learning a few appropriate phrases.

___a___ 5. Each magazine and book was cataloged according to (a. its   b. their) subject.

___a___ 6. Failure to sign (a. his or her   b. your) tax form is the most common error made by the average taxpayer, according to the Internal Revenue Service.

___a___ 7. Many an inexperienced mountain climber has lost (a. his or her   b. their) life attempting to reach the top of Kilimanjaro.

___b___ 8. Both the painter and the carpenter have submitted (a. his or her   b. their) estimates.

___b___ 9. (a. These   b. This) kind of rose will not bloom in cold climates.

___a___ 10. Every new drug must pass rigorous tests before (a. it   b. they) can be approved by the Food and Drug Administration.

B. *In the space provided, write the letter corresponding to the kind of error in pronoun usage each sentence contains. If the sentence is correct, write "d."*
  a. shift in person   b. unclear pronoun reference   c. failure to agree in number   d. correct

___d___ 11. Max bought a bowling ball and a baseball bat and then returned them.

___b___ 12. Alexi was too shy to ask Magda for a date, and he was teased about it.

___a___ 13. Students who miss the registration deadline will be unable to enroll in all of the classes you want to take.

___d___ 14. Drivers who listen to music and talk on a cellular phone while driving a car run the risk of having an accident.

    c   15. A beginning reporter on a newspaper is assigned important stories after they demonstrate their ability.

    b   16. The reason that Pierre is such an expert at gardening is that he had once been one.

    b   17. Hugo has been transferred to the night shift, which pleases his wife very much.

    d   18. Many Vietnamese-Americans have succeeded in maintaining their ancient traditions while adjusting to life in the United States.

    a   19. Yang was disappointed to learn that you have to take a course in calculus in order to earn his degree in engineering.

    b   20. Both Nick and Zach were upset with his semester grade.

    c   21. Neither of his two daughters has their own telephone.

    d   22. Bettors who boast of their winnings at Las Vegas often do not mention their losses.

    b   23. Jasmine worked hard and saved her money, which surprised her parents.

    c   24. Everyone is entitled to their own opinion with respect to the best candidate.

    b   25. Many people in this country are alcoholics, which is unfortunate.

REVIEW TEST 7-B
Common Errors in Pronoun Agreement and Reference

A. *In the space provided, write the letter corresponding to the correct pronoun.*

__a__ 1. The faculty of the engineering school was praised by the president for (a. its b. their) dedication to the college.

__a__ 2. (a. That b. Those) kind of television program tends to glamorize violence.

__a__ 3. Each of the workers was responsible for furnishing (a. his or her b. their) own tools.

__a__ 4. When studying a foreign language, one should avoid translating each word separately into (a. his or her b. your) own language.

__a__ 5. Each dog and cat was classified according to (a. its b. their) breed.

__a__ 6. Every airline passenger must walk through a metal detector before (a. he or she b. they) may board the airplane.

__b__ 7. (a. That b. Those) kinds of puzzles drive me crazy.

__b__ 8. Both Tyrell and Ana have completed (a. his b. their) homework.

__a__ 9. Many a speculator in the stock market has lost (a. his or her b. their) entire fortune.

__b__ 10. Cracking your knuckles or tapping your fingers is often a sign that (a. one is b. you are) nervous.

B. *In the space provided, write the letter corresponding to the kind of error in pronoun usage each sentence contains. If the sentence is correct, write "d."*
   a. shift in person b. unclear pronoun reference c. failure to agree in number d. correct

__d__ 11. The oboe, a member of the woodwind family, has many beautiful concertos written for it.

__b__ 12. The new sales clerk did not know how to use a cash register, but he denied it.

__a__ 13. Statistics have clearly demonstrated that drivers who do not use their seatbelts are more likely to suffer an injury if you have an accident.

__d__ 14. Beginning skiers who have not taken lessons run the risk of injury if they try to ski on the expert ski runs immediately.

__d__ 15. The identity of the witness was concealed in order to protect her.

___b___ 16. Joaquin's ability to solve difficult math problems is partly due to the fact that his father had been one.

___c___ 17. Neither of the two suspects could afford their attorney.

___c___ 18. When the typical male watches television, they jump from one channel to another.

___b___ 19. Dmitri painted his garage and installed new garage doors, which surprised his wife.

___c___ 20. Anyone who claims that they overpaid their bill may file a claim with the manager.

___b___ 21. The loggers complain that the new regulations have harmed their industry, which is controversial.

___b___ 22. Both Ramon and Tim agree that he was cheated.

___a___ 23. I was surprised to discover that you have to present two forms of identification before cashing a check at my bank.

___d___ 24. Many students who watched the television series on astronomy were better able to understand the theories of Galileo.

___b___ 25. Mark plays golf five days a week, which angers his wife.

Go to www.ablongman.com/yarber to complete Review Test 7-C.

WRITING PARAGRAPHS

DEVELOPING A PARAGRAPH BY USING EXAMPLES

One of the most common weaknesses in college writing is thin and underdeveloped paragraphs. While there is no exact rule about the minimum number of sentences required in a paragraph, a short paragraph is often a sign that the writer did not follow through in his or her thinking about the topic. Many weak paragraphs consist of little more than a topic sentence and one or two generalities, as if the writer hoped that the reader would complete the thought for the writer. In general, it is a good rule to examine carefully any paragraphs that you have written that contain only one, two, or three sentences. The chances are good that they are too thin and skimpy.

The length of a paragraph depends on the topic. The best measuring stick is your topic sentence: what promise did you make in it to your reader? As a result of your topic sentence, are a series of examples expected? Is a definition of a term used in the topic sentence promised? Or do you imply that you will present a comparison or contrast between two objects or people? The expectations raised by your topic sentence determine, to a great degree, the length and the kind of development required of your paragraph.

Here is a student-written paragraph describing the last few minutes in a grocery store before it closes for the weekend. The paragraph is underdeveloped because the writer makes a few vague observations but nothing that we can see or hear—nothing that makes the topic sentence come alive.

> ■ The last few minutes before closing time are chaotic at the Vons market where I work. There is confusion everywhere, and everyone is trying to leave on time. Customers and clerks are frantic, and there is always a problem at the last minute.

Notice how vague the paragraph is: "there is confusion everywhere," "customers and clerks are frantic," and "there is always a problem." But what kind of confusion? Why are the customers and clerks frantic? And what kinds of problems erupt at the last minute? We do not know the answers to these questions, and as a result, the paragraph is blurred and indistinct.

The student was asked to revise his paragraph, and here is his revision. Notice how he has developed the topic sentence with details that make the scene more vivid.

> ■ The last few minutes before closing time are chaotic at the Vons market where I work. As the checkout clerks begin to total their registers, the store is invaded by last-minute shoppers desperate for cigarettes, milk, or bread. A few customers are still in the vegetable section squeezing each tomato or cantaloupe as the manager paces by nervously. The butcher and his assistants are removing the meat from the display case and putting it in the freezer, slamming the doors like guards at Fort Knox. A little

boy is running up and down the aisles calling out for his mother who returns to the store hysterically looking for him. My friend Manuel, who restocks the shelves, waits impatiently for all of us to leave so that he can bring out his carts full of boxes of canned goods. Finally, the last customer is escorted to the door, and I sit down on an upturned soda case to rest for a few minutes before changing my clothes. In the stockroom a transistor radio begins to blare out rock lyrics. Suddenly there is a tap on the front door of the store. A customer says he didn't get his deposit back on the soda bottle he had returned.

As you can easily see, the revised paragraph is fully developed. It offers the sights and sounds of closing time, helping us to see and hear the chaos mentioned in the topic sentence. By comparing the two versions you can appreciate the difference between an undeveloped and a developed paragraph.

One of the most common ways to develop a paragraph is by using *examples*. A paragraph developed in this manner begins with a generalization, which it then supports with specific cases or examples. The examples should be typical, to the point, and supportive of the generalization.

In the following paragraph, Maya Angelou, the African American poet, uses examples to help you to see and hear the children as well as to smell the evening's refreshments.

■ The weeks until graduation were filled with heady activities. A group of small children were to be presented in a play about buttercups and daisies and bunny rabbits. They could be heard throughout the building practicing their hops and their little songs that sounded like silver bells. The older girls (nongraduates, of course) were assigned the task of making refreshments for the night's festivities. A tangy scent of ginger, cinnamon, nutmeg and chocolate wafted around the home economics building as the budding cooks made samples for themselves and their teachers.

—Maya Angelou, *I Know Why the Caged Bird Sings*, p. 146.

The next paragraph, written by a student, develops its topic sentence with a series of examples of the ways in which the climate phenomenon called El Niño affects weather and people worldwide.

■ El Niño is a naturally occurring climate event that brings warmer-than-normal ocean temperatures and affects weather and people throughout the world. The prolonged El Niño of 1997–1998, for example, contributed to crippling crop loss in Argentina and New Zealand and to wildfires in Indonesia. People, livestock, and crops were lost in floods across Chile, Peru, and Brazil. In the United States, El Niño's heavy rains caused mudslides and floods in California, Texas, and the southeastern states of the country. Because warm ocean temperatures make fish less plentiful, the livelihood of many of the world's fishermen and the coastal villages who depend on them was ruined.

165

Write a paragraph of at least six sentences on one of the topics below, using examples to develop your paragraph. Begin by writing your topic sentence and then listing specific examples to make the topic sentence clear. Then write your paragraph.

- the benefits of coming from a large family
- athletes who do not fit the image
- immigrants who have overcome handicaps
- corruption in public office
- outstanding local attractions to visit
- a friend with many accomplishments
- people to avoid at a party
- advice to a kid brother or sister
- some stereotypes that are true
- commercials that are actually enjoyable

Write a paragraph of at least six sentences on one of the topics below, using examples to develop your paragraph. Begin by writing your topic sentence and then listing at least three examples to support the topic sentence. Then write your paragraph.

- someone who helped you improve your life
- types of ethnic foods
- benefits of the Internet
- an acquaintance with bad manners
- free or inexpensive places to take a date
- an ideal vacation

Writing Tips For Example . . .

A paragraph developed by using examples may be based on one example, or it may be developed by using a series of examples that support the topic sentence. In either case, you should follow certain guidelines:

- Don't cite exceptions or rare instances as examples to prove your point.
- The best examples are often taken from your own experience. Personal examples aren't always available, of course, but when they are, they have an impact.
- Don't present your examples in a haphazard, random order. Follow a plan.

Writing Tips **Tougher Than Mount Everest . . .**

Do you have a case of writer's block that you can't seem to conquer? The best way to resume writing is to *forget* about writing—that is, for a while. Exercise can help, so take a short jog, walk briskly, or lift some weights. Watch a funny television show to relax your mind. Take a nap: maybe your block is the result of fatigue. If all of these tricks fail, your instructor will have some ideas about how to move your paper along.

Computer Activity

Follow the directions for writing about one of the topics listed in Exercise B on page 166.

When you have finished, transfer your file to another student whom you have selected as a writing partner.

Ask your classmate to list the three examples found in your paragraph. Do the same for his or her paragraph.

CHAPTER 8

COMPOUND AND COMPLEX SENTENCES

CHAPTER PREVIEW

In this chapter, you will learn about:

- Using a variety of sentence types
- Using and punctuating compound and complex sentences
- Recognizing three types of dependent clauses
  Adverb clauses
  Adjective clauses
  Noun clauses
- Writing paragraphs: Developing a paragraph by comparison and contrast

One of the marks of a good writer is the ability to use a variety of sentence types. The simple sentence is an important weapon to have in your writing arsenal, but it is limited in the ways it can be used and in the jobs it can perform. Compound and complex sentences give you additional alternatives for expressing your ideas, usually in more precise ways.

In Chapter 3 you were given a brief introduction to compound and complex sentences. In this chapter you will learn more about them, including how to form and punctuate them. Becoming familiar with compound and complex sentences and knowing when to use them will help you to make your writing more exact and interesting.

Compound Sentences

You will recall from Chapter 3 that a **simple sentence** consists of an independent clause—in other words, a subject–verb combination that stands alone and makes sense.

- Cold Play performed dozens of songs.
- Cold Play performed and recorded dozens of songs.
- Cold Play and the Rolling Stones performed dozens of songs.
- Cold Play and the Rolling Stones performed and recorded dozens of songs.

A **compound sentence** consists of two or more simple sentences (or **independent clauses**) containing closely related ideas and usually connected by a comma and a coordinating conjunction (*and, but, so, for, nor, or,* and *yet*). Notice how each of the following compound sentences consists of two independent clauses with related ideas joined with a comma and a coordinating conjunction:

- The average income of young American couples has increased, *but* many of them cannot afford to buy a home.
- Johnny Depp is my favorite actor, *and* his movie *The Pirates of the Caribbean* is my favorite movie.
- Vince offered to help cook dinner, *so* Janet asked him to make the salad.

When these sentences are divided into halves, each half can stand as an independent clause or simple sentence.

- The average income of young American couples has increased. Many of them cannot afford to buy a home.
- Johnny Depp is my favorite actor. *The Pirates of the Caribbean* is my favorite movie.
- Vince offered to help cook dinner. Janet asked him to make the salad.

By combining these simple sentences with commas and coordinating conjunctions, the results are longer, smoother compound sentences. But remember: the independent clauses in a compound sentence must contain closely related ideas, and they are usually joined with a coordinating conjunction. Never try to combine two independent clauses with *only* a comma. The result will be a **comma-splice,** a serious sentence fault. (See Chapter 9 for ways to avoid and to correct comma-splices.)

EXERCISE 8-1

Below is a series of independent clauses, each followed by a comma. Change each clause into a compound sentence by adding a second independent clause containing a related idea and combining the two clauses with a coordinating conjunction ("and," "but," "so," "for," "nor," "or," or "yet"). Try to use each of the coordinating conjunctions at least once.   **Student responses will vary.**

1. Elvis Presley's grave site at his former home, Graceland, is visited by more than 700,000 tourists each year, _____.

2. Charles Schulz drew the *Peanuts* cartoon strip for nearly fifty years,

    _____.

3. The senator resigned after being convicted of fraud,_____.
4. Everyone has trouble spelling certain words, _____.
5. Many people are willing to pay high prices to eat greasy snails in French restaurants,_____.
6. A growing number of drivers are forsaking traditional sedans and wagons for large all-terrain vehicles,_____.
7. Theresa gave up her habit of eating a huge bag of potato chips every day,

    _____.

8. Most people do not pay the entire balance on their credit card account every month, _____.
9. Climax, Colorado, is the highest settlement in the United States,

    _____.

10. Taj has not seen a movie since *Possession,* _____.

Most independent clauses are connected by coordinating conjunctions. You may, however, use a semicolon (;) to connect the clauses if the relationship between the ideas expressed in the independent clauses is very close and obvious without a conjunction. In such cases the semicolon takes the place of both the conjunction and the comma preceding it. For example:

■ Robert Penn Warren was this country's first official Poet Laureate; he was named on February 26, 1986.

■ I love enchiladas and chile rellenos; they are my favorite kinds of Mexican food.

When using a semicolon, be certain that a coordinating conjunction would not be more appropriate. Using a semicolon in the following sentence would be confusing because the relationship between the two clauses would not be clear:

■ **Confusing**: I have never played hockey; I like to watch hockey games on television.

By substituting a coordinating conjunction (and a comma) for the semicolon, you can make clear the relationship between the clauses:

■ **Revised**: I have never played hockey, *but* I like to watch hockey games on television.

Punctuating Compound Sentences

1. If the independent clauses in a compound sentence are connected by a coordinating conjunction, place a comma in front of the conjunction. Do not try to combine independent clauses with only a comma—the result would be a comma-splice, a serious sentence error. Notice the following.

■ **Comma-splice:** Calcium is important in one's diet, it is particularly important for pregnant women.

■ **Standard:** Calcium is important in one's diet, and it is particularly important for pregnant women.

2. Do *not* place a comma before a coordinating conjunction if it does not connect independent clauses.

■ **Nonstandard:** Herbs add flavor to salads, and are easy to grow.

■ **Standard:** Herbs add flavor to salads and are easy to grow.

■ **Nonstandard:** My cousin Phil was born in Syracuse, but later moved to Buffalo.

■ **Standard:** My cousin Phil was born in Syracuse but later moved to Buffalo.

In both sentences above, the conjunctions do not connect independent clauses, and therefore, they should not be preceded by commas. In Chapter 11 you will learn the rules for using the comma.

EXERCISE 8-2

Place a comma before any conjunction connecting independent clauses in the following sentences. Some sentences do not need commas.

1. Millions of Americans use the Internet daily, and they are relying on it for more than e-mail and chatrooms.
2. Many of them access the Internet to read the news and to read magazines that are online.
3. Others take courses on the Internet, and they study for degrees without attending class sessions.
4. The use of the Internet for conducting business and financial transactions is also skyrocketing.
5. Consumers are also shopping online, for they find it easy and convenient.
6. Not only are they spending more on purchases, but they are using the Internet to research products for later purchases in traditional stores.
7. Consumers can also sell things over the Internet, or they can make purchases on online auctions.
8. It is possible to book air flights, cruises, hotel reservations, and rental cars online, and it is often possible to find bargains unavailable from the traditional travel agent.
9. Online banking is many people's favorite online convenience.
10. Online banking allows customers to check their balances and pay bills while seated at their home computer.

> **Reminders** **for Compound Sentences**
> 1. A compound sentence consists of two or more independent clauses connected by a semicolon or a coordinating conjunction (a word like *and, but,* or *or*).
> 2. If the independent clauses in a compound sentence are connected by a coordinating conjunction, place a comma in front of the conjunction.
> 3. Independent clauses must never be combined with a comma *only.* You must use a comma *and* a coordinating conjunction.

Complex Sentences

Because their ideas can be shifted around to produce different emphases or rhythms, **complex sentences** offer the writer more variety than do simple sentences. Complex sentences are often more precise than compound sentences because a compound sentence must treat two ideas equally. Complex sentences, on the other hand, can establish more exact relationships. In Chapter 3 you learned that there are two kinds of clauses: independent and dependent. An **independent clause** can stand alone and form a complete sentence. A **dependent clause,** however, cannot stand alone. Even though it has a subject and a verb, it fails to express a complete thought. It must be attached to an independent clause in order to form a grammatically complete sentence.

You can recognize dependent clauses by the kinds of words that introduce them, making them dependent. The technical terms for these words are **subordinating conjunctions** and **relative pronouns.** Notice that each of the following dependent clauses begins with such a word.

- *after* we reached our motel that night
- *if* you speak a foreign language
- *because* baldness is inherited
- *that* shocked everyone

Although these clauses contain subjects and verbs, they do not express complete ideas; therefore, they are dependent clauses. By adding an independent clause to each, however, you can change them into complete, grammatically correct *complex* sentences.

- After we reached our motel that night, we called our children.
- If you speak a foreign language, you have an advantage when applying for many jobs.
- Because baldness is inherited, Steve and his brothers lost their hair while in their late twenties.
- The graduation speaker made a vulgar gesture that shocked everyone.

Note: A dependent clause is often followed by a comma when it begins a sentence. If an independent clause comes first, no comma is needed.

The following list contains words that most commonly introduce dependent clauses. Whenever a clause in a complex sentence begins with one of them (unless it is a question), it is a dependent clause.

**Most Common Words That
Introduce a Dependent Clause**

after	than
although	that
as, as if	though
as though	unless
because	what, whatever
before	when, whenever
how	where, wherever
if	whether
in order to	which, whichever
once	while
since	who, whose, whoever
so that	whom

EXERCISE 8-3

If the italicized clause in each sentence is a dependent clause, write "dep" in the blank; if it is an independent clause, write "ind."

__dep__ 1. Several Soviet women are among the heroic pilots *who flew missions in World War II.*

__ind__ 2. *Russians still talk* about how Lily Litvak shot down a dozen German planes during her brief career.

__dep__ 3. While pursued by enemy planes, Litvak would quickly maneuver *until she was behind her foes and able to attack freely.*

__dep__ 4. Many German pilots kept an eye out for the white rose painted on Litvak's plane *because they wanted the honor of downing the famous Russian ace.*

__ind__ 5. *Litvak's final skirmish came* when she was surrounded by a squadron of German planes and shot down by eight of them.

__ind__ 6. During another famous air battle, *two Soviet women pilots faced forty-two German pilots* who were planning an attack on a town.

___dep___ 7. *After the two aces destroyed some German planes*, the other German pilots turned back for home.

___ind___ 8. After that encounter one of the Soviets parachuted from her exploding plane, and *the other pilot landed safely*.

___dep___ 9. Perhaps the most stunning story is that which features Irs Kasherina, *who had to stand up and fly through enemy fire while holding her co-pilot's lifeless body off the controls.*

___ind___ 10. *The Soviet women pilots were respected and feared by their German enemies*, who renamed them the "night witches of the skies."

EXERCISE 8-4

Add an independent clause to each of the following dependent clauses, thereby creating a complex sentence.   **Student responses will vary.**

1. Whenever I visit my family, _____.
2. Because her work schedule has changed, _____.
3. _____, whose birthday is tomorrow.
4. _____ if you want to join us for a movie tonight.
5. Although we studied hard for the exam, _____.
6. _____ whether she wants to major in business or not.
7. Before you quit your job, _____.
8. _____ in order to save money for next semester's tuition.
9. _____ since his car is at the mechanic's shop.
10. After you finish your homework, _____.
11. While you get a manicure, _____.
12. As if losing her money in Las Vegas weren't enough, _____.
13. _____ as though someone were chasing him.
14. _____, unless you know of a better place to eat.
15. _____, though I don't know how to swim.

Three Kinds of Dependent Clauses

Now that you can recognize dependent clauses in complex sentences, it is time to take a closer look at them so that you will know how to use them correctly and make your own sentences more interesting and mature.

> **Reminders** **for Complex Sentences**
> 1. Dependent clauses begin with words like *after, if, although,* and the other words on the list on page 173. A dependent clause cannot stand alone—it must be combined with an independent clause in order to be complete.
> 2. When a dependent clause begins a sentence, it is often followed by a comma. If the independent clause comes first, no comma is needed.
> 3. A complex sentence is one that contains a dependent clause.

All dependent clauses share three traits: they have a subject and a verb, they begin with a word that introduces the dependent clause, and they must be combined with independent clauses to form complete sentences. So much for the similarities; let us now consider the differences among them.

Dependent clauses can be used in sentences in three different ways: as adverbs, as adjectives, and as nouns. Consequently, we label them adverb clauses, adjective clauses, and noun clauses.

Adverb Clauses   **Adverb clauses** act as adverbs in a sentence—they modify verbs, adjectives, and adverbs. Like single-word adverbs, they can be recognized by the questions they answer. They tell *when, where, why, how,* or *under what conditions something happens.* They can also be recognized because they begin with subordinating conjunctions. In the following sentences the adverb clauses are italicized.

- *When I was a senior in high school,* I broke my arm playing basketball. (The adverb clause tells *when.*)
- Jack's dog follows him *wherever he goes.* (The adverb clause tells *where.*)
- *Because she could speak Spanish fluently,* Edith was hired as an interpreter at the courthouse. (The adverb clause tells *why.*)
- She threw the shot put *as if it were a tennis ball.* (The adverb clause tells *how.*)
- I would help you *if I could.* (The adverb clause tells *under what conditions.*)

Adverb clauses can usually be moved around in a sentence. In the first sentence above, for example, the adverb clause can be placed at the end of the sentence without affecting its basic meaning.

- I broke my arm playing basketball *when I was a senior in high school.*

Notice that an adverb clause is followed by a comma when it comes at the beginning of a sentence; when it comes at the end of a sentence, it is not preceded by a comma.

EXERCISE 8-5

Underline all of the adverb clauses in the following sentences, and supply any missing commas.

1. <u>Although interest rates on credit cards are high,</u> many cardholders do not mind paying hundreds of dollars a year in interest.
2. <u>Because credit cards are a profitable business for banks,</u> the competition for new customers is heating up.
3. More than ten million consumers applied for cards <u>when AT&T introduced its Universal card.</u>
4. <u>Because more than six thousand financial institutions issue cards,</u> many issuers of cards are trying to stand out from the competition.
5. They offer such benefits as travel discounts, contributions to charities, and other features <u>when cardholders use their cards to charge anything from meals to vacations.</u>
6. Studies have shown that the use of charge cards stimulates spending <u>because it is not necessary to have cash at hand.</u>
7. Fast-food customers, for example, spend twice as much on average <u>when they use a credit card.</u>
8. <u>Although most U.S. consumer spending is by cash and checks,</u> the use of plastic cards is increasing.
9. <u>Though economists talk about the cashless society,</u> it will be a few years before such a phenomenon occurs.
10. <u>If the card companies have their way,</u> the cashless society will come about sooner rather than later.

Adjective Clauses   Adjective clauses modify nouns and pronouns in a complex sentence. Like all clauses, they have subjects and verbs. But as dependent clauses, they must be attached to independent clauses to express complete ideas and to form grammatically complete sentences.

Most adjective clauses begin with the relative pronouns *which, whom, that, who,* and *whose,* but a few are introduced by *when, where, why,* and *how.* Adjective clauses usually immediately follow the noun or pronoun they modify. In the following sentences the adjective clauses are italicized.

■ Anne Frank's diary, *which she began in 1942,* was terminated by her capture and death in 1945. (The adjective clause modifies *diary.*)

■ Min-Hua's father, *whom you met last night,* is from Baltimore. (The adjective clause modifies *father.*)

■ Many of the monuments *that have survived in ancient Egypt through thousands of years* were built at a terrible cost in human suffering and death. (The adjective clause modifies *monuments*.)

■ Any pitcher *who deliberately hits a batter* will be ejected. (The adjective clause modifies *pitcher*.)

■ Drivers *whose cars are left unattended* will receive citations. (The adjective clause modifies *drivers*.)

EXERCISE 8-6

Underline the adjective clauses in the following sentences. In the space before each sentence, write the noun or pronoun modified by the clause.

<u>game</u>   1. The modern pinball machine is a game <u>that challenges you to score points without losing the ball or tilting the game.</u>

<u>technology</u>   2. Despite the electronic technology, <u>which has been added to attract players</u>, the goals of the game remain the same: score points and keep the ball from going down the drain.

<u>components</u>   3. Despite the various types of machines, they have three components <u>that are common to all of them</u>: the flippers, the pinball, and the drain.

<u>flippers</u>   4. The flippers, <u>whose purpose is to keep the ball out of the drain and propel it toward the bumpers and ramps in order to score points</u>, are usually located at the bottom of the playfield.

<u>buttons</u>   5. The flippers are controlled with two buttons <u>that are located on either side of the machine.</u>

<u>pinball</u>   6. The traditional steel pinball, <u>which weighs 2.8 ounces</u>, flies around the table hitting bumpers and targets to score points.

<u>ball</u>   7. A ball <u>that fails to hit a target</u> falls down the drain, and you move on to your next ball.

<u>ball</u>   8. The third ball <u>that goes down the drain</u> means that the game is over, unless you've scored a replay or a match.

<u>art</u>   9. The back portion of the table usually contains art <u>that is carefully crafted to draw the player to a certain machine over any other in the arcade.</u>

<u>speaker</u>   10. The back of the table also contains a speaker <u>that produces musical scores to accompany game play.</u>

> ## Reminders for Punctuating Adjective Clauses
> 1. If the adjective clause is essential to the meaning of the sentence, do *not* set it off with commas.
> 2. If the adjective clause is *not* essential to the meaning of the sentence, set it off with commas.

Perhaps you noticed that the adjective clauses in sentences 2, 4, and 6 in Exercise 8-6 and those in the two examples on page 176 (*which she began in 1942* and *whom you met last night*) are set off by commas. That is because they are nonessential adjective clauses. **Nonessential** (or **nonrestrictive**) **modifiers** merely give additional information about the nouns and pronouns they modify. If we were to omit the adjective clauses in the two examples on page 176, those sentences would still convey their central ideas.

The punctuation rule for nonessential adjective clauses is easy: they should be set off by commas. **Essential** (or **restrictive**) **modifiers**—those needed to identify the subject—should not be set off by commas.

- ■ Anne Frank's diary, *which she began in 1942,* was terminated by her capture and death in 1945. (The adjective clause provides nonessential information.)
- ■ Anne Frank's diary was terminated by her capture and death in 1945. (Although the adjective clause has been removed, we still can identify the subject.)
- ■ Min-Hua's father, *whom you met last night,* is from Baltimore. (The fact that you met her father last night is nonessential.)
- ■ Min-Hua's father is from Baltimore. (By identifying the subject as *Min-Hua's father,* the writer is able to delete the nonessential clause without destroying the sentence.)

If in the sentence in the first example on page 177, the adjective clause were omitted, the resulting sentence would be confusing.

- ■ Many of the monuments were built at a terrible cost in human suffering and death. (This is a complete sentence, but the adjective clause is essential because it tells the reader *which* monuments the writer is referring to.)

Therefore, the adjective clause is needed to identify the subject and is not set off with commas.

- ■ Many of the monuments *that have survived in ancient Egypt through thousands of years* were built at a terrible cost in human suffering and death.

The punctuation rule for essential adjective clauses, therefore, is simple: They should *not* be set off by commas. Chapter 11 gives additional examples concerning the punctuation of essential and nonessential clauses.

EXERCISE 8-7

Underline all adjective clauses in the following sentences, and supply any missing commas.

1. Woody Harrelson, who is familiar to most people as an actor, is also an active environmentalist.
2. Anyone who has fair skin should avoid prolonged exposure to the sun.
3. The bus driver, whom I recalled knowing in high school, apologized for arriving ten minutes late.
4. A couple of orange crates that served as shelves for our stereo and speakers when we were students also held our books.
5. The letter, which did not bear a return address or postmark, aroused great curiosity and a little fear.
6. Mary Robinson, who was the first woman president of the Republic of Ireland, later served the United Nations.
7. The chemistry lab, which had inadequate ventilation, was closed by health inspectors.
8. The volcano that erupted in the Philippines did millions of dollars of damage.
9. Oil paintings that are worthless during a painter's lifetime are sometimes valuable many years later.
10. Sunspots that are observed only by astronomers can affect weather patterns throughout the year.

Noun Clauses **Noun clauses** do the same things in sentences that single nouns do: they function as subjects or objects, or they complement or complete the sense of the subject. Unlike adjective clauses and adverb clauses, noun clauses do not join independent clauses to form complete sentences. Instead, they replace some of the nouns in independent clauses. As a result, they function as subjects, objects, or subject complements of independent clauses. They are usually introduced by such words as *that, who, what, where, how,* and *why.*

■ **Subject:**   *Why a particular material reacts with light in a particular way* requires a complicated explanation.

■ **Direct object:**   I have just finished reading a book that promises *that the reader can improve his or her IQ by following its suggestions.*

■ **Object of a preposition:**   When selecting courses, you should be guided by *what your counselor recommends.*

■ **Subject complement:**   The sticker price of the car was *more than I expected.*

EXERCISE 8-8

Underline the noun clauses in the following sentences. Some sentences may have more than one noun clause.

1. Can you explain <u>how a laser beam translates digital data into music?</u>
2. <u>Where we spend our honeymoon</u> will be determined by <u>how far our ancient Volkswagen can take us.</u>
3. I will never forget <u>where I was when I learned of the *Columbia* space shuttle accident.</u>
4. Who knew <u>that the life story of Louis Pasteur became a popular film in the 1930s?</u>
5. No one could believe <u>that a bee sting had caused our neighbor's heart attack.</u>
6. Quick! Tell me <u>where you want me to set down this piano!</u>
7. <u>How humans will stop or reverse the polluting of Earth</u> remains to be seen.
8. We are curious about <u>who recently paid $104 million for a Picasso painting.</u>
9. I'd like to know <u>who among my neighbors sings Beyonce songs at dawn each day.</u>
10. Come see <u>how my pet cobra can spell out my first name with his body.</u>

EDITING EXERCISES

The paragraph below compares and contrasts two types of people: "morning people" and "night people." The subsequent paragraph describes how to choose a melon at the produce stand. You will notice that the sentences in each paragraph lack variety and the use of transitions. As a result, each paragraph seems to be a series of unrelated sentences. Revise each paragraph by combining ideas where appropriate through the use of compound and complex sentences, as well as transitions. Revise the sentences as necessary.

Morning people and night people often clash. Morning people function best in the early hours of the day while night people work better during the evening hours. Morning people are up at dawn to start their day. Night people see the sunset at the beginning of their day. Morning people are cheerful at early hours when night people are still not awake or ready to speak to other humans. Morning people have some advantages over night people. Most work shifts start in the morning. They end in the early evening. This arrangement is perfect for morning people. Night people, however, may find it hard to adjust to rising early.

They may suffer low productivity in the mornings. That problem may make them seem lazy or apathetic. Night people, however, have some advantages over morning people. They can use the quiet, late hours of the evening to get work done. They can also enjoy amusements such as nightclubs and parties without tiring. It would be ideal to maintain an energetic pace from the start of a day to its close. Yet most people can manage enthusiasm only during one or the other.

Choosing a smooth-skinned melon is difficult. It doesn't have as many features to observe as a rough-skinned melon. Look at its color. You want a creamy color. You don't want a green or white color. A creamy color means that the melon is ripe. Sugar spots are brown flecks that appear on the melon's surface. They're the best sign of readiness. You may see the flecks only on melons that you find at a fruit stand or farmers' market. You probably won't see them at supermarkets. Supermarket managers think that the flecks look bad. They usually wash the flecks off the melons. Press the melon gently. If there's a slight give, the fruit is ready for serving. Sometimes the melon looks ripe but feels hard. Leave it out at room temperature for a day or two. It will soften just right. Don't refrigerate a melon unless it's already ripe.

WRITING SENTENCES Using a Variety of Sentence Types

As you saw in this chapter, one of the marks of a good writer is the ability to use a variety of sentence types. This exercise asks you to try your hand at writing exact and interesting sentences.

1. Write a compound sentence in which the independent clauses are combined with a comma and a coordinating conjunction.
2. Write a compound sentence in which the independent clauses are combined with a semicolon.
3. Write two complex sentences, each containing an independent clause and an adverb clause. Underline the adverb clause in each.
4. Write two complex sentences containing an independent clause and a noun clause in each. Underline the noun clause in each.

5. Write two complex sentences containing essential (restrictive) adjective clauses. Underline the adjective clause in each.
6. Write two complex sentences containing nonessential (nonrestrictive) adjective clauses. Underline the adjective clause in each, and be sure to punctuate them correctly.

Language Tips

You should know how to punctuate compound and complex sentences.

1. If the clauses in a compound sentence are connected by a coordinating conjunction (a word like *and, but,* and *or*), place a comma in front of the conjunction.
2. If an adverb clause begins a complex sentence, it is followed by a comma.

For more uses of the comma, see pages 237–246.

REVIEW TEST 8-A
Compound and Complex Sentences

A. *Each of the following sentences contains one or two blanks. If a comma should be inserted in one or both blanks, write "a" on the line in front of the sentence. If no commas are needed, write "b."*

___b___ 1. The Cardinals flew home from a road trip ____ and greeted the crowd of proud fans.

___a___ 2. To pass the bar exam on her first try ____ Carla took a leave from work in order to study.

___a___ 3. Depending on the weather ____ and the price of airfares ____ Blanca will either fly or drive to San Juan next month.

___b___ 4. A flock of pigeons ____ that had gathered around the park fountain ____ fled when the rain began.

___b___ 5. The guitarist stopped playing and replaced a string ____ that had snapped.

___a___ 6. After Erika receives her B.S. degree from the University of Wisconsin ____ she wants to work for an accounting firm ____ in Ohio.

___a___ 7. Though he doesn't earn much money ____ Yuri sends a helpful check to his mother each month.

___a___ 8. I'm trying to diet ____ but having just one cookie won't hurt much ____ right?

___a___ 9. Although they were hungry and tired ____ the children behaved well and did not gripe or cry.

___b___ 10. Miguel is attending next week's Passover services ____ because his new girlfriend is Jewish.

___b___ 11. The young Frenchman reminded me that ____ I should use the phrase *bon soir* only in the evening.

___b___ 12. Please let me know ____ if you need anything at the office supply store.

___a___ 13. Eva and Katia ____ who are majoring in Latin American literature ____ will tour El Salvador and Bolivia next month.

___a___ 14. Chen Liu predicted that a huge snow storm would spoil our snowboarding trip ____ and he was right.

___b___ 15. We enjoy the pizza at Vito's Grotto ____ and the whitefish at Rachael's Deli.

B. *If the italicized group of words in each of the following sentences is an independent clause, write "a" on the line; if it is a dependent clause, write "b"; and if it is not a clause, write "c."*

   b   16. I finally received a postcard from a friend *who has lived in Paris for a year.*

   a   17. *Order a burger for my brother* and some Thai Rad Na noodles for me.

   c   18. Tyrone is the lead singer *in our grunge band.*

   a   19. *The monkeys have lived in the rain forest* for thousands of years.

   c   20. *Choosing three shirts and a pair of boots,* Kumar clearly enjoyed his shopping spree.

C. *Use the appropriate letter to identify the structure of the following sentences.*
        a. simple sentence   b. compound sentence   c. complex sentence

   b   21. Jason bought some Legos for his daughter, but he left them on the bus.

   c   22. I can't believe you ate the whole garlic chicken.

   c   23. Since her luggage was lost at the airport, Nadia faced the Moscow winter night without a coat.

   c   24. If Basma runs the marathon this Sunday, we'll make her a big steak dinner afterward.

   a   25. Many cancers caught early can be treated successfully.

REVIEW TEST 8-B
Compound and Complex Sentences

A. *Each of the following sentences contains one or two blanks. If a comma should be inserted in one or both blanks, write "a" on the line in front of the sentence. If no commas are needed, write "b."*

___b___ 1. Anyone ____ who wants to lose weight ____ must exercise as well as diet.

___a___ 2. We wanted to thank our guide ____ but we didn't know how to express it in Italian.

___b___ 3. Her parents prepared their wills ____ and placed their assets in a trust.

___a___ 4. When the summer was over ____ few traces of the vacation crowd were visible.

___a___ 5. The process of impeachment of a president is a serious act ____ and it has rarely been attempted in our history.

___b___ 6. Can you name an American president and vice president ____ who served together but were not elected?

___b___ 7. Many women ____ who marry today ____ retain their maiden names.

___b___ 8. The jury ruled that Dominic was responsible for the damage to the car ____ that he struck.

___a___ 9. Before you return the videotape to the video store ____ be sure to rewind the tape.

___b___ 10. Many commercials for food feature cats ____ and dogs.

___a___ 11. Her eldest daughter ____ whom you met last night ____ will attend Smith College next fall.

___a___ 12. Dan Vogel ____ who was my neighbor in Des Moines ____ taught me how to dance the tango.

___a___ 13. Shopping for clothes bores my husband ____ so I select his new suits.

___a___ 14. The Mach ____ which is a unit used to measure sound ____ is named for Austrian physicist Ernst Mach.

___b___ 15. Mercury is one of the planets ____ that can be seen without the aid of a telescope.

B. *If the italicized group of words in each of the following sentences is an independent clause, write "a" on the line; if it is a dependent clause, write "b"; and if it is not a clause, write "c."*

___c___   16.   Peru has suffered political turmoil *in recent years*.

___b___   17.   Chip saw a strange orange streak in the sky last night, and he believes *that it was a UFO*.

___a___   18.   Once you've finished eating, *please wash your dishes and put them away*.

___a___   19.   *The right bait makes all the difference in fishing*, the guide told me.

___c___   20.   *After visiting the Grand Canyon*, we plan to visit the Dollhouse Museum in Dallas.

C. *Use the appropriate letter to identify the structure of the following sentences.*
    a. simple sentence   b. compound sentence   c. complex sentence

___b___   21.   The opera singer Leontyne Price has retired, but she continues to give voice lessons.

___c___   22.   Various cultures have different gestures to indicate contempt or anger, a fact that confuses the foreign visitor.

___c___   23.   President John F. Kennedy was making a political trip to Dallas in 1963 when he was assassinated.

___a___   24.   Oh, I see a bug!

___c___   25.   If you are not careful, the dog will eat your taco.

Go to www.ablongman.com/yarber to complete Review Test 8-C.

WRITING PARAGRAPHS

DEVELOPING A PARAGRAPH BY COMPARISON AND CONTRAST

In many of your college classes you will be asked to write paragraphs in which you are to point out the similarities and differences between two subjects. Technically speaking, comparisons reveal similarities and differences, and contrasts are concerned only with differences. In practice, however, comparisons suggest likenesses, and contrasts point out differences.

When organized and developed carefully, a paragraph of *comparison and contrast* has a unity and logic that helps the reader understand the writer's ideas. If your paragraph, however, is only a series of scrambled likenesses and differences that leads nowhere, the result will be chaos.

Your first job in organizing your comparison-and-contrast paragraph is to decide what you want to emphasize: the differences or the similarities between the two subjects. This can best be done by making two lists, one for the differences and the other for the similarities. The next step is to reorder the lists of differences or similarities in their order of importance, beginning with the least significant and building up to the most dramatic and important.

To be certain that your paragraph has clarity and coherence, you should organize it in one of the following ways: point-by-point or the block method.

Point-by-Point Method

When you compare or contrast each subject point by point, you move back and forth between the two subjects, as in the following paragraph.

■ College freshmen are often surprised by the differences between their high school days and their experiences in college. In high school, attendance was taken daily and a school secretary often called the missing students' homes to verify that students were not truant. In college, many instructors never take attendance, nor do they make any effort to contact parents concerning absences or failing work. In high school, counselors and teachers gave individual help and attention to students who needed it, and after-school sessions were available for extra tutoring. In college, students are responsible for their own academic performance, and it is up to students to seek help. In most high schools the students are approximately the same age, but in a typical college class the students range in age from teenagers to grandmothers. Social life is important in high school, but in college it is squeezed in only when possible. Finally, students in high school are often treated as children, but they are assumed to be responsible adults in college.

Block Method

The second way to organize a comparison-and-contrast paragraph is to use the block method, which first presents all of the relevant details or aspects of one subject and then all of the corresponding qualities of the other.

The following paragraph follows this pattern and describes first the skills needed for the piano and then those required for the typewriter or computer keyboard.

■ Students of the piano often find that their dexterity at the keyboard aids them when learning to use the typewriter or computer. Playing the piano requires the ability to coordinate the movements of the eyes and hands, as the pianist reads the musical score and places her fingers on the appropriate keys. And if the pianist hopes to play with any measure of success, she also needs a sense of rhythm. Using the keyboard of the typewriter or computer requires these same skills. An accurate typist must read carefully the material she is typing, scarcely glancing at her hands on the keyboard. If she wishes to type rapidly, she must develop a rhythmic pattern in the movements of her fingers. It is not surprising, then, that many pianists are excellent typists.

The point-by-point pattern is particularly helpful for complex comparisons and for longer paragraphs. The block pattern (or subject-by-subject) should be used only when there are few points to be cited.

Regardless of the method of organization you use, transitions will help your reader follow your ideas. Words like *however, too, alike, in common, moreover, on the other hand, but, similarly, instead, both,* and so on show relationships between ideas.

EXERCISE   Using Comparison and Contrast

Write a paragraph of at least six sentences using either the block or the point-by-point method of arrangement. The following pairs may serve as topics, or you may choose your own. In either case, write a topic sentence for your paragraph and underline it.

- *two popular comedians or entertainers*
- *two friends or relatives*

- *two instructors*
- *two different sports*
- *two religions*
- *two political parties*
- *two views of a controversial subject such as capital punishment*

Writing Tips Could You Eat Pizza at Every Meal?

Your sentences need variety for the same reason your daily diet does: repetition breeds boredom. You should use a variety of sentence types: Mix shorter with longer sentences; use compound and complex sentences as well as simple sentences; vary the length of your sentences; don't begin every sentence with the subject; and make sure your vocabulary doesn't become stale. Use a thesaurus or dictionary to find alternatives for words you tend to overuse.

Computer Activity

Using the block arrangement, write a paragraph of comparison and contrast for one of the topics listed in the exercise on page 188.

When you have completed your paragraph, exchange files with your writing partner.

Ask your classmate to rewrite your paragraph by using the point-by-point method and arranging the statements in an ascending or descending order of importance. For example, comparing automobiles involves model, price, comfort, size of engine, and so forth. Which of these is most important? What is next in importance?

Do the same kind of rewriting for your classmate's paragraph.

CHAPTER 9

CORRECTING SENTENCE FRAGMENTS, RUN-ON SENTENCES, AND COMMA-SPLICES

CHAPTER PREVIEW

In this chapter, you will learn about:

- Recognizing three kinds of sentence errors
  Sentence fragments
  Run-on sentences
  Comma-splices
- Conjunctive adverbs
- Writing paragraphs: Developing a paragraph by classification

The purpose of writing is to communicate facts, ideas, and feelings in a clear and effective manner. If we make serious mistakes in sentence structure or grammar, our readers are confused and irritated, and communication fails. This chapter deals with ways to remedy three serious kinds of errors a writer can make: sentence fragments, run-on sentences, and comma-splices. Fortunately, these errors are easy to spot and easy to fix.

Sentence Fragments

A **sentence** is a group of words containing at least one independent clause. It has a subject and a verb, and it conveys a certain sense of completeness. A **sentence fragment,** on the other hand, is a group of words lacking an independent clause. Although it looks like a sentence because it begins with a capital letter and ends with a period or other end punctuation, it leaves the reader "hanging," waiting for more to follow.

Sentence fragments are common in conversation, particularly in responses to what someone else has said or as additions to something we have just said. Their meanings and missing parts are usually clear because of the context of the conversation and the speaker's gestures. In writing, however, it is best to avoid sentence fragments. Although professional writers occasionally use them for special effect, fragments usually suggest that the writer is careless and unable to formulate a complete thought.

One of the best ways to avoid sentence fragments is to read your written work *aloud.* Your voice will often detect an incomplete sentence. Another tip: Don't be fooled by the length of a so-called sentence. A long string of words without an independent clause is still a sentence fragment, despite its length. Here is an example of such a fragment.

■ The election of Nelson Mandela, an end to news censorship, abolition of executions, and power sharing with former white leaders, among other dramatic changes for South Africa.

At first glance this "sentence" is complete—after all, it begins with a capitalized word and concludes with a period. Despite its length, however, it is a sentence fragment because it does not contain an independent clause and therefore cannot convey a complete thought.

The following list contains the most common types of fragments that people write:

1. Prepositional phrase fragments
2. Infinitive phrase fragments
3. Participle phrase fragments
4. Noun phrase fragments
5. Dependent clause fragments

By understanding each type of fragment, you can eliminate them from your writing. Now we will look at the various types of sentence fragments and the ways to correct them.

Phrases as Fragments

One of the most common kinds of sentence fragments is the phrase. (A **phrase,** you recall, is a group of words lacking a subject and a verb and acting as a single part of speech within a sentence.) Prepositional phrases, infinitive phrases, and participle phrases are often confused with complete sentences.

Prepositional Phrases as Fragments   A prepositional phrase never contains a subject and a verb. Therefore, it can never stand alone as a sentence. The following sentences are followed by prepositional phrases masquerading as sentences.

- ▨ **Fragment:**   Some of the world's fastest boats raced for the cherished America's Cup. *Off the coast of southern California.*

- ▨ **Fragment:**   Whitey Ford won a record ten World Series games. *During his career as a pitcher for the New York Yankees.*

- ▨ **Fragment:**   After delaying it several weeks, Jeff finally began his term paper. *On the subject of religious cults in America.*

Because prepositional phrases are parts of sentences, the best way to correct this kind of fragment is to join it with the sentence to which it belongs. Notice how the fragments above are eliminated when they are joined to the preceding sentences.

- ▨ **Sentence:**   Some of the world's fastest boats raced for the cherished America's Cup off the coast of southern California.

- ▨ **Sentence:**   Whitey Ford won a record ten World Series games during his career as a pitcher for the New York Yankees.

- ▨ **Sentence:**   After delaying it for several weeks, Jeff finally began his term paper on the subject of religious cults in America.

Infinitive Phrases as Fragments   An infinitive is the "to" form of the verb: *to help, to see, to start*, and so on. Many fragments are the result of the writer trying to use an infinitive as the verb in a sentence.

- ▨ **Fragment:**   *To save money for a new car.* Hyo-Min works an extra shift every week.

- ▨ **Fragment:**   After final exams, we're going camping at Yosemite. *To relax, catch some fish, and breathe fresh air.*

- ▨ **Fragment:**   Scientists have repeatedly warned us. *To stop polluting our water before it is unsafe for human use.*

Most fragments consisting of infinitives can be corrected by combining them with the sentence they belong to.

- ▨ **Sentence:**   To save money for a new car, Hyo-Min works an extra shift every week.

- ▨ **Sentence:**   After final exams, we're going camping at Yosemite to relax, catch some fish, and breathe fresh air.

- ▨ **Sentence:**   Scientists have repeatedly warned us to stop polluting our water before it is unsafe for human use.

Participle Phrases as Fragments   The present participle is the "-ing" form of the verb: *helping, seeing, starting,* and *walking.* Present participles can never serve as verbs in a sentence unless they have helping verbs with them (words like *can, could, may, might, will, does*, *am*, *is*, *are*, and *were*). See pages 16–17 in Chapter 2 for a review of helping verbs. Like the infinitive, the present participle is often confused with the main verb in a sentence, and the result is a fragment.

Fragment: *Growing up in a large, poor family in the Appalachian Mountains.* He feared that a college education would be an impossibility.

Fragment: Madame Tussaud's Wax Museum is a popular tourist attraction in London. *Featuring likenesses of historical personages reproduced in lifelike poses.*

Fragment: *Exercising every day, cutting down on calories, and avoiding ice cream and other desserts.* I was able to lose twenty pounds last summer.

Fragments like these can be corrected by attaching them to the independent clauses preceding or following them.

Sentence: Growing up in a large, poor family in the Appalachian Mountains, he feared that a college education would be an impossibility.

Sentence: Madame Tussaud's Wax Museum is a popular tourist attraction in London, featuring likenesses of historical personages reproduced in lifelike poses.

Sentence: Exercising every day, cutting down on calories, and avoiding ice cream and other desserts, I was able to lose twenty pounds last summer.

Another way to correct fragments like these is to supply them with their missing subjects or verbs (or both).

Sentence: He grew up in a large, poor family in the Appalachian Mountains, and he feared that a college education would be an impossibility. (Supplying the missing subject and verb and combining the fragment with another sentence fixes the fragment.)

Sentence: Madame Tussaud's Wax Museum is a popular tourist attraction in London. It features likenesses of historical personages reproduced in lifelike poses. (Supplying the missing subject and verb and creating two separate sentences fixes the fragment.)

Sentence: Because I exercised every day, cut down on calories, and avoided ice cream and other desserts, I was able to lose twenty pounds last summer. (Changing the fragment into a dependent clause and adding it to another sentence, changing the sentence into a complex sentence, fixes the fragment.)

EXERCISE 9-1

Some of the following word groups contain sentence fragments. Underline the fragment, writing on the line the kind of fragment it is. Then correct the fragment by one of the methods explained above. If the group does not contain a fragment, write "C." (Incorrect sentences may be corrected by any of the methods described on pages 192–193.)

<u>prepositional phrase</u> 1. Kite flying has been a popular pastime. <u>Throughout much of human history.</u>

<u>C</u> 2. Kites were invented in China about three thousand years ago.

<u>participle phrase</u> 3. The earliest kites must have been very lightweight and elegant. <u>Consisting of silk sails stretched across bamboo frames.</u>

<u>infinitive phrase</u> 4. Simple and convenient, kites were often used. <u>To perform a variety of tasks.</u>

<u>participle phrase</u> 5. <u>Measuring weather, delivering love notes, and carrying signals.</u> Kites proved to be accurate, multipurpose tools.

<u>C</u> 6. In fact, one of the Wright brothers' earliest flights was conducted in a sort of motorized kite.

<u>infinitive phrase</u> 7. Modern kitebuilders are able to make kites that have a special ability. <u>To fly in stunt formations or even hover.</u>

<u>infinitive phrase</u> 8. Instead of silk, most kites are now made of ripstop nylon, which was originally used. <u>To make parachutes for American soldiers in World War II.</u>

<u>dependent clause</u> 9. It is called "ripstop" because holes and tears will not spread. <u>Throughout the fabric after the kite is accidentally punctured.</u>

<u>participle phrase</u> 10. <u>Coming in a variety of complex styles and costing as much as a hundred dollars or more.</u> Kites aren't just child's play anymore.

Noun Phrases as Fragments   Another type of fragment is a noun followed by a modifier with no main verb.

■ **Fragment:** The planet Venus, known to have a rough surface scarred by volcanoes and quakes.

■ **Fragment:** A newly invented crib, comforting babies by imitating movements of the womb.

■ **Fragment:** The annual Candace Awards, given for leadership and achievement by the National Coalition of 100 Black Women.

Tips **for Avoiding Sentence Fragments**

1. Read your sentences aloud. You will usually be able to hear whether or not you have written a fragment.
2. Be sure that every word group has a subject and a verb.
3. Look for the most common types of fragments:
   • Phrase fragments (prepositional phrases, "to" phrases, and "-ing" phrases)
   • Noun fragments (a noun followed by modifiers but without a verb)
   • Dependent-clause fragments

Most noun fragments can be corrected by supplying the missing verbs.

■ **Sentence:** The planet Venus is known to have a rough surface scarred by volcanoes and quakes.

■ **Sentence:** A newly invented crib comforts babies by imitating movements of the womb.

■ **Sentence:** The annual Candace Awards are given for leadership and achievement by the National Coalition of 100 Black Women.

Dependent Clauses as Fragments

Dependent clauses cannot stand alone. But because they contain subjects and verbs, they often end up as fragments. Dependent clauses can be spotted by the kinds of words that introduce them: subordinating conjunctions like *after, although, as, because,* and *if* or relative pronouns like *who, which,* and *that* (see page 173 for a list of words that introduce dependent clauses).

A dependent clause set off as a complete sentence can be corrected by combining it with the independent clause preceding or following it. Another method is to delete the subordinating conjunction or relative pronoun, thereby converting the dependent clause to an independent clause.

■ **Fragment:** The world's oldest living trees are the bristlecone pines. *Which grow in California.*

■ **Revised:** The world's oldest living trees are the bristlecone pines, which grow in California.

■ **Fragment:** Opera is one of the most appealing of the arts. Although it is also one of the most complex and difficult.

■ **Revised:** Opera is one of the most appealing of the arts. It is also one of the most complex and difficult.

■ **Fragment:**   Slave importation was outlawed in 1808. *Although 250,000 more were imported illegally in the next fifty years.*

■ **Revised:**   Slave importation was outlawed in 1808, although 250,000 more were imported illegally in the next fifty years.

EXERCISE 9-2

Correct any sentence fragments in the following word groups, using any of the methods explained earlier. If the sentence is correct, write "C" in front of it. (Incorrect sentences may be corrected by any of the methods described on pages 192–195.)   **Student responses will vary.**

1. Believe it or not, there is a set of rules about how to display the American flag. Which the War Department wrote in 1923.
2. Citizens may display their flags any time they want to. Although it is traditional to fly them only from sunrise to sunset.
3. The White House, unusual because its flag flies both day and night.
4. **c** The awesome sight of the flag above Baltimore's Fort McHenry inspired Francis Scott Key to write "The Star Spangled Banner."
5. No other flag may be flown above or to the right of the U.S. flag. Except at the United Nations headquarters in New York City.
6. A rule that most Americans are familiar with, that the flag should never touch the ground or floor.
7. A flag may cover the casket of military personnel or other public officials. If it is not permitted to touch the ground or be lowered into the grave.
8. Disposal of a worn or damaged flag in a dignified way, preferably by burning.
9. **c** The U.S. Supreme Court's decision to allow destruction of the flag as a means of political protest was a disappointment to many Americans.
10. Politicians still debate whether American schoolchildren should be required to pledge their allegiance to the flag. Although reciting that oath is not mandatory now.

Run-on Sentences

A **run-on sentence** is just the opposite of a sentence fragment. It is a group of words that *looks* like one sentence but is actually two sentences run together without punctuation. Normally, of course, two or more independent clauses are separated by a coordinating conjunction or a semicolon. But if the conjunction or the semicolon is omitted, the result is a run-on sentence.

Run-on sentences can be corrected in four ways.

1. By inserting a comma and a conjunction (*and, but, for, or, yet, nor, so*) between the independent clauses:

    ■ **Run-on:** Years ago I took calculus I have forgotten practically all I once knew about the subject.

    ■ **Revised:** Years ago I took calculus, but I have forgotten practically all I once knew about the subject.

2. By changing one of the independent clauses into a dependent clause:

    ■ **Run-on:** In the first inning the Rockies were losing six to two three innings later they were winning twelve to eight.

    ■ **Revised:** Although in the first inning the Rockies were losing six to two, three innings later they were winning twelve to eight.

3. By inserting a semicolon between the two independent clauses:

    ■ **Run-on:** St. Augustine, Florida, is America's oldest city it was settled by Spain in 1565.

    ■ **Revised:** St. Augustine, Florida, is America's oldest city; it was settled by Spain in 1565.

4. By using a period or other end punctuation between the independent clauses, making them two separate sentences:

    ■ **Run-on:** The Gideon decision is one of the landmark cases of the U.S. Supreme Court it grants all poor defendants the right to free counsel.

    ■ **Revised:** The Gideon decision is one of the landmark cases of the U.S. Supreme Court. It grants all poor defendants the right to free counsel.

Tips for Avoiding Run-on Sentences

1. Read your sentences aloud. Listen for a break marking the end of each thought.
2. Be sure that every independent clause is followed by a period or other end punctuation, a semicolon, or a comma and a coordinating conjunction.

EXERCISE 9-3

Using any of the methods explained above, correct any run-on sentences in the following word groups. If a sentence is correct, mark "C" in front of it. (Incorrect sentences may be corrected by any of the methods described on page 197.)   **Student responses will vary.**

1. **C** *Mona Lisa* is likely the world's most famous painting, partly because of the mysteries associated with it.
2. Leonardo da Vinci began the painting in 1503 and finished several years later meanwhile he carried it with him while traveling to many European cities and parted with it only at his death.
3. The model's identity is uncertain most scholars think that she is Lisa Gherardini, the second wife of Francesco del Giocondo, an Italian nobleman.
4. Leonardo used a technique called *sfumato*, in which hard lines are blurred and facial features fade into each other the expression and meaning in Mona Lisa's eyes and smile are hard to read.
5. The model is positioned much closer to the painter than in other portraits of the era it was also unusual to show a model from only the waist up, rather than full-length.
6. Adding to the mystery is the faint light portrayed in the painting we can't even tell what time of day it is.
7. **C** Not immediately noticeable, the background is also odd: a two-story structure that features a road, riverbed, and hot reddish rocks below and a frosty, glacial, mountainous region above.
8. **C** Perhaps Leonardo wanted to create a contrast between Mona Lisa's playful smile and her more foreboding background.
9. *Mona Lisa* was stolen in 1911 when a Louvre Museum employee simply hid it in his coat and walked out two years later it was recovered when the thief tried to sell it.
10. In late 2005, the painting was moved to a special wing of the Louvre Museum now the mysterious woman shows her smile behind unbreakable, nonreflective glass in a climate-controlled enclosure.

Comma-Splices

A **comma-splice** consists of two independent clauses connected ("spliced") by only a comma instead of being joined with a comma *and* a coordinating conjunction or with a semicolon. A comma-splice is only slightly less irritating to a reader than the run-on sentence; the writer made some attempt (although mistakenly) to separate two independent clauses. Nevertheless, a comma-splice is a serious error in sentence construction because it is difficult to read. Furthermore, it suggests, like the fragment and the run-on sentence, that the writer cannot formulate or recognize a single, complete thought.

Comma-splices can be corrected in the same ways as run-on sentences.

1. By using a period or other end punctuation between the independent clauses, making them two separate sentences:

    ■ **Comma-splice:** For many years sociologists referred to the United States as a "melting pot," that term has been replaced by the term "pluralistic society."

    ■ **Revised:** For many years sociologists referred to the United States as a "melting pot." That term has been replaced by the term "pluralistic society."

2. By inserting a comma and a coordinating conjunction between the independent clauses:

    ■ **Comma-splice:** Dennis enrolled in a course in hip-hop dancing, now all of the women want to dance with him.

    ■ **Revised:** Dennis enrolled in a course in hip-hop dancing, and now all of the women want to dance with him.

3. By inserting a semicolon between the two independent clauses:

    ■ **Comma-splice:** Sue told me I'd like the new Dixie Chicks CD, she was right.

    ■ **Revised:** Sue told me I'd like the new Dixie Chicks CD; she was right.

4. By changing one of the independent clauses into a dependent clause:

    ■ **Comma-splice:** Miguel studied classical music at a conservatory in New York, he plays drums in a rock group.

    ■ **Revised:** Although Miguel studied classical music at a conservatory in New York, he plays drums in a rock group.

Tips for Avoiding Comma-Splices

1. Do not use a comma alone to separate your sentences.
2. Read your sentence aloud. When you signal a new thought, use a period or other end punctuation, a semicolon, or a comma *and* a coordinating conjunction.

EXERCISE 9-4

Using any of the methods explained above, correct any comma-splices in the following word groups. If a sentence is correct, mark "C" in front of it.   **Student responses will vary.**

1. Lipstick has existed in some form since early history, the ancient Egyptians painted their lips with henna.
2. Modern lipstick contains a variety of pigments, waxes, oils, and moisturizers, the process of making a lipstick is actually quite scientific.
3. The wax is often from bee honeycombs or Brazilian palm trees, the Mexican candelilla plant is also used.
4. The wax gives a lipstick its shape and durability, oils give it a moisturizing quality.
5. Many kinds of oils are used, including olive oil, castor oil, and cocoa butter, in recent years makers have added aloe and vitamin E to keep lips moist.
6. **C** Many dyes are used to add color, mostly various red hues and bromo acid.
7. The ingredients are finely ground, then heated and poured into cold metal molds, then they're chilled.
8. The formula changes with the style, for example, matte lipsticks have more wax and less moisturizer, and shimmery lipsticks have mica or silica particles
9. Lipstick has not always been an attribute for its user, in 1770 Britain outlawed its use because of its seductive powers, which the government likened to witchcraft.
10. During World War II, the movie industry made lipstick and other cosmetics not only respectable but necessary for beauty, around that same time, beauty salons began to open throughout the United States.

Comma-Splices and Conjunctive Adverbs

Some comma-splices are the result of the writer's confusing a **conjunctive adverb** with a coordinating conjunction. A conjunctive adverb is a kind of connecting word that looks like a conjunction but is actually an adverb.

Some Conjunctive Adverbs			
accordingly	also	besides	consequently
furthermore	hence	however	moreover
nevertheless	nonetheless	otherwise	therefore

When one of these words appears *within* an independent clause, it is usually set off by commas.

- It was obvious from her face, *however,* that she was disappointed.
- I believe, *nevertheless,* that Maxim will continue to play.
- Iran and Iraq, *moreover,* also plan to sign the treaty.

When a conjunctive adverb appears *between* main clauses, it must be preceded by a semi-colon or a period (and often followed by a comma). If the semicolon or period is omitted, the result is a comma-splice.

- **Comma-splice:** Hershey is famous for its chocolate, *however,* the company also makes pasta.
- **Revised:** Hershey is famous for its chocolate; *however,* the company also makes pasta.
- **Revised:** Hershey is famous for its chocolate. *However,* the company also makes pasta.

Remember: Conjunctive adverbs are not conjunctions and can never be used by themselves to link clauses or sentences.

EXERCISE 9-5

Correct any comma-splices in the following groups of words. Use any of the methods presented in the chapter. If a sentence is correct, mark "C" in front of it.   **Student responses will vary.**

1. The easiest way to become an American citizen is to have been born here, however, natives of other countries may become citizens through the process of naturalization.
2. **C** To begin this process, aliens must first obtain application forms from local offices of the Immigration and Naturalization Service or from the clerk of courts that handle naturalization cases.
3. There are several requirements for those who seek citizenship, nevertheless, it is not altogether impossible.
4. Applicants must be at least eighteen years old, moreover, they must be able to prove at least five years of lawful residence in the United States.
5. **C** For spouses of U.S. citizens, on the other hand, the required residence period is usually only three years.
6. Applicants must also show an understanding of the English language, therefore, many aspiring citizens take night classes in English.

7. Knowledge of America's history and government is also required, in fact, the applicants will take a test on these subjects.
8. A fee must be paid by the applicants when they turn in their citizenship applications, subsequently, they receive appointments for a hearing.
9. Applicants may bring attorneys with them to their hearings, however, it is optional.
10. There is a thirty-day waiting period after the hearing, eventually the court may approve the applicant's application and finally administer the official oath of citizenship.

EDITING EXERCISE

The paragraph below describes the various types of cactus that grow throughout the Southwest. The paragraph is developed by using classification as an organizing device. Rewrite the paragraph, eliminating the sentence fragments, comma-splices, and run-on sentences. Revise the sentences as necessary.

No symbol of the great American desert is more recognizable than the cactus. Thriving in dryness and heat that would kill most other plants. Cactuses can live for long stretches without water, precious rainwater is stored in their stems. Although a bane to humans, the narrow needles on most kinds of cactus shield the plants from attack by animals. Several types of cactus common throughout the Southwest. Opuntias, usually called prickly pears, the oldest known cactus. They grow broad pads that are flavorful they are used in many Southwestern and Latin American recipes. The graceful organ pipe species, also prized for its tasty fruit. Chollas are common hikers and campers hate them because their long and painful thorns break off easily and are difficult to remove from flesh. The giant saguaro is often likened to a human standing with arms raised and bent at the elbow. The saguaro can grow as high as fifty feet, it may live for more than two hundred years. All of these common types of cactus are endangered as human settlements inch ever closer, bringing pollution and clearing entire groves. Disease, worms, and a growing rodent population, all additional threats to the silent strength and defiant beauty of desert cactus.

WRITING SENTENCES Avoiding Fragments, Run-on Sentences, and Comma-Splices

This writing exercise requires that you be able to recognize and correct three of the most serious kinds of errors a writer can make: sentence fragments, run-on sentences, and comma-splices.

1. Write a prepositional phrase fragment. Next, correct it by using one of the methods recommended in this chapter.
2. Write an infinitive fragment. Next, correct it by following the suggestions in this chapter.
3. Write a participle fragment. Next, correct it by one of the methods explained in this chapter.
4. Write a dependent clause fragment. Next, correct it by following one of the suggestions in this chapter.
5. Write a run-on sentence. Correct it by inserting a comma and a conjunction between the independent clauses.
6. Write a run-on sentence. Correct it by changing one of the independent clauses into a dependent clause.
7. Write a run-on sentence. Correct it by inserting a semicolon between the two independent clauses.
8. Write a comma-splice. Correct it by using a period or other end punctuation between the independent clauses, making them two sentences.
9. Write a comma-splice. Correct it by inserting a comma and a conjunction between the independent clauses.
10. Write a comma-splice. Correct it by changing one of the independent clauses into a dependent clause.

Language Tips

Be sure that a main or helping verb isn't missing from your sentences.

1. A missing main verb:

    Her memories of the accident very painful. (nonstandard)

    Her memories of the accident *were* very painful. (standard)

2. A missing helping verb:

    For the past semester Tara been absent only once. (nonstandard)

    For the past semester Tara *has* been absent only once. (standard)

REVIEW TEST 9-A
Correcting Sentence Fragments, Run-on Sentences, and Comma-Splices

In the space provided, write the letter corresponding to the kind of error each sentence contains. If a sentence is correct, write "d" in front of it.

    a. sentence fragment   b. run-on sentence   c. comma-splice   d. correct

__c__   1.   Stop doing that, you're choking me.

__d__   2.   A faulty fuel sensor postponed the space shuttle's launch.

__b__   3.   Honestly, honey, I don't know how you manage to keep your grades up and keep a full-time job please tell me the secret to your energy.

__a__   4.   Fireworks, legal in some states but not in others.

__a__   5.   A dab of cologne behind your ears to make him notice as you walk past.

__c__   6.   The reporter was threatened with jail time for not revealing her source, nonetheless, she mentioned no names.

__b__   7.   The water skier was badly wounded he had hit a rock in shallow water.

__a__   8.   Picking blueberries in summer and apples in fall, at their grandparents' farm in Vermont.

__a__   9.   Unable to set aside her Harry Potter book, even though it was two hours past her bedtime.

__c__   10.   I just received your text message about watching the football game, has it started yet?

__d__   11.   Gee, I haven't seen a *Captain Kangaroo* episode in twenty years!

__b__   12.   Kevin keeps his childhood tonsils in a jar in the garage his wife won't allow them in the house.

__d__   13.   Jessica likes *Nancy Grace*, *Jerry Springer*, and a few other TV shows.

__a__   14.   In a heated state of excitement since winning the Mustang at bingo last night.

__d__   15.   After dinner, we usually take a walk, unless the weather is too chilly.

__c__   16.   I don't care what you say, Britney Spears is the greatest talent that this planet has ever known.

__a__   17.   Saying that our German Shepherd is beautiful, and wanting to paint her portrait.

b 18. On Wednesdays our streets are cleaned on Thursdays our garbage is collected.

d 19. The withdrawal of his name from the city council election shocked all of us.

a 20. The Arabian Peninsula, home of some of the world's hottest and most beautiful beaches.

c 21. No, Santos isn't home right now, you might call again in an hour.

b 22. Nothing made his father angrier than losing the tool chest it had been passed from father to son for four generations.

b 23. We checked both Wal-Mart and Kresge's neither sells the battery we need for our camera.

d 24. All in all, a good sandwich and a long nap are hard to beat.

a 25. A mastermind of the largest corporate fraud in history, cheating hundreds of ordinary people out of their life savings.

REVIEW TEST 9-B
Correcting Sentence Fragments, Run-on Sentences, and Comma-Splices

In the space provided, write the letter corresponding to the kind of error each sentence contains.
If a sentence is correct, write "d" in front of it.

a. sentence fragment   b. run-on sentence   c. comma-splice   d. correct

___a___ 1. To seek a cure for depression and to determine its causes.

___b___ 2. The closing ceremonies of the Olympics were impressive music and fire-works were everywhere.

___c___ 3. Jacqueline apparently does not have a "green thumb," none of the flowers that she planted has lived.

___d___ 4. Thanksgiving is not a national holiday in Mexico.

___c___ 5. Financial advisors recommend that credit card balances be paid as soon as possible, some even urge that credit cards be destroyed.

___a___ 6. A large pizza with anchovies, onions, sausage, and mushrooms.

___d___ 7. Believing that the threat of flooding had passed, the villagers returned to their homes.

___c___ 8. Our town has an airport, however, it is too small to accommodate passen-ger planes and commercial flights.

___a___ 9. Spending hours surfing the Internet, like someone casually flipping the pages of an encyclopedia.

___d___ 10. Roy's grandmother is ninety-four, and she continues to mow her own lawn.

___c___ 11. The storm continued throughout the night, in the morning we discovered that all of our food was soaked with water.

___b___ 12. The motorboat sank in the lake its propeller had become entangled on a submerged cable.

___b___ 13. Francisco goes hunting however, he carries a camera, not a gun.

___c___ 14. A position was advertised for someone who could speak Spanish and use a computer, over two hundred people applied.

___a___ 15. Because the current was swift and the girl could not swim.

___a___ 16. The state of Maine, which boasts of its rich history.

___d___ 17. The Chinese and Japanese smoke more cigarettes per capita than Americans do, according to recent studies.

___d___ 18. Realizing that he was uncoordinated and possessing no sense of rhythm, Kolya gave up his dream of being a dancer.

___c___ 19. Keep an eye on the mainsail, meanwhile, we will repair the tiller.

___b___ 20. Many words have interesting histories "anecdote," for example, comes from a Greek word meaning "unpublished."

___d___ 21. Phil's career goals are a good-paying job, a beautiful wife, and a home in Miami Beach.

___d___ 22. Soccer is the most popular sport in Europe, where it is called football.

___d___ 23. Many American presidents did not graduate from college, said Freddie, citing this fact as his reason for dropping out of college.

___a___ 24. The sale of carbon paper, having declined in recent years because of the advent of photocopying and the computer.

___b___ 25. Michele finally completed painting her garage she painted it the same color as her house.

Go to www.ablongman.com/yarber to complete Review Test 9-C.

Writing Paragraphs

Developing a Paragraph by Classification

College instructors often ask their students to sort things or ideas according to their individual characteristics. You might be asked by your literature or drama teacher to show how Shakespeare's plays have traditionally been divided into three large groupings. Your biology instructor may ask you to explain the various types of pollution. Or your political science instructor may want you to contrast the powers granted to the three branches of the federal government. In all of these assignments, you will be showing how parts of a whole are different. The method of development used is *classification*.

The following paragraph uses classification as a developmental device to show the various types of personality disorders according to the particular characteristic most prominent in each.

■ Several types of personality disorders have been identified by psychologists and psychiatrists. It must be kept in mind that in given cases the dividing lines are often unclear and that an individual will have some characteristics of more than one type. Nevertheless, three clusters of personality disorders have been devised. Paranoid, schizoid, and schizotypal personality disorders are associated with individuals who often seem odd or eccentric. Histrionic, narcissistic, antisocial, and borderline personality disorders cause their sufferers to be dramatic, emotional, and erratic. Their behavior is more colorful, more forceful, and more likely to get them into contact with mental health or legal authorities than is true of disorders in the first cluster. The final classification includes those who have avoidant, dependent, compulsive, and passive-aggressive personality disorders. In this cluster of disorders, unlike the others, people often experience anxiety and fearfulness, and individuals suffering from them are more likely than the others to seek help.

In the next paragraph the author classifies the five basic types of sacrifice as they are presented in the book of Leviticus in the Bible.

■ The book of Leviticus describes five basic types of sacrifice among the ancient Hebrews. The first was the burnt offering, in which the entire carcass of an animal was sacrificed by fire. The second type was the cereal offering, an offering of a product of the field and obviously not of such serious character as a burnt offering. Third was the peace offering, apparently the form of animal sacrifice for ordinary occasions. Fourth was the sin offering, made for sins committed unwittingly. Fifth was the sacrifice required when one committed a breach against God or against his neighbor through deception, perjury, or robbery.

When writing a paragraph based on classification, you will probably need to use words and phrases like the following:

Words and Phrases Used in Classification Paragraphs

There are *several types of* reactions to . . .

There are *numerous kinds of* . . .

Skin cancers *can be classified as* . . .

The judicial system *is composed of* . . .

Facial muscles *comprise* . . .

One type of engine . . .

Another *type of* engine is . . .

Finally, there is . . .

EXERCISE A Using Classification

Select one of the following topics and develop it into a paragraph based on classification. Underline your topic sentence.

- *campus types*
- *bores*
- *part-time jobs*
- *daytime television*
- *commercials*
- *gifts*
- *bosses*

Writing Tips Writing with Class . . .

When you develop a paragraph by classification, you are sorting things or ideas according to similar characteristics. It is one way of answering the question, "What (or who) is it and where does it belong?" To classify, therefore, is to group things in categories. In this kind of paragraph, be certain that your categories are logical and do not overlap. To divide your student body into "men, women, and athletes," for instance, would be inaccurate because "athletes" obviously includes individuals from the first two groups. Be certain that your parts account for all elements of the object. To divide the federal government into the judicial and legislative branches would be incomplete because the executive branch is omitted. Finally, when classifying, make certain that every item fits into a category and that there are no items left over.

EXERCISE B Using Classification

Select one of the following subjects and develop it into a paragraph based on classification. Be sure that your topic sentence lets your reader know how your paragraph is developed.

- *clubs on your campus*
- *flowers in your garden*
- *neighborhoods in your city*
- *favorite foods*
- *types of popular music*
- *methods of relaxation*
- *computer games*

Writing Tips What's Another Word for . . . ?

Consider investing in a thesaurus to keep your word choice fresh, exact, and colorful. A thesaurus is a book that lists numerous synonyms of words in various arrangements. Thesauruses do not define words; they give words of similar meaning. Consequently, you have to be careful about selecting a synonym from the lists supplied. *Roget's International Thesaurus,* with 256,000 words and phrases, is the most popular thesaurus and is available at most libraries and booksellers. Most word-processing programs include a thesaurus feature that can replace designated words instantly.

Computer Activity

Using the words and phrases that are suggested on page 209, select a topic from Exercise A or B, and write a paragraph.

Be sure to explain your basis for classification in your paragraph. When you have finished your paragraph, divide your computer screen, and list in the bottom pane the categories into which the general subject of your paragraph has been divided.

Are the categories sufficient to include all items within your general subject, or do they overlap? If they overlap, rewrite your paragraph to make clear distinctions.

CHAPTER 10

CONFUSED SENTENCES

CHAPTER PREVIEW

In this chapter, you will learn about:

- Writing clear and correct sentences
  Avoiding misplaced and dangling modifiers
  Avoiding illogical comparisons
  Avoiding confusing adjectives and adverbs
  Using parallel structure
- Writing paragraphs: Developing a paragraph
  by process and analysis

To write sentences that are not confusing, we have to make certain that they are grammatically correct. This means, for example, that their subjects and verbs agree and that their pronouns and antecedents are linked without confusion. But clarity and correctness depend on other considerations as well. In this chapter we will look at some of the other ways to avoid illogical, inexact, or confused sentences.

Misplaced and Dangling Modifiers

Modifiers are words that describe other words in sentences. They may be single words, phrases, or clauses; they may come before the word they modify, or they may follow it. In either case, a modifier should appear near the word it modifies, and the reader should not be confused about which word it modifies.

A **misplaced modifier** is one that is not close to the word it modifies and as a result modifies the wrong word. Sentences with misplaced modifiers are usually confusing and often result in unintended, though sometimes humorous, meanings.

Notice the unintended meanings in the following sentences. In each sentence, the modifier has been misplaced.

- The bank robber was described as a short man wearing a baseball cap weighing 175 pounds.
- Growing at the bottom of the swimming pool, Kevin found some mold.
- On the wall above his desk is a photograph of his daughter in a gold frame.

By placing the modifiers next to the words they modify or by rewording the sentences, we can make the meaning of these sentences clear.

- The bank robber was described as a short man weighing 175 pounds and wearing a baseball cap.
- Kevin found some mold growing at the bottom of the swimming pool.
- On the wall above his desk is a photograph in a gold frame of his daughter.

EXERCISE 10-1

Rewrite any of the following sentences that contain misplaced modifiers. If a sentence is correct, write "C" in front of it.

1. Crying frightened tears, the policeman helped the toddler find his mother at the beach.

   Crying frightened tears, the toddler found his mother at the beach, with the help

   of a policeman.

2. Our teacher announced that we would have a test as we filed out the door.

   As we filed out the door, our teacher announced that we would have a test.

3. Please tell James that he should hurry and eat his dinner in the oven.

   Please tell James that he should hurry and eat his dinner, which is in the oven.

4. Last week I discussed my low skills in playing tennis with my neighbor.

   Last week I discussed with my neighbor my low skills in playing tennis.

5. Lisa promised a new computer to her daughter with a fast modem.

   Lisa promised her daughter a new computer with a fast modem.

6. We saw the plane crash on our new widescreen television.
   On our new widescreen television, we saw the plane crash.

   _____

7. Rigoberto bought a diamond ring for his wife in a shiny gold setting.
   Rigoberto bought a diamond ring in a shiny gold setting for his wife.

   _____

8. Lance Armstrong had an interview about his seven Tour de France rides with a writer from *Sports Illustrated*.
   Lance Armstrong had an interview with a writer from *Sports Illustrated*,

   about his seven Tour de France rides.

9. With dimples and rotted spots all over, I could see that the canteloupe had spoiled.
   I could see that the canteloupe, with dimples and rotted spots all over,

   had spoiled.

10. **C** Hungry and dehydrated, Gilda ate a huge meal after her hike in the desert.

    _____

    _____

A variation of the misplaced modifier is the **squinting modifier,** a modifier that usually appears in the middle of a sentence so that it can modify either the word that precedes it or the one that follows it. As a result, the squinting modifier makes the sentence ambiguous. We will discuss two sentences that contain squinting modifiers.

Notice the confusion caused by the placement of the modifier in our first sentence.

■ His doctor encouraged him regularly to diet and exercise.

In this sentence, it is unclear whether *regularly* modifies *encouraged him* or *to diet and exercise*. Here are two improved alternatives.

■ His doctor regularly encouraged him to diet and exercise.
■ His doctor encouraged him to diet and exercise regularly.

Confusion also exists in our second sentence.

■ Applicants who can already dance normally are placed in an advanced class.

In this sentence, which applicants are placed in the advanced class? Applicants who dance normally? More probably, it is applicants who already dance who are normally placed in an advanced class. Here are two improved alternatives.

- Applicants who can already dance are normally placed in an advanced class.
- Applicants who dance normally are usually placed in an advanced class. (Notice the difference in meaning in this alternative.)

To avoid a squinting modifier and the confusion it creates, you will usually find it best to place the modifier immediately before the word it modifies.

EXERCISE 10-2

Rewrite any of the following sentences that contain squinting modifiers. If a sentence is correct, write "C" in front of it.   **Student responses will vary.**

1. Students who study carefully pass the state examination.

    _____

2. Jogging remarkably shed my extra pounds.

    _____

3. Going to the movies often is expensive.

    _____

4. Paddling through the Everglades lazily relaxed us.

    _____

5. **C** Hong Kong is under the control of China after more than a century of British rule.

    _____

6. Those who gamble secretly take chances with their finances.

    _____

7. Elena's story about her vacation in Hawaii that she told slowly put us to sleep.

    _____

8. Anyone who sings occasionally hits a wrong note.

    _____

9. **C** The tax lawyer advised his clients early in the year to establish a trust fund.

    _____

10. Donna reminded her husband regularly to get a physical examination.

    _____

A **dangling modifier** is a modifier that has no word in the sentence for it to modify. It is left "dangling," and as a result it ends up accidentally modifying an unintended word, as in the following example.

- After reviewing my lecture notes and rereading the summaries of each chapter, the geology examination was easier than I had thought.

Tips **for Correcting Misplaced and Dangling Modifiers**

1. Place every modifier close to the word it modifies.
2. If the word meant to be modified is not in the sentence, insert it close to its modifier.
3. Reword or punctuate the sentence so that the intended meaning is clear.

According to this sentence, the geology examination reviewed the lecture notes and reread the summaries of each chapter. But this is obviously not the meaning intended. To correct this sentence, we must first determine *who* was doing the action. By supplying the missing subject, we can then improve the sentence.

■ After reviewing my lecture notes and rereading the summaries of each chapter, I found that the geology examination was easier than I had thought. (**Or:** After I reviewed my lecture notes and reread the summaries of each chapter, the geology examination was easier than I had thought.)

Here are some more sentences with dangling modifiers.

■ Sound asleep, the alarm clock was not heard by Frank.

■ Arriving home after midnight, the house was dark.

■ Frightened by the noise, the barks of the dog woke us up.

By supplying subjects and rewording these sentences, we can make their meanings clear.

■ Sound asleep, Frank did not hear the alarm clock.

■ When we arrived home after midnight, the house was dark.

■ Frightened by the noise, the dog woke us up by its barking.

EXERCISE 10-3

Rewrite any of the following sentences that contain dangling modifiers. If a sentence is correct, write "C" in front of it.   **Student responses will vary.**

1. When watching an exciting movie on television, commercials are especially irritating.

    _____

2. Raised in Colorado, it is natural to miss the snow-covered mountains.

    _____

3. Although only a sophomore, the field hockey team selected Kathy as its captain.

    _____

4. **C** Although it was nearly finished, we left the concert early because we had to study for our biology exam.

_____

5.   As a child, his father bought him a violin in the hope that he would become a violinist.

_____

6.   Walking on the beach, the sand warmed my bare feet.

_____

7.   While walking across the manicured golf course yesterday, the sprinklers suddenly came on.

_____

8.   After offering a toast to the guest of honor, dinner was served.

_____

9. **C** Breathless and exhausted, the winner of the marathon could not talk.

_____

10.   Driving across the country last summer, the differences in regional accents could be detected.

_____

Illogical Comparisons

A **comparison** is a statement about the relationship between two (or among more than two) things.

- ■ Wal-Mart is larger than any other retailer in the United States.
- ■ My father's 1990 Chevrolet runs as well as my new Honda.
- ■ Tiger Woods won the Masters golf tournament with a lower score than any other golfer in the annual event's history.

When making a comparison, be certain that the things being compared are similar and that your comparison is complete. Omitted words often make the comparison unclear, illogical, or awkward.

- ■ **Unclear:** Tulsa is closer to Oklahoma City than Dallas.

This sentence is not clear because the comparison is not stated fully enough. Be sure that the comparisons are full enough to be clear.

- ■ **Revised:** Tulsa is closer to Oklahoma City than it is to Dallas.

Why is the following sentence illogical?

■ **Unclear:** The population of Mexico City is growing at a faster rate than that of any major city in the world.

Because Mexico City is a major city, this sentence is illogical because it compares its subject with itself. When comparing members of the same class, use *other* or *any other*.

■ **Revised:** The population of Mexico City is growing at a faster rate than that of any *other* major city in the world.

Why is the following sentence unclear?

■ **Unclear:** The average hourly wage for a woman is lower than a man.

This sentence is unclear because it compares the hourly wage with a man. Be sure that items being compared are comparable.

■ **Revised:** The average hourly wage for a woman is lower than a *man's.*

EXERCISE 10-4

Revise any of the following sentences that contain illogical comparisons. If a sentence is correct, write "C" in front of it.

1. I enjoy pizza much more than Garth.
   I enjoy pizza much more than Garth does.

2. The Tim McGraw CD is more expensive than Faith Hill.
   The Tim McGraw CD is more expensive than the Faith Hill CD.

3.**C** There's less rain today than there was yesterday.

4. Clothes are more fashionable at Tommy Hilfiger than other stores.
   Clothes are more fashionable at Tommy Hilfiger than at other stores.

5. We'd rather listen to blues than other musicians.
   We'd rather listen to blues than other kinds of music.

6. The neighbors near our new house in Brownsville are friendlier than our old house in Boston.

   The neighbors near our new house in Brownsville are friendlier than the neighbors near our old house in Boston.

7. Sipping coffee with my English instructor is more enjoyable than a super model.

   Sipping coffee with my English instructor is more enjoyable than sipping coffee with a super model.

8. **C** Jose is younger than most professional guitarists.

9. The defense attorney's case is stronger and more interesting than the prosecutor.

   The defense attorney's case is stronger and more interesting than the prosecutor's.

10. Judy's flu has grown worse than yesterday.

    Judy's flu has grown worse than it was yesterday.

Confusing Adjectives and Adverbs

Adjectives and **adverbs** are modifiers; they limit or describe other words.

- ■ **Adjective:** *Moderate* exercise suppresses the appetite.
- ■ **Adverb:**   The surgeon *carefully* examined the sutures.

Many adverbs end in *-ly* (*hurriedly*, *graciously*, and *angrily*); some of the most common, however, do not (*here*, *there*, *now*, *when*, *then*, and *often*). Furthermore, some words that end in *-ly* are not adverbs (*silly*, *manly*, and *hilly*).

Using Adjectives after Linking Verbs

You will recall from Chapter 2 that the most common linking verbs are *be*, *appear*, *become*, *grow*, *remain*, *seem*, and the "sense" verbs (*feel*, *look*, *smell*, *sound*, and *taste*). Words that follow such verbs and refer to the subject are adjectives—never adverbs. In the following sentences, the adjective (called a *predicate adjective* because it follows the verb and modifies the subject) comes after a linking verb.

- ■ Pablo's ideas are *exciting*. (*Exciting* modifies *ideas*.)
- ■ Their wedding reception was *expensive*. (*Expensive* modifies *wedding reception*.)
- ■ That detergent makes my hands feel *rough*. (*Rough* modifies *hands*.)

The rule for deciding whether to use an adjective or an adverb after a verb, therefore, is simple: if the verb shows a condition or a state of being, use an adjective after it. Here are some additional examples that illustrate the rule.

- The hamburger smells *tantalizing.*
- Mike's girlfriend appeared *nervous.*
- The math final seemed *easy.*
- Rimsky looked *handsome* in his new suit.

Most of us would not write or say, "This soup is warmly," or "She is beautifully." In both cases we would instinctively use an adjective rather than an adverb. The choice is not so obvious with "bad" and "well," however. Study carefully the use of these words in the sentences below.

- **Nonstandard:**   Ibrahim had some of my homemade soup and now he feels *badly.* (*Badly* is an adverb following a linking verb; it cannot modify the pronoun *he.*)

- **Standard:**   Ibrahim had some of my homemade soup and now he feels *bad.* (*Bad* is an adjective modifying *he.*)

- **Nonstandard:**   I feel *badly* about that. (As in the first example above, *badly* is an adverb and therefore cannot modify the pronoun *I.*)

- **Standard:**   I feel *bad* about that. (*Bad* is an adjective modifying *I.*)

- **Nonstandard:**   That hat looks very *well* on Barbara. (*Looks* is a linking verb, and therefore, we need an adjective after the verb to modify the noun *hat.* *Well* is an adverb except when it means "to be in good health.")

- **Standard:**   That hat looks very *good* on Barbara. (*Good* is an adjective modifying the noun *hat.*)

- **Standard:**   Although Kate has been sick, she looks *well* now. (*Well,* as noted above, is an adjective when it means "to be in good health." In this sentence it follows the linking verb *looks* and modifies *she.*)

Tips **for Choosing Adverbs or Adjectives**

The choice of an adverb or an adjective depends on the kind of verb in the sentence:

1. If the verb is a *linking verb* and you want to describe the subject, an *adjective* is correct.
2. If you want to modify a verb that shows *action,* an *adverb* is correct.
3. If you want to modify an adjective, an *adverb* is correct.

Using Adverbs to Modify Verbs

When a verb expresses an action by the subject, use an adverb after it—not an adjective. Study the following sentences.

- **Nonstandard:** Because Jack was unfamiliar with the city, he drove *careful.*
- **Standard:**   Because Jack was unfamiliar with the city, he drove *carefully.*

- **Nonstandard:** Lorraine spoke very *quiet* of her many accomplishments.
- **Standard:**   Lorraine spoke very *quietly* of her many accomplishments.

- **Nonstandard:** Teesha picked up the expensive glass *delicate.*
- **Standard:**   Teesha picked up the expensive glass *delicately.*

Verbs that sometimes show condition or state of being in one sentence but an action by the subject in another sentence can be troublesome:

- The dog smelled the meat *carefully.* (*Smelled* is an *action* verb.)
- The meat smelled *rotten.* (*Smelled* is a *linking* verb.)
- The alarm sounded *suddenly.* (*Sounded* is an *action* verb.)
- His cries sounded *pitiful.* (*Sounded* is a *linking* verb.)
- Claire appeared *abruptly.* (*Appeared* is an *action* verb.)
- Claire appeared *tired.* (*Appeared* is a *linking* verb.)

EXERCISE 10-5

Write the letter of the correct word on the line preceding the sentence.

___b___   1. Screw on the lid (a. tight   b. tightly), or the applesauce will not stay fresh.

___b___   2. Please make your dog stop staring so (a. strange   b. strangely) at me.

___a___   3. I wish the group chatting behind us at the theater had been more (a. quiet b. quietly).

___b___   4. Because of her unreliable car, she rarely arrives (a. punctual   b. punctually) at work.

___b___   5. Because Sheila has never studied physics, she believes that these experiments are (a. awful   b. awfully) difficult.

_____b_____ 6. Because of his wrenched knee, Sam cannot walk as (a. quick   b. quickly) as his buddies.

_____a_____ 7. Franco felt (a. bad   b. badly) about crashing his girlfriend's new car.

_____b_____ 8. Bridget was (a. bad   b. badly) hurt in the rugby scrum.

_____a_____ 9. Although Louis's jambalaya tasted (a. delicious   b. deliciously), it contained many calories and grams of fat.

_____b_____ 10. Jerry had thought he would pass the driving test (a. easy   b. easily), but he failed it twice.

Parallel Structure

When writing about items in a series, be sure that you present each item in the same grammatical form. In other words, each item should be an adjective, or each item should be a prepositional phrase, or each item should be an infinitive, and so on. When all items in a series are in the same grammatical form, the sentence or passage is said to have **parallel structure.**

Notice the use of parallel structure in the following sentences:

- Edward *approached* the plate, *tugged* at his belt, *adjusted* his grip, then *swung* the bat. (parallel past-tense verbs)

- Tanya sang *softly, confidently,* and *seductively.* (parallel adverbs)

- *To lose weight, to study conscientiously,* and *to spend less time on the telephone*— these were Ken's New Year's resolutions. (parallel infinitive phrases)

- Ahmad quit smoking *because it was an expensive habit, because his wife had quit,* and *because his doctor had urged him.* (parallel dependent clauses)

Parallel structure is a writing technique worth acquiring because it makes sentences smoother and shows the connection between ideas. For these reasons, professional writers and public speakers often make use of parallel structure. It helps to "bind up" a sentence, making its parts and meaning much easier to grasp.

Contrast the rhythm and clarity of the following pairs of sentences:

- **Faulty:** The president claimed that he wanted to *clean up the environment, improve the public schools,* and *reducing crime in the streets.* (infinitive, infinitive, and participle)

- **Parallel:** The president claimed that he wanted *to clean up the environment, to improve the public schools,* and *to reduce crime in the streets.* (three infinitives)

■ **Faulty:**   Our new fax machine is *efficient, inexpensive,* and *it is easily operated.* (two adjectives and a clause)

■ **Parallel:**   Our new fax machine is *efficient, inexpensive,* and *easily operated.* (three adjectives)

■ **Faulty:**   Her baby has already started *walking* and *to talk.* (participle and infinitive)

■ **Parallel:**   Her baby has already started *walking* and *talking.* (two participles)

You can also achieve effective parallel construction by using correlative conjunctions. As mentioned in Chapter 2, correlatives are connectives used in pairs, and therefore they are handy tools for linking similar grammatical patterns with ideas of similar importance. The most common correlatives are *either/or, neither/nor, not only/but also,* and *both/and.*

Here are some examples of correlative conjunctions used to achieve parallel structure:

■ Sheila is proficient *not only* on the clarinet *but also* on the saxophone.

■ *Neither* the musicians *nor* the producers could have predicted the success of rock music on television.

■ The president's remarks were addressed *both* to Congress *and* to the American people.

When using correlative conjunctions, be sure to place them as closely as possible to the words they join.

■ **Nonstandard:**   She *neither* wanted our advice *nor* our help.

■ **Standard:**   She wanted *neither* our advice *nor* our help.

■ **Nonstandard:**   Misha will be flying *both* to Minneapolis *and* Chicago.

■ **Standard:**   Misha will be flying to *both* Minneapolis *and* Chicago.

■ **Nonstandard:**   Richard would *neither* apologize *nor* would he admit that he was wrong.

■ **Standard:**   Richard would *neither* apologize *nor* admit that he was wrong.

EXERCISE 10-6

Rewrite any of the following sentences that contain faulty parallelism. If the sentence is correct, write "C" before it.   **Student responses will vary.**

1.   In computer class, Phuong learned to build Web pages, and also using the Internet.

_____

_____

2. Trisha complained that her counselor had neither an understanding of students' problems and he did not like people.

_____

_____

3. Owning a home not only requires a lot of maintenance but also it is expensive and it needs a lot of time.

_____

_____

4. Wally's ideas are clever, original, and they are practical.

_____

_____

5. The ambassador from Iran would neither apologize nor would he promise to accept the demands of the United Nations.

_____

_____

6. **C** Professor Gorra is brilliant, eloquent, and helpful.

_____

_____

7. **C** Winston Churchill said that victory would require blood and sweat and toil and tears.

_____

_____

8. The governor said that his hobbies were fly-fishing and to play video games with his grandchildren.

_____

_____

9. Many people join health clubs for exercise, for relaxation, and sometimes to find romance.

_____

_____

10. Nicolas Cage is admired as an actor because he is not only a dramatic actor but also he is good in comedy roles.

_____

_____

EDITING EXERCISES

The paragraphs below contain dangling modifiers, illogical comparisons, incorrectly used adjectives or adverbs, and other weaknesses. Rewrite each paragraph, eliminating any confusing constructions and revising unclear sentences.

Removing an insect from a child's ear can be real frightening. Sometimes it is difficult to know if an insect is in the ear or something else. Although tempting, the insect should not be killed by poking something in its ear because you may damage the child's ear or make the bug more difficult to remove. Because insects love light, use it to coax the bug out. Pull the child's earlobe real gentle so the light can reach the ear canal easy. You can also shine a flashlight into the ear and tugging its lobe, the insect may emerge from the child's ear. Pouring a few drops of mineral oil into the ear carefully makes the insect float out. You must be sure that it is a bug before trying this method; if it is a piece of popcorn or other expanding item, you may have caused the object to swell and become more difficult to remove. If the insect does not emerge still, or if you are no longer sure that the object is an insect, call a health care professional before anyone else.

Look for a few signs and you'll be able to tell pretty good if your date is truly interested in you. Subtle but universal, you can look for body language clues. Something called symbolic reaching is more common than others. For example, instead of resting on your date's lap, he or she might rest an arm on the table with fingers pointed in your direction. Even more bold, he or she may touch you during your conversation. Concealing or sitting on your hands usually means he or she isn't interested. Mimicking each other's body language, vocal tone and volume, talking speed, or gestures is another real good sign of interest. Humans subconsciously do this when attracted. Does your date blink really frequent? Another sign of interest, we tend to blink more when we're nervous from trying to make a good impression. Feet tell more about one's feelings than most body parts: the more direct they're pointed at you, the more certain your date is attracted to you. There's an old saying: where the feet point, the heart follows quick. Finally, mind the distance between you and your date; sitting or standing two feet or closer to you signifies attraction more than other things. Of course, some people are physical shy even when they're total in love, but most will show at least one or two of these signs when interested.

WRITING SENTENCES   Avoiding Confused Sentences

Illogical, inexact, or confused sentences not only irritate your reader; they also fail to make your meaning clear. This writing exercise will help you avoid such sentences.

1. Write two sentences, each containing a misplaced or dangling modifier. Using the suggestions in this chapter, revise each sentence.
2. Write two sentences, each containing an illogical comparison. Using the suggestions in this chapter, revise each sentence.
3. Write two sentences, each illustrating the correct use of adjectives after linking verbs.
4. Write two sentences, each illustrating the correct use of adverbs modifying verbs.
5. Write two sentences, each using faulty parallel structure. Using the suggestions in this chapter, revise each sentence so that it has parallel structure.

Language Tips

Using adjectives and adverbs correctly can often be tricky for nonnative speakers of English. Here are some suggestions.

1. Many adverbs are made from an adjective + *-ly.*

    quick/quick*ly,* serious/serious*ly,* careful/careful*ly,* quiet/quiet*ly,* heavy/heavi*ly,* and bad/bad*ly*

2. Not all words ending in *-ly* are adverbs, however.

    friendly, lively, lonely, silly, and lovely

3. An adjective tells us more about a noun. Note that adjectives may appear after a few verbs (especially forms of *to be*).

    interesting book, *light* snow, *confusing* question

    Professor Jenkins's lecture was *funny.*

4. An adverb tells us more about a *verb.*

    Tom *walked quickly* to the front of the room. (*verb + adverb*)

    We stayed home because it *snowed heavily.* (*verb + adverb*)

    Be sure the modifier is an adverb. Compare the following sentences.

    She *speaks* English *perfectly* (*verb + object + adverb*)

    Beatrice speaks *perfect English.* (*adjective + noun*)

5. We also use adverbs before adjectives and other adverbs.

    very cheap (*adverb + adjective*)

    very quickly (*adverb + adverb*)

R E V I E W   T E S T   1 0 - A
Confused Sentences

A. *Write the letter of the correct word in the space provided.*

___b___ 1. Hummingbirds move so (a. quick b. quickly) that their beauty is hard to see.

___a___ 2. We felt (a. bad b. badly) about missing Elizabeth's birthday party.

___b___ 3. Suki has become (a. real b. really) good at her job in the appliance store.

___b___ 4. Maximina looked at me pretty (a. serious b. seriously) when I told her that the test is tomorrow, not next week.

___a___ 5. Daniel felt very (a. happy b. happily) about being invited to the party.

B. *In the space before each sentence, write the letter corresponding to the kind of error the sentence contains.*

   a. *misplaced or dangling modifier*   b. *illogical or incomplete comparison*
   c. *adjective or adverb used incorrectly*   d. *faulty parallel structure*

___b___ 6. The price of Mariska's car is higher than Cody.

___a___ 7. Bruised and tackled viciously, Tran found it difficult to watch his wife play rugby.

___a___ 8. To enroll in a college course, your application must be complete.

___d___ 9. Armando likes jogging on Saturdays and to do crossword puzzles on Sundays.

___c___ 10. Su Lan rides her bicycle very careful to class each day.

___b___ 11. Mosquito bites are much more common than fleas.

___d___ 12. Uma said her hobbies were reading good novels and to help children who struggle in school.

___b___ 13. Physiologically, pigs and orangutans are more like humans than other animals.

___d___ 14. Zombie movies, cooking, and to skateboard make up my ideal weekend schedule.

___a___ 15. Spinning in its wheel and living on spoiled cabbage, Robin's grandson thought that the hamster had a pretty good life.

___c___ 16. Karen drives dangerous when she's late to work.

c   17. Do you recall when a computer company asked consumers to "think different" and buy its product?

d   18. I'd like a sandwich, a cup of soup, some pie, and to drink a lemonade.

c   19. It's been months since the refrigerator has had a real thorough cleaning.

a   20. Extremely loyal viewers, *CSI: Las Vegas and Law & Order* are Olga and Ramon's favorite TV shows.

c   21. A beginning driver, Mani can't shift smooth yet.

b   22. Kwesi makes fifteen dollars an hour at the supermarket, which is as much as the electronics store.

a   23. Having never seen a basketball game, the star player's name was unfamiliar to me.

d   24. This weekend we should make pancakes and to dice some walnuts into them.

b   25. Dr. Martinez said that surgery on a foot is generally less painful than a spine.

R E V I E W   T E S T   1 0 - B
Confused Sentences

A. Write the letter of the correct word in the space provided.

___a___   1. Although Carla had never played in a championship game previously, she did not appear (a. nervous   b. nervously) on the mound.

___b___   2. As the time approached for the announcement of the winner's name, Larry became (a. real   b. really) excited.

___b___   3. Because I didn't have time to proofread my essay, I didn't notice that two words in the title were spelled (a. incorrect   b. incorrectly).

___b___   4. Miguel waved good-bye to his friends and walked (a. slow   b. slowly) to the train.

___a___   5. Because the refrigerator was disconnected, the meat smelled (a. bad b. badly).

B. In the space before each sentence, write the letter corresponding to the kind of error the sentence contains.

        a. misplaced or dangling modifier   b. illogical or incomplete comparison
          c. adjective or adverb used incorrectly   d. faulty parallel structure

___b___   6. To her surprise, Lupe made higher grades in chemistry class than her brother.

___b___   7. Art says that life in Las Vegas is not much different from any city its size.

___b___   8. Prices at a military commissary are usually lower than other retail establishments.

___d___   9. Many people join a political party because of family tradition, economic reasons, or because they like a particular candidate.

___a___   10. Featuring an electric starter and a four-stroke engine, the salesperson claimed that the lawn mower was the best on the market.

___a___   11. Waving and smiling to their friends, the television camera panned slowly across the crowd.

___b___   12. The natives of the small Pacific island are taller than any of the inhabitants of the area.

___c___   13. Despite its small size, the dog barked very ferocious at the mail carrier.

___a___ 14. To receive the discount, the advertisement states that we must purchase the lamp before next Monday.

___c___ 15. The firefighters responded very quick when the alarm sounded at the old fireworks factory.

___a___ 16. Trying to think of a way to begin my speech, a funny story came to mind.

___d___ 17. The attorney was tall, slender, and seemed to be middle-aged.

___a___ 18. Barking at passing cars and inspecting the shrubbery of the neighborhood, we found the dog that had escaped from its kennel.

___a___ 19. Selling shoes during the summer and waiting on tables during the school year, my tuition was paid without the help of my parents.

___a___ 20. Having misread the assignment, my term paper received a low grade.

___c___ 21. The supermarket manager felt happily about the sales campaign.

___c___ 22. Tanya has a good sense of humor and can tell a joke really good.

___b___ 23. In my opinion, staying up all night to review before an examination is a handicap than if you get a good night's sleep.

___c___ 24. The advertisements for the computer claim that it is real easy to operate.

___b___ 25. Mr. Conley said that students of his generation worked harder than the schools today.

Go to www.ablongman.com/yarber to complete Review Test 10-C.

WRITING PARAGRAPHS

DEVELOPING A PARAGRAPH BY PROCESS AND ANALYSIS

"How is it done?" "How did it happen?" These are the questions answered by paragraphs developed by *process and analysis*. Some process-and-analysis paragraphs tell the reader how to change a tire, train a puppy, mix concrete, or plant a tree. Others explain how something happened or how it takes place: how the pyramids of Egypt were built, how the blood circulates through the body, or how the Roman Catholic Church elects a pope. In all cases, the purpose is to provide information to the reader as clearly and directly as possible.

Because all process-and-analysis paragraphs essentially explain how an act is done or how a process happens, their ideas are presented chronologically. Every idea follows the preceding one in a *time sequence*. If the ideas are presented out of order, the results are chaotic. Imagine trying to put together a transistor radio from a kit whose instructions began, "After receiving a radio signal, adjust the aerial to improve reception." The first requirement, then, is to make certain that all the steps are presented in a clear sequence.

When writing the process-and-analysis paragraph, you should include more than a list of steps. A paper giving such a list would be technically correct but would have all the excitement of a set of directions for assembling a bicycle. Give your paragraph direction by giving it a topic sentence. For instance, instead of just listing in order the steps in taking a blood sample, write a topic statement that lets the reader see an overall pattern. "Taking a blood sample is more painful for the nurse than the patient" is more inviting than "There are three steps to follow in taking a blood sample." In this way your paragraph has a point of view; it catches the reader's interest.

The following paragraph explains how the four-stroke engine works. Notice that it is arranged in time order.

■ The four-stroke engine employs four distinct operations spread over four full strokes of each of its pistons. The first, the intake stroke, begins with the intake valve open and the piston at the top of its cylinder. As the rotating crankshaft drives the piston down, the resulting suction draws a mixture of air and fuel into the cylinder. Near the bottom of the stroke the intake valve closes, and the piston is forced upward by the crankshaft. The air-fuel mixture is compressed, and near the top of the piston's stroke a spark plug ignites the compressed charge of air and fuel. The temperature and pressure in the cylinder increase dramatically, forcing the piston down and transferring power to the crankshaft. Just before the piston reaches the bottom of the power stroke, the exhaust valve opens, releasing most of the burned mixture. After the high pressure blows down, the low-pressure exhaust gas remaining in the cylinder is driven out when the crankshaft forces the piston up again. The exhaust valve then closes, the intake valve opens, and the entire cycle begins again.

231

The next paragraph explains how a product is made—in this case a chocolate bar. Notice that the steps are presented chronologically.

■ Chocolate makes life more enjoyable for nearly everyone around the world—in fact, an average American eats about ten pounds of chocolate each year. How is that magnificent delight, the chocolate bar, created? It starts with the cacao tree, which grows in tropical regions such as Africa and South America. The tree produces reddish-yellow, pineapple-sized fruit, which contain cocoa beans within. The cocoa beans are fermented, then dried in open air and sun for a week. Next, they're shipped to the chocolate maker, who roasts the beans to heighten their flavor. Since beans from different regions have different flavors, the maker blends them to produce the exact flavor for which it is known. The beans are then ground, and, because of their fat content, they make a liquid that is bitter. The chocolate maker pours the liquid into a mold where it cools. Using its secret recipe, the maker adds various ingredients such as sugar, vanilla, or milk. Conching comes next: it's a blending method in which the ingredients are mixed for a few days. Afterward, the chocolate is heated slowly in its mold, then cooled slowly, so that the chocolate will harden and keep its shape. Once the chocolate has cooled, it is ready for distribution to eager customers.

EXERCISE   **Using Process and Analysis**

Select one of the subjects below, and write a paragraph explaining how to do something or how something happened or came about. Write at least 125 words, and underline your topic sentence.

- *the signs of spring's arrival*
- *how a particular discovery was made*

- *how to tune a motorcycle or car*
- *how to give a speech*
- *how to organize a musical group*
- *how to write a term paper*
- *the formation of the solar system*

Writing Tips **Yikes!**

Have you ever opened a book, seen a sea of unending print, and felt a wave of dread? The appearance of your paragraphs can affect your reader's response in a similar way. Extremely long paragraphs can intimidate or discourage a reader. On the other hand, short paragraphs can make a reader feel that no single idea has been developed sufficiently. While there is no exact rule about the minimum number of sentences required in a paragraph, a short paragraph is often a sign that the writer did not follow through in his or her thinking about the topic. As a result, many weak paragraphs consist of little more than a topic sentence and one or two generalities, as if the writer hoped the reader would complete the thought for him or her. Newspapers often employ brief paragraphs, and brief paragraphs are also used to show a division or shift in a section of an essay or to draw attention to a startling fact or an important statement. In general, however, paragraphs that have only one, two, or three sentences are probably too thin and underdeveloped.

Computer Activity

Choose one of the subjects from the exercise above, and follow the directions. When you finish your paragraph, exchange it with a classmate.

Some word-processing programs permit written or voice annotations to be added during peer evaluation without changing the original text. If your computer program does not have this feature, use the SAVE, COPY, and PASTE commands to make a second copy.

E-mail the file to a classmate. Ask him or her to rearrange any sentences that violate the sequential order of your paragraph.

Make comments on your classmate's paragraph in the same manner.

When your paragraph is returned to you, compare your original with the peer-edited copy.

CHAPTER 11

PUNCTUATION AND CAPITALIZATION

CHAPTER PREVIEW

In this chapter, you will learn about:

- Making your meaning clear
  Using the correct endmarks
  Using the correct internal punctuation
  Using the correct capitalization
- Writing paragraphs: Developing a paragraph
  by cause and effect

When we speak, we make our meaning clear with more than just words. We pause at certain times, raise our voices for emphasis, and use various body movements. When we write, we use punctuation marks for the same purpose: to make our meaning intelligible to the reader. Every mark of punctuation carries some meaning and gives hints about how to read and interpret the sentence. Similarly, the capitalization of words serves as a guide to their meaning. In this chapter we will look at the most common situations in written English that require punctuation and capitalization.

End Marks

End marks—periods, question marks, and exclamation points—are used to indicate the purpose of a sentence.

The Period

1. Use the period to end a sentence that states a fact (called a **declarative sentence**), an indirect question, or a command (called an **imperative sentence**) that is mild.

■ **Declarative sentence:** Toni Morrison, the African-American novelist, won the Nobel Prize for Literature in 1993.

■ **Indirect question:** Mr. Riley asked me whether I wanted to give an oral report on one of Toni Morrison's novels.

■ **Mild command:** Please help me make a poster for my presentation.

2. Use a period after most abbreviations.

■ Dr.   ■ A.D.

■ Jr.   ■ oz.

■ etc.   ■ A.M.

Periods do not usually follow acronyms, abbreviations of well-known organizations and governmental agencies, and certain other abbreviations, including two-letter state abbreviations when ZIP codes are included.

■ UFO   ■ NATO

■ TV   ■ UN

■ IL   ■ UCLA

If an abbreviation comes at the end of a statement, do not use an additional period as an end mark.

■ The Smithsonian Institution is in Washington, D.C.

The Question Mark

1. Use a question mark after a direct question.

■ What did she want?

■ "What did she want?" he asked.

2. Use a question mark to indicate uncertainty about the accuracy of a word, phrase, or date.

■ The Greek philosopher Plato (427?–347 B.C.) was a disciple of Socrates.

Do not use a question mark after an indirect question.

■ Patti asked if we wanted to stay for lunch.

Remember that if an abbreviation comes at the end of a statement, you do not use an additional period as an end mark. However, use a question mark if one is needed.

■ Have you ever visited Washington, D.C.?

The Exclamation Point

1. Use an exclamation point after strong imperative sentences or requests.

   ■ Stop making that noise!

   ■ Get out of here!

2. Use an exclamation point after an emphatic interjection or statement showing strong emotion.

   ■ Wow! I won the lottery!

   Be careful not to overdo use of the exclamation point. When overused, it creates an almost hysterical tone in writing. Use a comma or a period instead of an exclamation point after a mild interjection.

   ■ Yes, I'd like more coffee, please.

   ■ No, I don't care for any dessert.

   Remember that if an abbreviation comes at the end of a statement, you do not use an additional period as an end mark. However, use an exclamation point if one is needed.

EXERCISE 11-1

Supply question marks, periods, or exclamation points where needed.

1. Renee asked me whether I needed a ride to class **class.**
2. Is the meeting at 8:30 AM or PM **a.m. p.m.?**
3. Dr Reilly earned his PhD at UCLA and now works in Washington, DC **Dr. Ph.D. D.C.**
4. Louise asked me, "Do you want anchovies on your pizza" **pizza?"**
5. Someone yelled, "Fire" **"Fire!"**
6. Please wash your hands before touching the dough **dough.**
7. The reporter asked whether forces from NATO would be sent to enforce the truce **truce.**
8. The Rev Martin Luther King Jr. was known for his oratorical skills, wasn't he **Rev. King, he?**
9. I did not see a UFO on my front lawn last night **night.**
10. The audience shouted "Encore" when the singer took her bows **"Encore!" bows.**
11. Professor Merwin asked me what is the difference between longitude and latitude **latitude.**
12. My father prefers to use an IBM typewriter instead of the computer that I bought when I was a student at the U of Idaho **U. Idaho.**

13. Please turn out the lights when you leave the office, will you <u>you?</u>

14. Rafael's address is 5730 Warren St, St Paul, MN 65101 <u>St., St.</u> <u>65101.</u>

15. Did you know that the first alphabet was developed by the Sumerians around 3000 BC <u>B.C.?</u>

Internal Punctuation

The Comma

The comma is the punctuation mark most frequently used inside a sentence. It also offers the widest range of individual choice. As a result, many writers are uncertain concerning its proper use, and they sprinkle commas indiscriminately through their sentences. Do not use a comma unless you have a definite reason for doing so. The rules below will help you avoid cluttering your sentences with unnecessary commas while at the same time making certain you use commas that make your meanings clear.

1. Use a comma to separate independent clauses joined by a coordinating conjunction (*and, but, for, nor, or, so,* and *yet*).

   ■ Rhode Island is the smallest state, and Alaska is the largest.

   ■ Raul has a beautiful tenor voice, but he is too shy to sing publicly.

   ■ Her parents have been divorced for two years, yet they remain friends.

   You may omit commas before the conjunction if one or both independent clauses are short.

   ■ Takeesha left but Ramon stayed.

   ■ I was exhausted but I couldn't sleep.

   Note: Do not use a comma between two independent clauses that are not joined by a coordinating conjunction. This error creates a **comma-splice** (see Chapter 9). Use a semicolon, add a coordinating conjunction, or start a new sentence.

   ■ **Comma-splice:** The chief mechanic examined the engine, his assistant checked the tires.

   ■ **Correct:** The chief mechanic examined the engine, and his assistant checked the tires. (**Or:** The chief mechanic examined the engine. His assistant checked the tires. **Or:** The chief mechanic examined the engine; his assistant checked the tires.)

Do not use a comma before a coordinating conjunction linking two words or phrases.

■ **Nonstandard:** Shelly wrote a term paper on the history of jazz, and hip hop.
(The conjunction *and* does not join two independent clauses.)

■ **Standard:** Shelly wrote a term paper on the history of jazz and hip hop.

EXERCISE 11-2

Add commas to the following sentences wherever needed. If no comma is needed in a sentence, write "C" in front of it.

1. Making your diet healthier can be difficult, but it'll be easier if you make just a few small changes.
2. **C** Make one change at a time; allow yourself to get used to it before you try more changes.
3. Nothing can replace the thrill and flavor of a big bowl of potato chips while you study or watch DVDs, yet you may find some pleasure in a bowl of low-calorie popcorn, carrot coins, or mango slices.
4. Have a big breakfast, and you'll eat fewer calories throughout the day.
5. **C** Make sure your dish is half-full of fruit and vegetables, and you'll still have room for the entrée and a little dessert.
6. Many people aren't big fans of vegetables, so it's nice to know that flavorful fruit is just as healthy as vegetables.
7. It may be tempting to replace a soda pop with fruit juice, but did you know that most juices have *more* calories than most sodas?
8. Many people lose weight just by cutting down on soft drinks, diluting juice with water, and limiting alcohol to weekends.
9. Soup counts as a vegetable serving, and the noncreamy kind is filling but low-fat and low-calorie.
10. Promise yourself that you won't supersize your meals when you eat out, or you might also need to supersize your pants!

2. Use a comma to separate an introductory adverb clause from the main part of the sentence.

■ *When we visited Los Angeles last summer,* we went to a baseball game at Dodger Stadium.

■ *Although Japan lost World War II,* the nation's economy recovered within a few years of its defeat.

3. Use a comma after a long introductory prepositional phrase and its modifiers.

   - *After an arduous trek over snowcapped mountains and scorched desert floors,* the Mormons finally reached Utah.
   - *In preparing your annual report to the board of directors,* be sure to include predictions for next year's sales.

4. Use a comma to set off an introductory participial phrase.

   - *Remembering the promise made to his wife,* Marco carefully kept a record of his expenditures and entered each purchase in his checkbook.
   - *Pleased by the initial reaction from the customers,* the owner of the hardware store extended its sale another week.

   Do not put a comma after participial phrases that are actually the subject of the sentence.

   - **Nonstandard:** Playing golf once a week, was Carl's only exercise.
   - **Standard:**   Playing golf once a week was Carl's only exercise.

   - **Nonstandard:** Reading about the lives of the Acadians, made me want to visit Cajun country in Louisiana.
   - **Standard:**   Reading about the lives of the Acadians made me want to visit Cajun country in Louisiana.

5. Use a comma to set off an introductory infinitive phrase unless the phrase is the subject of the sentence.

   - To make a best-selling CD, you must overcome tremendous obstacles.
     (**But:** To win the jackpot in Las Vegas was his dream.)
   - To impress his future in-laws, Marty wore a suit and tie.
     (**But:** To impress his future in-laws was Marty's goal.)

EXERCISE 11-3

Add commas to the following sentences wherever needed. If no comma is needed in a sentence, write "C" in front of it.

1. **C** Nearly two million Native Americans live and preserve their tribal cultures in every part of the United States.
2. Dozens of tribes across the country host pow-wows every year, and visitors are often encouraged to attend them.

3. A huge gathering, open to the public, a typical pow-wow features parades, dancing, singing, and other Native American customs.

4. After a pageant in which young tribal women's beauty and achievements are admired by all, one contestant is crowned as princess.

5.**C** Remembering old tribal ways and customs and passing them on to younger members are the main aims of tribal pow-wows.

6. Reflecting the influence of the surrounding U.S. culture, some pow-wows feature golf tournaments and games of softball or volleyball.

7. Employing a variety of dance styles and costumes, the dance contests are crucial parts of any pow-wow.

8. Circling the drummers and bobbing in a slow, smooth rhythm, the female dancers sway gracefully.

9.**C** Lids of snuff cans decorated and hung from women's dresses for the Jingle Dance produce tinny tones that are light and musical.

10.**C** Performers of the men's Traditional Dance are said to be reenacting the stealth of a warrior seeking his foe.

11. Unless you are a Native American, you must remember that you are visiting a different culture with its own etiquette.

12.**C** It is important to bring your own seating and avoid sitting on benches reserved for dancers.

13. When the Blanket Dance is done, you will be expected to join the custom of placing at least a dollar on the blanket.

14.**C** Standing respectfully during solemn songs is an important custom.

15. From the Oneida of New York to the Chumash of California, a tribe is planning a pow-wow within a day's drive from virtually everywhere.

6. Use a comma after an introductory request or command.

   ■ *Remember,* tomorrow is the deadline for filing your tax return.

   ■ *Look,* we've been through all of this before.

7. Use a comma to separate words, phrases, or clauses in a series unless all of the items are joined by *and* or *or*.

   ■ She was young, attractive, and talented. (**But:** She was young and attractive and talented.)

   ■ The job requires one to travel constantly, to be separated from one's family, and to work long hours with little hope of advancement.

   ■ Huynh made some sandwiches, Carolyn brought her guitar, and Tara furnished the soft drinks.

8. Use a comma to separate interrupting elements (words, phrases, and clauses) when they break the flow of a sentence.

   ■ It is a fact, *isn't it,* that the spleen filters the blood?

   ■ Jorge will stay, *if possible,* with his brother in Laredo.

   Other interrupting elements (also called parenthetical elements or transitional expressions) include the following: *as a matter of fact, at any rate, for instance, nevertheless, of course, therefore, in my opinion, on the other hand,* and *that is.* These and similar phrases are usually set off by commas when they appear in a sentence.

   ■ Cleveland, on the other hand, is situated on a lake.

   ■ The store had three good reasons, nevertheless, for going bankrupt.

   ■ The Lakers and the Spurs, for example, acquired new managers.

9. Use a comma to set off direct address and words like *please, yes,* and *no.*

   ■ You should wear a helmet, Roxanne, when you ride your motorcycle.

   ■ Will you get off my foot, please.

   ■ Yes, I collect old fishing reels.

EXERCISE 11-4

Add commas to the following sentences wherever needed. If no comma is needed in a sentence, write "C" in front of it.

1. Physics, literature, economic science, and peace efforts are among the categories for which the Nobel Prize is given.
2. No, James did not attend Grambling State University in Louisiana; he attended Tennessee Technological University in Cookeville.
3. Remember, Lakisha, that we agreed to meet Heather and Sean for dinner tonight.
4. We can't decide whether to tour Hungary, Poland, or Ukraine for our graduation trip.
5. Michael Jordan, Wilt Chamberlain, Elgin Baylor, and Jerry West scored more points per game in their careers than any other NBA player.
6. The best places to meet men, if you ask me, are record stores, cafes, sports bars, and jazz clubs.
7. **C** English majors often make fruitful careers as lawyers or broadcasters or advertising executives.
8. Tell me, please, how to download these songs to my MP3 player.

9. The U.S. population is approaching three hundred million; therefore, we need better public transit.

10. Most of the fireworks used for Fourth of July shows are made in China, not the United States.

Additional Uses of the Comma

1. Use a comma to set off modifiers that are not essential to the sense of the sentence. **Nonessential** (or **nonrestrictive**) **modifiers** add information to the sentence, but they modify things or people clearly identified in the sentence. In other words, they could be removed from the sentence, and the reader would still know who (or what) the sentence was about. As you saw in Chapter 8, nonessential clauses are set off by commas.

   ■ Bob Costas, *who was born in New York City,* is a well-known television journalist and sports commentator. (The adjective clause *who was born in New York City* is not essential to the identity of the subject *Bob Costas,* nor is it required for the central meaning of the sentence. Therefore, it is nonessential and is set off by commas.)

But, as you also saw in Chapter 8, if a clause is an essential (or restrictive) modifier, it is not set off by commas.

   ■ Anyone who was born in New York City is eligible to apply for the scholarship. (The adjective clause *who was born in New York City* is essential to the meaning of the sentence. Not everyone is eligible to apply for the scholarship—just those born in New York City. The clause is therefore essential and is not set off by commas.)

Nonessential appositives are set off by commas. An **appositive** is a word or phrase following a noun or pronoun that renames or explains it. Most appositives are nonessential and require commas.

   ■ Alexander Hamilton, the first secretary of the Treasury of the United States, was killed in a duel. (The fact that Alexander Hamilton was the first secretary of the Treasury gives further information about the subject, but it is not essential to the meaning of the sentence. Therefore, the appositive is set off with commas.)

   ■ Mr. Murphy, my physics instructor, has won several national bodybuilding titles. (Like the preceding appositive, *my physics teacher* gives additional but nonessential information about the subject and is therefore set off with commas.)

Some appositives are restrictive, or serve as **essential modifiers**—that is, they are needed in the sentence to identify the element they rename. In such cases they are not set off with commas.

■ The rapper Hammer once worked for the Oakland A's baseball team. (Which rapper worked for the Oakland A's baseball team? We would not know unless the appositive *Hammer* were included. Therefore, the appositive is essential and commas are not used.)

2. Use a comma to set off **coordinate adjectives.** Adjectives are coordinate if *and* can be placed between them. They describe different qualities of the same noun and may be separated by a comma rather than *and*.

■ a long, boring movie (a long *and* boring movie)

■ an expensive, rare gem (an expensive *and* rare gem)

Some adjectives are not coordinate, and therefore no commas are used to separate them.

■ dirty blue jeans

■ a retired staff sergeant

■ an exciting volleyball game

Notice that you would not write the following.

■ dirty and blue jeans

■ a retired and staff sergeant

■ an exciting and volleyball game

Adjectives usually precede the word they describe; when they follow the word they describe, they are set off with commas.

■ **Usual order:**   The loud and unruly crowd stormed the soccer field.

■ **Inverted order:** The crowd, loud and unruly, stormed the soccer field.

EXERCISE 11-5

Add commas to the following sentences wherever needed. If no comma is needed in a sentence, write "C" in front of it.

1. The rain, unexpected and drenching, forced us to cancel the homecoming parade.
2. C Anyone who arrives after the start of the play will not be seated until the intermission break.
3. Maya Angelou, the African American poet, was our commencement speaker.
4. Moreno's older brother, who owns a Mexican restaurant, has written a popular cookbook.
5. C The first step in solving the problem is to find the lowest common denominator.

6. A damp, piercing wind cut through her thin jacket.
7. Our guide, who spoke five languages, explained the meaning of the carving on the wall.
8. **C** The actor Liam Neeson was born in Northern Ireland.
9. **C** Many professional hockey players who formerly played for the Soviet Union or Russia now play on American teams.
10. The policeman, frowning and shaking his head, refused to let us park in front of the theater.

3. Use a comma to set off contrasted elements and opposing expressions.

- Lou's birthday is in June, not July.
- Mr. Mather gets a hotel room downtown, never in the suburbs.

4. Use a comma to set off quoted material.

- "My wife just gave birth to triplets," Bill said.
- Georgia announced proudly, "I've been named vice president of the company."

5. Use commas to set off the year in complete dates.

- September 11, 2001, is a day that everyone living at the time will always remember.
- On August 6, 1945, the first atomic bomb was dropped.

When only the month and year are given, the comma is usually omitted.

- The first commercial telecast took place in April 1939.
- The Great Depression began in October 1929 in the United States.

6. Use a comma to separate the elements in an address.

- United Nations Plaza, Riverside Drive, New York, New York

Within a sentence, place a comma after the final element in an address.

- Her office at the United Nations Plaza on Riverside Drive, New York, is five city blocks from her apartment.

7. Use a comma to set off abbreviations standing for academic degrees when they appear within a sentence.

- Judith Walsh, M.D., was awarded a plaque recognizing her contributions to the community.

Notice that only one period is necessary at the end of a sentence.

▪ A plaque recognizing her contributions to the community was given to Judith Walsh, M.D.

8. Use a comma to prevent misreading. In some sentences it is necessary to use a comma even though no rule requires one.

▪ **Confusing:** To Mary Jane was very special.
▪ **Clear:** To Mary, Jane was very special.

▪ **Confusing:** While we ate the dog continued to bark.
▪ **Clear:** While we ate, the dog continued to bark.

EXERCISE 11-6

Add commas to the following sentences wherever needed. If no comma is needed in a sentence, write "C" in front of it.

1. Please send my order to 20 Coral Springs Road, Beverly Hills, California 90210.
2. **C** Romania was once part of the Roman Empire.
3. Michael Weiss and Johnny Weir are American figure skating champions, not Korean.
4. Sylvia Finkelstein, Ph.D., will lecture about Cottleville history tonight.
5. To Norman, Lois is the finest woman in the world.
6. On June 26, 2003, the family held the first of its annual reunions.
7. **C** We hope to finish our college degrees by June 2010.
8. "I don't want to," says Alexa when we tell her to clean her room.
9. Marcia Lopez, D.D.S., said that some of her patients have teeth that are more frightening than Dracula's.
10. If you eat, the cat will beg for a scrap.

Omitting Commas

When in doubt, many writers are tempted to add commas to their sentences. Too many commas, however, can slow down the thought or confuse the meaning. Here are some of the common situations that might tempt you to use the comma.

1. Do not use a comma after the last item in a series of adjectives preceding the noun.

▪ **Nonstandard:** She was a dedicated, imaginative, creative, painter.
▪ **Standard:** She was a dedicated, imaginative, creative painter.

2. Do not use a comma between two words joined by a coordinating conjunction.

    ■ **Nonstandard:** A good night's rest, and a healthy breakfast are the best prepara-
    tion for a test.

    ■ **Standard:** A good night's rest and a healthy breakfast are the best prepara-
    tion for a test.

3. Do not separate a verb from a restrictive *that* clause.

    ■ **Nonstandard:** The surgeon general has determined, that cigarette smoking
    is dangerous to your health.

    ■ **Standard:** The surgeon general has determined that cigarette smoking
    is dangerous to your health.

4. Do not use a comma to separate the subject from its verb.

    ■ **Nonstandard:** The American painter Whistler, is best known for his painting
    of his mother.

    ■ **Standard:** The American painter Whistler is best known for his painting
    of his mother.

5. Do not use a comma to separate independent clauses unless the comma is followed by
    a coordinate conjunction (see Chapter 9 for information about comma-splices).

    ■ **Nonstandard:** The blaze began at Barksdale Air Force Base, it burned out
    of control for nine hours.

    ■ **Standard:** The blaze began at Barksdale Air Force Base, and it burned out
    of control for nine hours.

The Semicolon

1. Use a semicolon to separate two related independent clauses when there is no coordi-
    nating conjunction to join them.

    ■ The law is clear; the question is whether it is fair.

    ■ Competition for admittance to medical school is intense; only one applicant
    in about twenty is admitted.

    If you use a comma instead of a semicolon for an omitted conjunction, you will create
    a comma-splice (see Chapter 9 and page 237 in this chapter). The exception to this
    rule is the case of compound sentences in which the clauses are very short.

    ■ I came, I saw, I conquered.

2. Use a semicolon to separate independent clauses joined by a **conjunctive adverb.** Conjunctive adverbs are words like *however, moreover, therefore, furthermore, nevertheless, consequently, otherwise, besides,* and *hence* (see Chapter 9).

Conjunctive adverbs are not conjunctions, and therefore they require more than a comma before them. When they come at the beginning of an independent clause, a semicolon or period should precede them. If they are not preceded by a semicolon or period, the result is a comma-splice.

- ■ **Comma-splice:** Puerto Rico is not a state, however, its residents are American citizens.
- ■ **Standard:** Puerto Rico is not a state; however, its residents are American citizens.

- ■ **Comma-splice:** The Rolls-Royce is an expensive automobile, moreover, its maintenance costs are higher than for most other cars.
- ■ **Standard:** The Rolls-Royce is an expensive automobile; moreover, its maintenance costs are higher than for most other cars.

3. Use a semicolon to separate items in a series if the items contain commas.

- ■ Copies of the report should be sent to our offices in St. Louis, Missouri; Spokane, Washington; Duluth, Minnesota; and Caldwell, Idaho.

EXERCISE 11-7

Add a semicolon or comma where needed in the following sentences, and delete any unnecessary punctuation. If a sentence is punctuated correctly, write "C" in front of it.

1. Cows will not eat hay that has a musty odor; therefore, farmers must make sure that it is dry before they bale it.
2. Professor Kgosi showed us slides of his trip to Zanzibar, Tabora, and Linga in Tanzanina; Mairobi, Nakum, and Mombasa in Kenya; and Jube, Waw, and Kartoum in Sudan.
3. I will have to find a job this semester, or I will have to get a loan to pay for my tuition.
4. **C** Eddie decided to leave before dinner because the roads were becoming icy.
5. Jessica quit her job at the bakery last week; she plans to move to Cedar Rapids to take over her father's farm.
6. The music that the disc jockey played was from the 1950s, so I decided to listen instead of dance.
7. Tran speaks English at school; at home, however, he speaks Vietnamese.

8. Monaco has no famous colleges or universities; however, it has a ninety-nine per-cent literacy rate.
9. Studies have demonstrated that wearing seatbelts reduces the likelihood of injury; however, many drivers refuse to wear them.
10. The striking workers demonstrated in front of the factory, but the company officials refused to meet with them.

The Colon

The colon can be thought of as an equal sign; it tells the reader that what follows it is equivalent to what precedes it.

1. Use a colon to introduce a list of items after an independent clause.

    ■ Three countries abstained from voting: Poland, Cuba, and Canada.
    ■ Yiddish is made up chiefly of words from four languages: Russian, German, Polish, and Hebrew.

2. Use a colon to introduce a word or phrase that renames or explains an earlier idea in the sentence.

    ■ The Hubble telescope soared into space despite a serious flaw: a distortion in one of its light-gathering mirrors.

3. Use a colon between two complete thoughts when the second explains the first.

    ■ It was becoming painfully obvious to him: he was being ignored.

    A less frequent use of the colon is after a list of items preceding an independent clause.

    ■ Cuba, Brazil, and Australia: these are the largest producers of cane sugar.

4. Use a colon after a salutation in a business letter and between the hour and minutes when referring to time.

    ■ Dear Senator Edwards:
    ■ 8:22 P.M.

    Do *not* place a colon between a verb and its objects or complements or between a preposition and its objects.

    ■ **Nonstandard:** Her favorite science-fiction writers are: Ursula LeGuin, Isaac Asimov, and Harlan Ellison.
    ■ **Nonstandard:** Charlie Chaplin was easily recognized by: his black mustache, his walk, and his black hat.

EXERCISE 11-8

Insert a colon wherever needed in the following sentences, and delete any colons that are unnecessary or incorrect. If a sentence is correct, write "C" in front of it.

1. Although Barbara and I were in Boston for just one day, we were able to achieve our goal: a tour of the city's historical sites.
2. **C** The Boston area is home to more than fifty colleges and universities, including Harvard University, Boston College, and the Massachusetts Institute of Technology.
3. The North End and Beacon Hill possess quaint features of a bygone era: cobbled streets, gaslights, and treacherous brick sidewalks.
4. **C** At the Congress Street bridge we saw a full-scale working replica of the Boston Tea Party ship and a colorful reenactment of the dumping of tea into the harbor.
5. **C** Barbara and I stopped for coffee at the Bull & Finch pub, whose facade and interior were featured in the television show *Cheers*.
6. I was amazed by the New England Aquarium's four-story circular glass tank, which houses the aquarium's main attractions: sharks, turtles, eels, and hundreds of tropical fish.
7. We next visited the Old North Church, whose steeple contained the two lanterns that sparked the famous midnight ride of Paul Revere.
8. Next we toured the 1713 Old State House to see tea from the Boston Tea Party, one of John Hancock's coats, and the east front where the Boston Massacre occurred.
9. Handwritten documents, tape recordings, and the actual Oval Office desk: these mementos at the John F. Kennedy Library touched us deeply.
10. As dusk descended on Boston, Barbara and I strolled to the Public Garden for our final treat: a ride in one of the famous swan-shaped boats.

Parentheses

1. Use parentheses to enclose unimportant information or comments that are not an essential part of the passage. In this respect parentheses are like commas; the difference is that they evoke the reader's attention more than commas.

   ■ Mapmakers use a system of medians of longitude (from the Latin *longus,* "long") and parallels of latitude (from *latus,* "wide").

   ■ Zora Neale Hurston (who started out as an anthropologist) is one of the finest novelists in American literature.

2. Use parentheses to enclose dates that accompany an event or a person's name.

   ■ The Iran-Contra scandal (1988) involved several members of President Reagan's administration.

   ■ Louis Armstrong (1900–1971) invented the popular "scat" style of singing.

Note: Never insert a comma, a semicolon, a colon, or a dash before an opening parenthesis.

■ **Nonstandard:** Exposure to various chemicals, (including benzene, asbestos, vinyl chloride, and arsenic) increases risks of various forms of cancer.

The Dash

The dash is a forceful punctuation mark, but it must be used carefully. It often takes the place of the comma, the semicolon, the colon, or parentheses in a sentence in order to separate emphatically words or groups of words. The difference between the dash and these other marks is that it focuses attention on the items being separated.

1. Use a dash to mark an abrupt change in the thought or structure of a sentence.

    ■ I wonder if we should—oh, let's take care of it later.

2. Use a dash to make parenthetical or explanatory matter more prominent in the sentence.

    ■ George Halas—one of the founders of the National Football League—was known as "Papa Bear."
    ■ The family's belongings—their clothing, furniture, computer, and other possessions—were stolen during their weekend absence.

3. Use a dash to set off single words that require emphasis.

    ■ Sandra thinks about only one thing—money.

4. Use a dash to set off an appositive or an introductory series.

    ■ Only one professional wrestler—Jesse Ventura—has been elected governor of a state. (The use of dashes in this sentence emphasizes the appositive *Jesse Ventura;* parentheses would also be correct, but they would not present the same emphasis.)
    ■ Leonardo da Vinci, William the Conqueror, Alexander Hamilton, and Richard Wagner—they were all illegitimate children. (A colon could also be correct in this sentence after *Richard Wagner.*)

EXERCISE 11-9

Depending on what you believe is the desired emphasis, insert parentheses or dashes in the following sentences.   **An "X" in the following sentences indicates that the student may insert either a parenthesis or a dash, depending on the desired emphasis.**
1. MiaXmy pet dogXis not allowed to enter the house.
2. Law, navigation, politics, medicine, warXShakespeare wrote about all of these topics.

3. If we win the championship gameᐟand the critics say we won'tᐟit will be a tremendous victory for our athletic program.
4. My oldest brotherᐟthe computer programmer who lives in Menlo Parkᐟis unable to attend our cousin's wedding.
5. Earl claims that it was her intelligenceᐟnot her wealthᐟthat attracted him.
6. The most common American slang termsᐟaccording to an authority on languageᐟdeal with money, sex, and drinking.
7. Only one obstacle kept Con from a career in musicᐟtalent.
8. I read an article in the *Times*ᐟor maybe it was the *Post-Dispatch*ᐟdescribing the tornado in Kansas last week.
9. Kent's fatherᐟan acupuncturistᐟlives in San Antonio.
10. Our dinner last nightᐟsalad, steak, a vegetable, and dessertᐟcost only five dollars with a special coupon.

Quotation Marks

Quotation marks have three main functions: to indicate the exact words of a speaker, to call attention to words used in an unusual sense or in definitions, and to enclose the title of certain kinds of literary and artistic works. In every case, be sure that you use them in pairs; a common mistake is to omit the second set of quotation marks.

1. Use quotation marks for direct quotations; that is, use quotation marks around the exact words of a speaker.

■ "I guess I do," the nervous bride whispered.

■ Grandpa announced, "It's time to take my nap."

Notice that a comma precedes quotation marks in a direct quotation and that the first word of the quotation is capitalized if the quotation is a complete sentence. Do not use quotation marks for indirect quotations.

■ Grandpa announced that it was time to take his nap.

Always place commas and periods *inside* the end quotation marks.

■ "If you wait a few minutes," she said, "we will walk to the corner with you."

When the quotation is a question or exclamation, place the question mark or exclamation point *inside* the quotation marks.

■ Ben asked with a smile, "Who left this on my desk?"

■ "That music is too loud!" my father shouted.

When the question mark or exclamation point applies to the entire sentence and not just to the quotation, it should be placed *outside* the end quotation marks.

- Did she say, "I have to go to a sales meeting next Tuesday"?
- I'm tired of being told that my writing is "adequate"!

Always place semicolons *outside* the end quotation mark.

- O. Henry's most famous short story is "The Gift of the Magi"; like his others, it has a surprise ending.
- The Russian delegate's vote was a loud "Nyet!"; as a result, the resolution was vetoed.

Enclose quoted material *within* a direct quotation in single quotation marks.

- "We object to 'In God We Trust' on our currency," the lawyer stated.
- "My favorite poem is 'Chicago,'" said Imelda.

2. Use quotation marks for words and definitions; that is, use quotations marks to call attention to words used in an unusual sense and in definitions.

- I like the lyrics of some rap artists; my brother's term for them is "nonsense."
- The origin of the word "bedlam" is interesting.
- The Spanish expression "Adios" comes from another expression meaning "Go with God."

Note: Some writers prefer to italicize words when used in this sense.

3. Use quotation marks for titles of literary and artistic works; that is, use quotation marks to enclose titles of short works. These include titles of songs, essays, magazine and newspaper articles, television episodes, chapters of books, and short poems. Longer works appear in italics (or are underlined).

Poem:	"Lady Lazarus" "Birches"
Song:	"Every Breath You Take" "It's My Party and I'll Cry If I Want To"
Short Story:	"Raymond's Run" "The Dead"

Italics

1. Italicize (or underline) the titles of books, plays, magazines, newspapers, movies, long poems, paintings, and the names of ships, airplanes, and trains.

Book:	*Motherless Brooklyn*
Play:	*Romeo and Juliet*

- **Magazine:**   *The National Enquirer*
- **Newspaper:**   *Los Angeles Times*
- **Television:**   *The Simpsons*
- **Movie:**   *Million Dollar Baby*
- **Painting:**   *Mona Lisa*
- **Long Poem:**   *Song of Myself*
- **Ship, airplane, or train:** *Titanic, Spirit of St. Louis, Silver Bullet*

2. Italicize (or underline) foreign words and phrases that have not yet been adopted as English expressions. If you are not certain about the current status of a particular word or phrase, use a modern dictionary.

- *ad nauseam* (Latin*)*

- *sotto voce* (Italian)

- *nom de plume* (French)

3. Italicize (or underline) letters, numbers, and words when referring to the letters, numbers, and words themselves.

- Georgia received two *B*'s and two *A*'s this semester.

- Three Russian iceskaters received *10*s in the Olympic competition.

- The word *mischievous* is frequently mispronounced by speakers. (As you saw earlier, some writers prefer to enclose words used like this in quotation marks.)

4. Italicize (or underline) words that receive special emphasis.

- He lives in Manhattan, *Kansas,* not Manhattan, *New York.*

When words that would be italicized in a book are handwritten or typed, they are underlined.

EXERCISE 11-10

Supply missing quotation marks, and underline where appropriate in the following sentences.

1. Would you please translate the French phrase <u>noblesse oblige</u> for me?
2. Janice led a discussion of three poems by Audre Lorde titled "Hanging Fire," "The Woman Thing," and "Sisters in Arms."
3. We rode the <u>Ski Express</u> train to Vermont as a result of reading an article about it in <u>Yankee Magazine</u>.

4. "My favorite love song," said Darnell, "is 'Just the Way You Are,' as sung by Billy Joel."

5. The expression "to love, honor, and obey" has been dropped from some marriage ceremonies.

6. Have you read The Van and The Snapper, two novels by Roddy Doyle?

7. "Faster Than a Speeding Photon," an article by David Freedman in Discover magazine, discusses Einstein's theory of the speed of light.

8. Isabel Allende, the Chilean novelist, has written a humorous book about the pleasures of food titled Aphrodite.

9. Although the movie Field of Dreams was not believable, the references to baseball history were interesting.

10. Did you read the review of the movie Singin' in the Rain in the Louisville Herald?

11. When Frasier is on television, Oscar refuses to answer the telephone.

12. In the film The Postman the leading character wins a woman's heart by quoting from the poems "Walking Around" and "Leaning into the Afternoons" by the poet Pablo Neruda.

13. Stardust magazine recently published a poem titled "The Moment," which was about Perugino's painting titled Giving of the Keys to Saint Peter.

14. The story of the sinking of the Titanic is the subject of the movie The Titanic.

15. Song of Myself, Walt Whitman's famous long poem, was published in 1855.

The Hyphen

The most common use of the hyphen is to break a word at the end of a line when there is not enough room for the entire word. The hyphen has several other important uses, however.

1. Use a hyphen after *ex-*, *self-*, and *all-* when they are used as prefixes.

   ■ ex-husband
   ■ self-destructive
   ■ all-purpose

2. Use a hyphen after prefixes that precede a proper noun or adjective.

   ■ anti-Semitic
   ■ pro-French
   ■ pre-Christian

3. Use a hyphen between compound descriptions serving as a single adjective before a noun.

  ▪ wine-red sea
  ▪ soft-spoken cop
  ▪ slow-moving train

4. Use a hyphen to link compound nouns and verbs.

  ▪ father-in-law
  ▪ walkie-talkie
  ▪ president-elect

5. Use a hyphen between fractions and numbers from twenty-one through ninety-nine.

  ▪ one-third
  ▪ one-fifth
  ▪ fifty-four

The Apostrophe

The use of the apostrophe can be somewhat tricky at times, but by following the suggestions below, you will avoid the confusion that many writers have with this punctuation mark. The apostrophe is used for the possessive case (except for personal pronouns), and to indicate an omitted letter or number, specific words, and letters. In the following pages we will examine each of these uses.

1. Use the apostrophe to form the possessives of nouns and some pronouns.

  a. To form the possessive of a *singular* person, thing, or indefinite pronoun, add 's:

  ▪ the razor's edge
  ▪ the dog's bark
  ▪ everybody's obligation
  ▪ Giorgio's motorcycle

  If a proper name already ends in s in its singular form and the adding of 's would make pronunciation difficult, it is best to use the apostrophe only.

  ▪ Ulysses' return (Ulysses's would be difficult to pronounce but is acceptable.)
  ▪ Moses' teachings

b. To form the possessive of a plural noun ending in *s*, add an apostrophe only.

- the cities' mayors
- the soldiers' wives and husbands
- the cats' owners

c. To form the possessive of a plural noun not ending in *s*, add *'s*.

- women's rights
- children's television programs
- mice's tails
- alumni's representative

d. To form the possessive of compound words, use the apostrophe according to the meaning of the construction.

- Laurel and Hardy's movies (The *'s* is added to *Hardy* because the construction refers to the movies that Laurel and Hardy made together.)
- **But:** Chaplin's and Woody Allen's movies (The *'s* is added to *Chaplin* and *Allen* because the construction refers to the movies of Chaplin and Allen, respectively.)
- Her mother and father's home (the home of her mother and father)
- **But:** Her brother's and sister's homes (the separate homes of her brother and sister)

e. To form the possessive of most indefinite pronouns, add *'s:*

- someone's hat
- everybody's choice

The following indefinite pronouns can be made possessive only with *of: all, any, both, each, few, many, most, much, several, some,* and *such.*

- **Nonstandard:** Although I hadn't seen my two friends since grade school, I could remember each's name.
- **Standard:**   Although I hadn't seen my two friends since grade school, I could remember the name of each.

As shown in the following list, do not use an apostrophe with the possessive forms of personal and relative pronouns.

Correct	Incorrect	Correct	Incorrect
his	his'	theirs	their's, theirs'
hers	her's, hers'	whose	who's
ours	our's, ours'	its	it's
yours	your's, yours'		

Remember that *its* indicates ownership and *it's* is a **contraction** for *it is* or *it has*. Similarly, *who's* means *who is* or *who has*.

2. Use an apostrophe to indicate an omitted letter(s) in a contraction.

   ▓ Cannot→can't   ▓ it is→it's

   ▓ had not→hadn't   ▓ who is→who's

   ▓ you are→you're   ▓ have not→haven't

3. Use an apostrophe as needed to indicate the plural of an individual lowercase letter, an abbreviation, or a word used as a word.

   ▓ p's and q's

   ▓ Several V.I.P.'s

   ▓ five *and*'s and six *but*'s

   The apostrophe may be omitted when the *-s's* might be mistaken as a possessive.

   ▓ 11 ozs

   ▓ the SATs

   ▓ the CEOs

   The apostrophe may be omitted in forming the plural in many cases.

   ▓ the 1990s (or 1990's)

   ▓ 9s (or 9's)

   The first two numbers in a date are sometimes replaced with an apostrophe.

   ▓ '66 Mustang

   ▓ Spirit of '76

   ▓ "Summer of '98"

> ### Tips **for Forming Possessives of Nouns**
> 1. Make the noun singular or plural, according to your meaning.
> 2. If the noun is singular, add 's. If adding the 's makes the pronunciation difficult, add an apostrophe only.
> 3. If the noun is plural and ends in s, just add an apostrophe. If the noun is plural and ends in some other letter, add 's.

EXERCISE 11-11

Insert apostrophes in the following sentences where appropriate, and delete apostrophes that are incorrect. Reword any sentence as needed. If a sentence uses apostrophes correctly, write "C" before it.

1. Men's clothes are sold on the department store's fourth floor.
2. The girls' car was gone when they came out from the gym.
3. A snake's rattle is found at the end of it's tail.
4. He's traveling to Mali with the Peace Corps next year.
5. No one's safe when Gino practices his tennis serve.
6. Puerto Ricans are citizens of the United States.
7. Dave and Jen's house features a pool, while Ivan's and Alicia's houses do not.
8. **C** From whose tree did you pluck the limes for our margaritas?
9. Tyrell and Araceli's physics experiment won every award at the university's annual tournament.
10. If that doughnut is yours, you should either eat it or hide it before Uncle Donny's arrival.

Numbers

1. If a number requires no more than two words, the general practice is to spell it out.

   - ■ nine months later (not 9 months later)
   - ■ forty-one dollars (not 41 dollars)
   - ■ eighteen billion light-years (not 18,000,000,000 light-years)

2. If a number requires more than two words, the general practice is to use figures.

   - ■ 694 tons (not six hundred ninety-four tons)
   - ■ 4 1/2 pounds (not four and one-half pounds)
   - ■ 1372 pages (not one thousand three hundred seventy-two pages)

3. Write out a number beginning a sentence.

   ■ **Awkward:** 14 patients at Broadway Hospital were treated for food poisoning.

   ■ **Revised:** Fourteen patients at Broadway Hospital were treated for food poisoning.

EXERCISE 11-12

Insert any omitted hyphens or apostrophes in the following sentences, and make any necessary corrections in the use of numbers, quotation marks, underlining, hyphens, or apostrophes. If a sentence is correct, write "C" before it.

1. **twenty**
    There are about 20 species of cypress trees in North America.

2. **Who's**
    Gwen's father is listed in Whos Who in Science.

3. **C** Stephen Hawking, whose theories on black holes and the origin of the universe are debated by scientists, is an English physicist.

4. The coelacanth, a species of lungfish thought to have gone extinct **sixty thousand** 60,000 years ago, was discovered recently off Madagascar.

5. **C** Jason's father is a member of the Yale class of '80.

6. The surface area of the Earth is one hundred ninety-six million nine hundred fifty **196,950,711** thousand seven hundred eleven square miles.

7. **Thirty-one**
    31 ingredients were required in Aunt Hilda's recipe for fruitcake.

8. **b's   d's**
    Ben's bs and ds look alike in his handwriting.

9. **you're**
    You shouldn't drive a car when youre sleepy or intoxicated.

10. **It's   its**
    Its been difficult to make the dog sleep in it's house.

Writing Tips **Have Pen, Will Query**

Have you written an essay, a poem, or a story that you think would appeal to a broader audience? *Poets & Writers,* a magazine that lists names of book and magazine publishers in search of good writing, is available at most libraries and booksellers. The magazine will tell you how and where to submit your work. Many of the editors listed in *Poets & Writers* specifically look for writers who have never been published.

EDITING EXERCISES

Punctuate this passage from the novel Great Expectations *by Charles Dickens. The first speaker is an escaped convict. The second speaker is seven-year-old Pip, who is lingering at the gravestone of his deceased parents.*

Hold your noise cried a terrible voice as a man started up from among the graves at the side of the church keep still you little devil or Ill cut out your throat

He was a fearful man all in grey with a great iron on his leg his shoes were falling apart he had no hat and an old rag was tied around his head he had been soaked in water smothered in mud cut by stones and torn by briars he limped and shivered and glared and growled his teeth chattered as he seized me by the chin

Oh dont cut my throat sir I pleaded in terror pray dont do it sir

Tell me your name said the man be quick about it

Pip sir

Show me where you live said the man point to the place

I pointed to where our village lay a mile or more from the church

The man after looking at me for a moment turned me upside down and emptied my pockets there was nothing in them but a piece of bread he ate the bread ravenously

Now look here said the man who do you live with assuming I'm going to let you live which I havent made up my mind about

My sister sir Misses Joe Gargery wife of Joe Gargery the blacksmith sir

Language Tips

In spoken English we usually say "I'm," "you've," "didn't," and so on (for *I am, you have,* and *did not*). We also use these short forms in informal written English (for example, in letters to friends). When we write short forms, we use an apostrophe (') for the missing letter or letters.

I'm = I am   you've = you have   didn't = did not

1. When *'s* is added to a pronoun, it can replace the *i* in *is* or the *ha* in *has.*

He's late. (He *is* late.)

He's finished the job. (He *has* finished the job.)

2. When *'d* is added to a pronoun, it can replace the *woul* in *would* or *ha* in *had.*

I'd see a doctor if I were you. (I *would* see a doctor if I were you.)

I'd never been so scared in my life. (I *had* never been so scared in my life.)

WRITING SENTENCES Using Correct Punctuation

Careless punctuation can irritate your readers and often distort the meaning of your writing. In this exercise you are asked to write original sentences illustrating the correct use of punctuation.

1. Write a brief dialogue (five or six sentences) between two speakers, using quotation marks.
2. Write a sentence in which you correctly use the dash.
3. Write a sentence using a comma to set off an introductory participial phrase.
4. Write a sentence using a comma after a long introductory prepositional phrase.
5. Write a sentence in which commas are used to set off interrupting elements.

Capitalization

The capitalization of words helps the reader by serving as a guide to their meaning.

The rules for capitalization are based, in general, on the following simple principle: the names of *specific* people, places, and things (in other words, **proper nouns**) are capitalized; the names of *general* people, places, and things (**common nouns**) are not capitalized.

1. Capitalize the first word in every sentence, including direct quotations that are complete sentences.

- The average teenager watches almost twenty hours of television weekly.
- Do you know the name of last year's top-selling video game?
- Miss Foster said, "The first woman's rights convention was held in New York in 1848."

2. Capitalize the first and last words in a title and all other words except *a, an, the,* and unimportant words.

- Buffy the Vampire Slayer
- Lord of the Flies
- Midnight in the Garden of Good and Evil

3. Capitalize the titles of relatives and professions when they precede the person's name or when they are used to address the person.

- Congratulations, Uncle Ned.
- The most popular teacher on our campus is Professor Childress.

Do not capitalize titles of relatives and professions when they are preceded by possessives (such as *my, his, our,* and *their*) and when they are used alone in place of the full name. When a name follows, capitalize the title.

- My uncle won a prize for watercolor painting.
- The most popular professor on our campus teaches chemistry.
- My Uncle Will lives in Reno.
- I saw Professor Baer at the picnic.

4. Capitalize official titles of honor and respect when they precede personal names.

- Justice Ruth Bader Ginsburg
- United Nations Secretary General Kofi Annan
- Senator Edwards
- Mayor Williams

Do *not* capitalize titles of honor and respect when they follow personal names.

- Douglas Williams, a general in the United States Army
- Peter Riley, the senator from Illinois
- Sheila Tierney, the newly elected mayor of Chicago

An exception to this rule may be made for certain national officials (the President, Vice President, and Chief Justice) and international figures (the Pope, the Secretary General of the United Nations).

5. Capitalize the names of people; political, religious, and ethnic groups; languages; and nationalities and adjectives derived from them.

- Czechs
- Irish
- Protestantism
- Hispanic
- Democrats
- Puritans

6. Capitalize the names of particular streets, buildings, rivers, cities, states, nations, geographical features, and schools and other institutions.

- Main Street
- Empire State Building
- Coney Island
- Rio Grande River
- United Nations
- U.S. Senate
- Spellman College
- Catskill Mountains
- Washington University
- Belize

7. Capitalize directions when they refer to specific regions or are part of a proper name.

- the Southwest
- the East Coast
- Southern writers
- North Dakota
- the Mideast
- West Virginia
- immigrants from the Southeast
- refugees from the West

Do not capitalize these words when they merely indicate a direction or general location.

- the southern slope of the mountain
- the north of Italy

- southern Montana
- on the east side of town

8. Capitalize the days of the week, months of the year, and names of holidays and religious seasons.

   - Friday
   - Good Friday
   - September
   - the Fourth of July
   - Ramadan
   - Passover
   - Veterans Day

9. Capitalize the names of particular historical events, eras, and special events.

   - Super Bowl Sunday
   - World Series
   - World War II
   - the Roaring Twenties
   - Kristalnacht
   - Cannes Film Festival
   - the Civil War
   - the Great Depression
   - the Middle Ages
   - the Harlem Renaissance

10. Capitalize the names of school subjects only if they are proper nouns or if they are followed by a course number.

    - anthropology
    - Anthropology 101
    - Portuguese
    - Political Science 240
    - Asian studies
    - Asian Studies 152
    - psychology
    - Psychology 277

11. Capitalize all references to a supreme being.

- God
- the Buddha
- the Almighty
- a Higher Power
- Allah
- the Savior
- the Lord
- the Holy Ghost

EXERCISE 11-13

Circle every letter or word that should be capitalized.

1. Lou Gehrig played for the (new)(york)(yankees) and played in 2,130 consecutive games, a record that was broken by Cal Ripkin of the (baltimore)(orioles) in 1995.
2. Julia Roberts, the (american) film actress, won an (academy)(award) for best actress in the movie (erin)(brockovich) in 2000.
3. The 1964 (civil)(rights)(act) established as law equal rights for all citizens in voting, education, public accommodations, and federally assisted programs.
4. Who is the author of the expression, ("fish) and guests smell after three days"?
5. Margaret Michell is the author of the novel (gone)(with)(the)(wind.)
6. A book discussing the ethical aspects of cloning has been written by a professor from (vanderbilt)(university) and (professor) Jennings, who teaches at my college.
7. Happy birthday, (aunt)(mary.)
8. The commencement speaker was (chief)(justice)(souter) of the (supreme)(court.)
9. Colin Powell, a retired general in the (united)(states)(army,) was born in New York.
10. For many years the (irish,)(italians,) and (jews) were the dominant ethnic groups in (new)(york)(city.)
11. Many famous actors and actresses live near (mulholland)(drive) in the (hollywood) (hills.)
12. My (uncle) Dan told me many stories about fishing along the banks of the (mississippi)(river.)
13. Many (african)(americans) celebrate the festival called (kwanzaa,) which means "first fruits of the harvest" in the (african) language Swahili.

14. One of the required courses for a major in mathematics is (statistics) 201.
15. Munich is the capital of (bavaria) in southern Germany and is located on the (isar) (river.)

EXERCISE 11-14

Circle every letter or word that should be capitalized. If a sentence is correct, write "C" in front of it.

1. In 1533, (britain's) (king) (henry) (viii)—though already married to (catherine) of (aragon)—married (anne) (boleyn) and was excommunicated from the (roman) (catholic) church.
2. If I can't save enough money for tuition next semester, I'll not be able to join my family when they take their vacation to western (canada.)
3. One of the most important religious holidays in the (mideast) is (ramadan.)
4. Every (fourth) of (july) at our company's party, Mr. Dickerson sings ("you (give) (love) a (bad) (name") by the hard rock band (bon) (jovi.)
5. Thanks to their coach's tough training methods, the water polo team from (ukraine) won a gold medal at last year's (olympics.)
6. The former governor said that her memoir, (memories) of the (mansion,) was factually accurate.
7. We flew (pogo) (airlines) from (west) (virginia) to western (ireland) and then to southern (norway.)
8. Jennifer and her husband caught several trout in the (gulf) (stream) last spring.
9. A politician from the state of Mississippi revealed that he had been a member of the (klan.)
10. The oldest university in the (united) (states) is (harvard,) which was founded in 1636.
11. The (prince) of (wales) has a country estate at (balmoral) (castle.)
12. Floods in the northern part of (minnesota) damaged the fall crops.
13. Letters written by the explorers of the (south) (pole) were read to our geography class by (professor) (brink.)
14. **C** Mexico adjusts the value of its peso in accordance with the rise or fall of the American dollar.
15. Applicants for the sales position were required to pass written examinations in (english,) (spanish,) and (japanese.)

EDITING EXERCISES

Supply all missing capital letters in the following paragraph.

When I was a junior at mckinley high school, mr. chavez, our teacher, led our american history 101 class on a tour of washington, d.c., our nation's capital. The city was originally carved from the state of maryland. It is located at the head of the potomac river, which separates it from virginia to the southwest. The idea of a national capital city originated at a meeting of congress in 1783 in philadelphia shortly after the war for independence had been concluded. The cornerstone of the capitol was laid by george washington in september 1793, and in 1800 the offices of the government were moved to the new capital from philadelphia. The two most famous buildings are the capitol and the executive mansion, which came to be known as the white house. The senate and the house of representatives meet in the capitol, and the president and his family live in the white house. Both buildings are linked to the lincoln memorial by a mall, which was originally intended to be a broad, tree-lined avenue like the champs elysee in paris. The streets in Washington are lettered to the north and south and numbered to the east and west, and the avenues are named for the states. Among notable monuments are the lincoln memorial, the jefferson memorial, and the john f. kennedy center for the performing arts. Other impressive buildings include the supreme court, the library of congress, and the treasury. Two famous institutions of learning in the city are howard university and georgetown university. The oldest residential neighborhood is georgetown, where most of the foreign embassies are located. Washington hosts hundreds of national conventions of organizations such as the national association of manufacturers and the national education association. Tourism is also a major source of income, which benefits such nearby communities as chevy chase, bethesda, and silver spring in the state of maryland and alexandria, falls church, and arlington in virginia. Most tourists visit the city in the spring and summer months. While in the capital, we saw several members of congress, and we met senator wilson from our state. We also attended the musical play "phantom of the opera."

WRITING SENTENCES Using Correct Capitalization

As you saw in this chapter, a word can often be capitalized in one situation but not capitalized in another. In this exercise you will be asked to illustrate such situations.

1. Write a sentence in which "president" is capitalized. Next, write a sentence in which "president" is not capitalized.

2. As in the example above, use the following words in original sentences. For each word, write two sentences: one that requires the word to be capitalized, and one that requires that it not be capitalized.
   - uncle (or aunt)
   - professor
   - university
   - street
   - college
   - west (or another direction)
   - day
   - biology (or another subject)

Language Tips

We often use the following words with verbs.

on	back
off	over
in	about
out	around
up	forward
down	through
away	along

For example:

get on	The bus was full. We couldn't *get on*.
drive off	She got into the car and *drove off*.
come back	We're *coming back* next Saturday.
turn on	Please *turn on* the light so that I can see.

These italicized words (*get on, drive off, come back,* and *turn on*) are verb phrases. When words like *on, off, up, down,* and so forth, follow verbs, they give a special meaning to the verbs. For example:

Sorry I'm late. My car *broke down.*

Look out! There's a car coming.

I was very nervous as the plane *took off.*

Marino has *to get up* at five o'clock every morning in order to get to work on time.

For more information on verb phrases, see page 16.

REVIEW TEST 11-A
Punctuation

In the space provided, write the letter of the sentence that is correctly punctuated.

___b___ 1. a. Although the dog's collar was found on the beach the dog was never located by its owner.
   b. Although the dog's collar was found on the beach, the dog was never located by its owner.

___a___ 2. a. Richard Wright's novel *Black Boy* is about the racism that a young African American must overcome on the way to adulthood.
   b. Richard Wright's novel "Black Boy" is about the racism that a young African American must overcome on the way to adulthood.

___a___ 3. a. My neighbor often wakes me up early in the morning by singing "Home on the Range."
   b. My neighbor often wakes me up early in the morning by singing *Home on the Range*.

___b___ 4. a. Shakespeare's birthday, (April 23, 1564), was also the date on which he died, (April 23, 1616).
   b. Shakespeare's birthday (April 23, 1564) was also the date on which he died (April 23, 1616).

___a___ 5. a. Many people who are avoiding alcohol now socialize at coffeehouses instead of bars.
   b. Many people, who are avoiding alcohol, now socialize at coffeehouses instead of bars.

___a___ 6. a. Uncle Don said, "Sylvia's favorite short story, 'The Catbird Seat,' was written by my favorite author: James Thurber."
   b. Uncle Don said, "Sylvia's favorite short story *The Catbird Seat* was written by my favorite author: James Thurber."

___b___ 7. a. Buck burst into the room and shouted, "Help. I've been bitten by a snake."
   b. Buck burst into the room and shouted, "Help! I've been bitten by a snake."

___a___ 8. a. The examining physician noticed a three-quarter-inch scar on Rosa's right arm.
   b. The examining physician noticed a three quarter inch scar on Rosa's right arm.

___b___ 9. a. Mrs. Curry warned her students, "Expect a quiz on tonights reading when you come to class tomorrow."
  b. Mrs. Curry warned her students, "Expect a quiz on tonight's reading when you come to class tomorrow."

___a___ 10. a. The Earl of Sandwich, an English nobleman, gave his name to a well-known food item.
  b. The Earl of Sandwich, an English nobleman gave his name, to a well-known food item.

___b___ 11. a. Ramon said that his pulse ranges from 50 to 75, depending on how much coffee he has drunk.
  b. Ramon said that his pulse ranges from fifty to seventy-five, depending on how much coffee he has drunk.

___b___ 12. a. Nebraska's football team is having an unpredictable season, I can't predict the outcome of tomorrow's game.
  b. Nebraska's football team is having an unpredictable season; I can't predict the outcome of tomorrow's game.

___b___ 13. a. Dr. Blatz's course which emphasizes in-depth discussions and lengthy research projects, is difficult but rewarding.
  b. Dr. Blatz's course, which emphasizes in-depth discussions and lengthy research projects, is difficult but rewarding.

___a___ 14. a. The babysitter asked whether she could play our new stereo.
  b. The babysitter asked "whether she could play our new stereo?"

___b___ 15. a. The left headlight of Nadia's new car, was smashed in the accident.
  b. The left headlight of Nadia's new car was smashed in the accident.

___a___ 16. a. Who was it who said, "A penny saved is a penny earned"?
  b. Who was it who said, "A penny saved is a penny earned?"

___a___ 17. a. Although angry, Victor continued to play as if nothing had happened.
  b. Although angry Victor continued to play as if nothing had happened.

___b___ 18. a. Jon wanted to practice on his drums but his landlord complained, about the noise.
  b. Jon wanted to practice on his drums, but his landlord complained about the noise.

___b___ 19. a. As a birthday gift for Trish, I renewed her subscription to "Jet," her favorite magazine.
  b. As a birthday gift for Trish, I renewed her subscription to *Jet*, her favorite magazine.

___b___ 20. a. Hey, let's sing the song, "Happy Birthday!"
  b. Hey, let's sing the song "Happy Birthday"!

Capitalization

Below each sentence, put an "X" next to the letter of any word in the sentence that should be capitalized.

21. The pastor of the (a) church on Market (b) street is (c) father Murphy.

    (a) _____ (b) ____**X**____ (c) ____**X**____

22. One of the most important (d) moslem holidays is Ramadan, which is the ninth month of the Muhammadan (e) year and celebrated throughout the (f) world.

    (d) ____**X**____ (e) _____ (f) _____

23. Candidates for a position with the oil company must speak the French (g) language as well as (h) arabic.

    (g) _____ (h) ____**X**____

24. Jimmy Carter was the first president from the (i) deep (j) south since before the Civil (k) war.

    (i) ____**X**____ (j) ____**X**____ (k) ____**X**____

25. In the opening lines of the poem, the poet prays to the muses and to the (l) holy (m) spirit for (n) inspiration.

    (l) ____**X**____ (m) ____**X**____ (n) _____

REVIEW TEST 11-B
Punctuation

In the space provided, write the letter of the sentence that is correctly punctuated.

b   1.   a. This chocolate cake contains 65 grams of fat and three thousand five hundred calories.
           b. This chocolate cake contains sixty-five grams of fat and 3,500 calories.

a   2.   a. Have you finished wrapping Charles' gift yet?
           b. Have you finished wrapping Charles gift yet?

b   3.   a. It will be the two son's responsibility to cook dinner.
           b. It will be the two sons' responsibility to cook dinner.

a   4.   a. Theresa is moving to Wyoming next fall in order to attend college.
           b. Theresa is moving, to Wyoming next fall, in order to attend college.

a   5.   a. Although Rosa is a busy attorney, she handles many *pro bono publico* cases as well.
           b. Although Rosa is a busy attorney, she handles many pro bono publico cases as well.

b   6.   a. Amanda said "that she left her husband because he overcooked her dinner one night."
           b. Amanda said that she left her husband because he overcooked her dinner one night.

a   7.   a. Marco's oldest brother, whom you met last night, is an engineer in Toledo.
           b. Marco's oldest brother whom you met last night is an engineer in Toledo.

b   8.   a. Angela said that her new sports car is fun to drive, moreover, it fits into tiny parking spaces.
           b. Angela said that her new sports car is fun to drive; moreover, it fits into tiny parking spaces.

b   9.   a. Enclose: an essay, transcript, and financial aid form with your application.
           b. Enclose an essay, transcript, and financial aid form with your application.

___a___ 10. a. The program concludes with the quartet singing three songs: "Rhiannon," "The Real Slim Shady," and "Hound Dog."
           b. The program concludes with the quartet singing three songs, "Rhiannon," "The Real Slim Shady," and "Hound Dog."

___b___ 11. a. Phoenix not Tucson is the capital of Arizona.
           b. Phoenix, not Tucson, is the capital of Arizona.

___b___ 12. a. *Sailing to Byzantium*, by William Butler Yeats, is my favorite poem.
           b. "Sailing to Byzantium," by William Butler Yeats, is my favorite poem.

___a___ 13. a. Sylvia's brother, a member of the U.S. fencing team, won a bronze medal in the Olympics.
           b. Sylvia's brother, a member of the U.S. fencing team won a bronze medal in the Olympics.

___a___ 14. a. Shall we watch the UCLA game on NBC or the MIT game on CBS?
           b. Shall we watch the U.C.L.A. game on N.B.C. or the M.I.T. game on C.B.S.?

___a___ 15. a. Corine Griffin, M.D., who has a degree from Yale, is the new dean of the medical school.
           b. Corine Griffin M.D., who has a degree from Yale, is the new dean of the medical school.

___a___ 16. a. "Is the coffee ready?" Rita asked Bill.
           b. "Is the coffee ready"? Rita asked Bill.

___b___ 17. a. Please send the package to 602 Pico Boulevard Santa Monica California.
           b. Please send the package to 602 Pico Boulevard, Santa Monica, California.

___b___ 18. a. I enjoy the heat and openness of the desert, however, I also like the lush, cool forests.
           b. I enjoy the heat and openness of the desert; however, I also like the lush, cool forests.

___a___ 19. a. She asked me whether I wanted to borrow her copy of Adrienne Rich's new collection of poetry.
           b. She asked me "whether I wanted to borrow her copy of Adrienne Rich's new collection of poetry?"

___b___ 20. a. Jamal is a witty, intelligent, inspiring, community leader.
           b. Jamal is a witty, intelligent, inspiring community leader.

Capitalization

Below each sentence, put an "X" next to the letter of any word in the sentence that should be capitalized.

21. My (a) doctor received his degree from the (b) university of Michigan, which is in the (c) city of Ann Arbor.

   (a) _____ (b) _____X_____ (c) _____

22. Innsbruck is in the (d) western part of Austria and was the site of the 1976 (e) olympic ski competition.

   (d) _____ (e) _____X_____

23. While driving through the (f) midwest, we stopped at Carbondale to visit my (g) brother Elvis, who is majoring in (h) chemistry at Southern Illinois (i) university.

   (f) _____X_____ (g) _____ (h) _____ (i) _____X_____

24. A preacher from the (j) state of Washington gave the invocation at the inauguration of (k) mayor Morgan.

   (j) _____ (k) _____X_____

25. Letters by a Canadian explorer were the subject of an article by (l) professor Bennett and a (m) professor from Duke (n) university.

   (l) _____X_____ (m) _____ (n) _____X_____

Go to www.ablongman.com/yarber to complete Review Test 11-C.

WRITING PARAGRAPHS

DEVELOPING A PARAGRAPH BY CAUSE AND EFFECT

"Why did this happen?" "What will happen because of this?" When we ask questions like these, we are thinking in terms of *cause and effect*. The driver who wants to know why his engine keeps dying in traffic, the scientists who ponder the effects of cloning, and the cook who wonders why the soufflé has collapsed are all following a familiar way of thinking: leaping back and forth from effect to cause and from cause to effect.

To demonstrate a cause-and-effect relationship, two patterns can be used: the effects may be stated in the topic sentence, with the causes listed in the body of the paragraph; or the paragraph may move from causes to their effects. In either case, cause-and-effect paragraphs explore why something happened or explain what happened as a result of something else.

In the following paragraph, the cause—the meeting of humid air and cold, dry air—is stated in the topic sentence and is followed by its effects.

> When humid air moving north from the Gulf of Mexico meets cold, dry air streaming westward from the Rocky Mountains, the result is often a tornado. When a tornado strikes, it can cause the air pressure to drop as much as ten percent in a few seconds. It is this sudden drop in pressure that causes houses and other structures literally to explode. Although a tornado has less energy than most storms, the concentration of its energy makes it the most violent of storms. Tornadoes, commonly called twisters, hang from a dark cloud mass. They usually darken after hitting the ground, as the funnel cloud picks up dust and other debris. Smaller tornadoes often bounce across an area and cause damage only where they contact the ground.

The next paragraph works from *effects* to their *cause*, which is stated in the concluding sentence.

> Jennifer has difficulty sleeping, and she is often depressed. She has reduced her diet to two salads a day and has lost over thirty pounds. She weighs only eighty-two pounds and thinks she should lose even more weight. She has few friends and worries constantly about her appearance. Although emaciated, she continues to restrict her intake of food. Jennifer's condition is diagnosed as anorexia nervosa, an eating disorder in which a person loses one-fourth or more of her normal weight but feels fat and worries about becoming obese. Some researchers believe that this disorder stems from our culture, which emphasizes weight and which encourages young women to be always dieting.

Select one of the following topics and develop it into a paragraph, moving from causes to effects or from effects to causes.

- *religious conversions*
- *capital punishment*
- *the decline in voter registration*
- *the decline in reading scores*

- *the growth of conservatism*
- *the warming trend throughout the world*
- *the increase in date rape*
- *the decline of Detroit in the auto world*

Writing Tips   May the Force Be With You!

Passive verbs are not as forceful or strong as active verbs. For this reason, effective writers tend to avoid them when possible.

To change a passive verb to active, find the word that performs the action in the sentence and make it the subject:

	subject
Passive:	Senator Marshall was asked by the *dean* to speak at commencement.
	subject
Revised Active:	The *dean* asked Senator Marshall to speak at commencement.

Notice that the revised form is tightened up and more forceful.

When "who" did an action is less important than *to whom it was done,* or when you don't know who or what performed the action, passive verbs are useful constructions:

The *suspect* had been seen in nearby towns.

Helen was honored by her coworkers.

Counterfeit *money* was substituted for genuine bills.

Writing Tips **Dashing through the Snow . . .**

Students sometimes confuse the use of the dash with that of the hyphen. These points may help.

1. Use dashes to set off explanatory matter that you want to make more prominent.
2. Use a dash to indicate a sudden change in the thought or structure of a sentence. This use occurs chiefly in writing dialogue in a story or in letter writing.
3. Use a hyphen—not a dash—to set off certain prefixes, to separate certain compound words, and to show that a word is to be carried over to the next line.

To produce a dash with a typewriter or on a computer, key two hyphens, with no space before, between, or after them.

Computer Activity

With your writing partner, select one of the topics given in the exercise on page 276.

Each of you is to write a paragraph on the same topic but approach it from two different points of view. Decide who will write on *cause* and who will write on *effect*.

When you have finished your paragraph, make a copy and exchange computer files.

In tandem, you and your writing partner should have covered both aspects of the topic, that is, the causes and effects related to your topic. Discuss the relationships between these particular causes and effects.

A CHECKLIST FOR THE ESL WRITER

A P P E N D I X   P R E V I E W

- Learning to use articles (*a, an,* and *the*)
- Problems with verbs and tense
- Learning to use phrasal verbs
- Learning to use adjectives and adverbs
- Common expressions that can cause confusion
- Problems with word order and unnecessary words
- Other problems with grammar
- Additional reference books for ESL students

Students whose second language is English often have questions about grammar and usage that we have not discussed in the other sections of this book. This checklist is for such students. In it we will emphasize the areas in which ESL writers and speakers have frequent problems.

We realize that memorizing these pages would not solve all problems a student might have with English. Even native speakers of English encounter questions of grammar and usage that can be very confusing. Ask your instructor if he or she can provide *Longman ESL Worksheets*, which are available to students who use this textbook. The worksheets have been designed for individual use or independent study, and they can help you identify areas requiring additional attention. An equally important way to improve your mastery of English and become a confident, effective user of the language is by reading and listening to native English speakers.

Learning to Use Articles and Quantifiers

The use of articles (*a*, *an*, and *the*) and quantifiers (words like *a few*, *some*, *many*, and *a lot of*) can be confusing for anyone who speaks English as a second language. These guidelines will help you use articles and quantifiers in your speaking and writing.

Articles (*a/an* and *the*)

A and *an* are called *indefinite articles*. Use *a* when the word following it begins with a consonant sound. Use *an* when the word following it begins with a vowel sound.

- a *bear,* a *car,* a *unit;* an *apple,* an *argument,* an *hour*

The is called a *definite article*.

How do you know whether to use an indefinite article (*a* or *an*) or a definite article (*the*) before a noun? For example, when should you write or say "*a* bear" or "*the* bear"? "*A* fire" or "*the* fire"? "*An* orange" or "*the* orange"? Before you can decide which article to use before a noun—or whether none should be used—you have to know whether the noun is countable or uncountable.

Countable nouns are the names of things, people, and ideas that we can count or make plural; they have a singular and a plural form.

- a dog→six dogs
- the salesman→the salesmen
- a phobia→several phobias
- the saucer→three saucers

Uncountable nouns are the names of things we usually cannot count. Uncountable nouns have only one form: the singular.

- earth (we don't say "earths")
- weather (we don't say "weathers")
- health (we don't say "healths")
- information (we don't say "informations")

After deciding whether a noun is countable or uncountable, you are ready to decide the kind of article to use with it.

Whether you use *a/an* or *the* in front of a noun depends on the listener's (or reader's) familiarity with the thing being referred to and if the noun is countable or uncountable. In general, when referring to things that are countable and that are not already known to both the speaker and the listener, use the indefinite article (*a/an*) before the noun.

- *A* good mechanic is difficult to find.
- *An* apple is all I have for breakfast most mornings.

In these sentences the writer is not referring to a specific mechanic or apple.

When it is clear which thing you mean and you are referring to things known to your listener, use the definite article *the*.

- *The* mechanic who worked on my car said it needs new brakes. (The listener knows which mechanic is referred to.)
- *The* apple you gave me yesterday was rotten. (Not just any apple; the one you gave me.)
- I watched *a* program on television last night. *The* program was about incurable diseases. (In the first sentence, *a* is used because the listener does not know which program is referred to; in the second sentence, *the* is used before *program* because it has been identified.)

Using A/An

1. Use *a/an* before singular countable nouns.

    - This is *a* boring movie. (**Not:** "This is boring movie.")
    - Would you like *a* cup of coffee? (**Not:** "Would you like cup of coffee?")
    - I have *an* idea. (**Not:** "I have idea.")

2. Use *a/an* to refer to a particular person or thing when the listener doesn't know which one is meant, when it doesn't matter which one is meant, or in front of a singular countable noun when you are introducing it for the first time without having referred to it before (as explained in the third example above).

    - My cousin bought *an* expensive German car. (The listener or reader doesn't know which expensive German car it is.)
    - Alberto comes from *a* small town in Texas.
    - Could you give me *a* piece of paper?

3. Use *a/an* to refer to any one member of a class.

    - *A* professional musician must study for many years.
    - *An* isosceles triangle has three sides.

4. Use *a/an* before a noun when you say what something is or what something or someone is like.

   ■ That is *a* good idea.

   ■ Tony is *a* thoughtful person.

   ■ Stan has *a* great sense of humor.

   ■ This is *an* incredible view!

   Do not use *a/an* before uncountable nouns: *music, weather, gold,* and so forth, except when you are limiting the meanings of the nouns in some way.

   ■ He brings *a* certain excitement to his performances. (**Not:** He brings certain excitement.)

   ■ Kim has *an* incredible understanding of Asian politics. (**Not:** Kim has incredible understanding of Asian politics.)

Using **The**

1. Use the definite article (*the*) when it is clear which thing you mean.

   ■ We will need *a* shovel when we plant the rosebushes. (No specific shovel is meant.)

   ■ Please give me *the* shovel in the toolshed. (The listener knows which shovel is meant.)

2. Use *the* when there is only one of something.

   ■ London is *the* capital of England.

   ■ Bill Gates is *the* richest man in the United States.

   ■ Superman leaped from *the* top of the building.

3. Use *the* when you mean something in particular.

   ■ *The* singers at the concert last night were great. (The singers at the concert, not singers in general.)

   ■ *The* cookies I made yesterday were full of calories. (Not all cookies; a particular group of cookies.)

4. Use *the* to refer to things in general by using *the* with a singular countable noun.

   ■ *The* rose is my favorite flower.

   ■ *The* hippopotamus, despite its appearance, is a very fast animal.

5. Use *the* to refer to a noun and identify or limit it.

   ■ *The* argument that I had with my sister was over trivial matters. (*That I had with my sister* limits the argument to a specific one.)

   ■ *The* argument against the tax increase was delivered by the mayor. (*Against the tax increase* limits the argument to a specific one.)

6. Use *the* to refer to words denoting nationality and certain adjectives: *the rich, the poor, the Germans, the Irish,* and so forth.

7. Use *the* with a number of expressions referring to our physical environment: *the city, the country, the sea, the beach, the mountains, the wind, the weather, the universe, the future, the sunshine,* and so forth.

Do NOT use *the* in the following situations.

1. Do not use *the* with uncountable or plural nouns to talk about things in general.

   ■ Books are expensive. (**Not:** The books are expensive.)

   ■ Life in starving countries is precarious. (**Not:** The life in starving countries is precarious).

2. Do not use *the* with singular proper names.

   ■ Mike lives in Chicago. (**Not:** Mike lives in *the* Chicago.)

   Exception: Use *the* with certain geographical names (*the* Bronx, *the* Atlantic, *the* Pacific, *the* Mississippi River, and *the* Matterhorn).

3. Do not use *the* with the names of meals.

   ■ We usually eat lunch at noon. (**Not:** We usually eat *the* lunch at noon.)

   Exception: Use *the* if you are referring to a specific meal (*The* dinner that she prepared was delicious).

4. Do not use *the* when you are thinking of certain places and what they are used for.

   ■ Mrs. O'Reilly goes to church every Sunday. (**Not:** Mrs. O'Reilly goes to *the* church every Sunday.)

   ■ After graduation from high school, Sean joined the army. (**Not:** After graduation from *the* high school, Sean joined the army.)

   Note that there are some exceptions:

   ■ The fire at *the* church last week was caused by arson.

   ■ *The* new high school enrolled new students last week.

Generalizations

1. Use *a/an* or *the* to make generalizations with most singular nouns:

   - *A* gesture can often be misunderstood by visitors in a foreign country. (*A* can mean any gesture.)
   - *The* telephone is being replaced by the cellular phone in many homes. (*The* is used to mean telephones in general.)

2. Omit *a* and *the* and make a noun plural to make a generalization:

   - *Gestures* can often be misunderstood by visitors in a foreign country.
   - *Telephones* are being replaced by the cellular phone in many homes.

   These are not the only situations in which articles are used. As you continue to speak and write English, you will become familiar with other rules. In the meantime, consult one of the books mentioned on page 303 when you have questions about their use.

Quantifiers

Quantifiers are words that come before nouns and tell you *how many* or *how much*. Their use can sometimes be confusing, and when used incorrectly, they can change the meaning of a sentence. In this section we will examine some of the most confusing quantifiers.

Some and Any   Both *some* and *any* can refer to an indefinite or vague quantity or number. They are used when it is difficult or unimportant to specify exactly how much or how many of something we are thinking of.

1. In general, use *some* in positive sentences and *any* in negative sentences.

   - I have *some* money left from my shopping trip.
   - I don't have *any* money left to buy more gifts.
   - Helen said *something* to me about the matter.
   - I didn't understand *any* of her remarks.

2. Use *any* in questions.

   - Do you have *any* ideas for your term paper yet?
   - No, I don't have *any* ideas. (**Not:** No, I don't have *some* ideas.)
   - Has *anybody* heard from Luis?

3. If you expect the answer "Yes," use *some* in your questions.

   - Would you like *some* help with that package?
   - Would you like *some* coffee?

4. Use *any* in affirmative statements after words like *never, hardly, without,* and *little* that have a negative meaning.

    ■ We had *hardly any* problem in finding our way to the beach.

    ■ There are *never any* surprises in Professor Forrest's exams.

5. Use *any* (or *anyone, anybody, anything,* and *anywhere*) when it means "it doesn't matter *which, who, what,* or *where*."

    ■ You can use *any* of these scissors. They're all sharp.

    ■ Students may register *any* time before September 10.

    ■ I dreamed that I could have *anything* I wanted for my graduation gift.

    ■ Fianna said that *anybody* could request a song.

6. Use either *any* or *some* in *if* clauses.

    ■ If you hear *any/some* news, give me a call.

    ■ If you meet *any/some* of our neighbors, tell them we'll return home soon.

7. Use *some* in requests.

    ■ May I have *some* more paper, please?

Much, Many, Little, Few, a Lot, and *Plenty*

1. Use *much* and *little* with uncountable nouns.

    ■ *much* energy   ■ *much* optimism

    ■ *little* money   ■ *little* admiration

2. Use *many* and *few* with plural nouns.

    ■ *many* dreams   ■ *many* voters

    ■ *few* friends   ■ *few* parking spaces

3. Use *a lot of/lots of* and *plenty of* with uncountable and plural nouns.

    ■ *a lot of* energy   ■ *lots of* mail

    ■ *a lot of* visitors   ■ *lots of* tires

    ■ *plenty of* courage   ■ *plenty of* reasons

4. Use *much* and *many* chiefly in negative sentences and in questions.

    ■ Our car doesn't require *much* fuel.

    ■ Do you have *many* relatives here?

Much is not usually used in positive sentences. Most speakers and writers prefer *a lot (of)* in such constructions.

- Politicians spent *a lot of* money in the last election. (**Not:** spent *much* money)
- There has been *a lot of* thunder and lightning this week. (**Not:** *much* thunder and lightning)

5. Use *too much* and *so much* in positive sentences.

- There has been *too much* rain this week.
- I ate *so much* pasta that I couldn't finish my dessert.

We can omit a noun after *much* or *many* if the meaning is clear.

- You haven't talked *much* tonight.
- Have you seen any football games this season? Not *many*.

6. Use *little* and *few* for negative ideas.

- There's *little* interest in going on a trip next week.
- She has *few* memories of growing up in Nebraska.

Intensify the meaning of *little* and *few* by using *very* before them.

- There's *very little* interest in going on a trip next week.
- She has *very few* memories of growing up in Nebraska.

A little and *a few* are more positive; their meaning is closer to *some*.

- We have *a little time* before the bus leaves. (some time)
- *A few* of her records survived the fire. (some records)

Problems with Verbs

If you are not a native speaker of English, you probably run into situations in which deciding which tense or form of a verb to use is confusing. **Tense** refers to the form of the verb that indicates time. The tense forms do not always agree with divisions of actual time, however. The simple present tense, for example, is not limited to the present time. Furthermore, helping/auxiliary verbs and many adverbs and expressions are used with verbs to indicate time.

First, we will review the twelve verb tenses and their uses, as well as the ways they are formed. Then you will learn to distinguish among the more confusing tenses and to avoid mistakes that even native speakers of English sometimes make.

The Twelve Verb Tenses

1. **Simple Present Tense**—This is the simple present tense:

   ■ I/we/you/they study

   ■ He/she/it studies

   Use the simple present tense to speak of things that happen all the time or repeatedly, or are true in general.

   ■ The sun *rises* in the East.

   ■ "The Star Spangled Banner" *is* our national anthem.

   ■ Helen's father *works* in a bank.

2. **Simple Past Tense**—This is the simple past tense:

   ■ I/we/you/he/she/it/they studied

   The simple past tense often ends in *-ed*. But many common verbs are irregular. This means that their past tense does not end in *-ed* and must be memorized.

Some Irregular Verbs		
Present	**Past**	**Example**
buy	bought	We *bought* a house in the country last summer.
go	went	The police *went* with the doctor to the hospital.
hit	hit	A severe storm *hit* the area last week.
Note: See pages 96–97 for other examples.		

   Use the simple past tense to talk about actions or situations completed in the past.

   ■ Clark *worked* until eleven o'clock last night.

   ■ World War II *ended* in 1945.

   ■ Sherry *spent* her inheritance in Paris last month.

3. **Simple Future Tense**—The simple future tense takes two forms:

   ■ I/we/you/he/she/it/they will study

   ■ I am / he/she/it is / you/we/they are going to study

Use the simple future tense to describe an action in the future.

- I *will study* my biology notes tonight.
- I *am going to study* my lab notes tonight.

4. **Present Perfect Tense**—This is the present perfect tense:

- I/we/you/they have studied
- he/she/it/ has studied

Form the present perfect tense with *have/has* and the past participle of the verb. The past participle often ends in *-ed* (wait*ed*, hop*ed*), but many important verbs are irregular (*thought, written, done*, and so forth). See pages 96–97 for other examples of irregular past participles.

Use the present perfect tense to describe an action that occurred at an unspecified time in the past.

- Marta *has* already *mailed* her application for a passport.

Use the present perfect tense to describe an action that started in the past and continues up to the present.

- Marta *has lived* in North Carolina for three years.

5. **Past Perfect Tense**—This is the past perfect tense:

- I/we/you/he/she/it/they had studied

Form the past perfect tense with *had* and the past participle (see the present perfect tense above about irregular forms of the past participle).

Use the past perfect tense to describe something in the past that occurred before another action in the past.

- Fred was very nervous because he *had* never *been* on a blind date before.
- Sheila knew who the killer was because she *had seen* the movie last week.
- When I arrived home I discovered that I *had lost* my door key.

6. **Future Perfect Tense**—This is the future perfect tense:

- I/we/you/he/she/it/they will have studied

Form the future perfect tense by using *will have* and the past participle of the verb.

Use the future perfect tense to describe an action in the future that will be completed or achieved by a certain time in the future.

■ By next September we *will have lived* in this apartment three years.

■ Claudia *will have completed* the requirements for her degree by the time she is twenty.

■ By the time her treatment for rabies is completed, Michele *will have received* a dozen vaccination shots.

7. **Present Progressive Tense**—This is the present progressive tense:

■ I am studying

■ he/she/it is studying

■ we/you/they are studying

Form the present progressive tense by using the simple present form of *be* (*am*, *is*, and *are*) and the present participle form of the verb (the "ing" form).

Use the present progressive tense to describe something that is happening at or very close to the time of speaking.

■ They *are working* in the garden now.

■ Tony *is watching* the game on television.

■ Lou *is taking* a nap.

8. **Past Progressive Tense**—This is the past progressive tense:

■ I/he/she/it was studying

■ we/you/they were studying

Form the past progressive tense by using the simple past tense form of *be* (*was* and *were*) and the present participle form of the verb.

Use the past progressive tense to describe a continuous action that was going on around a particular past time.

■ What *were* you *doing* when I called you?

■ George *was painting* the kitchen when the doorbell rang.

■ The sun *was setting* on the horizon as our boat pulled out of the harbor.

9. **Future Progressive Tense**—This is the future progressive tense:

■ I/he/she/it/we/you/they will be studying

Form the future progressive tense by using the simple future form of *be* (*will be*) and the present participle form of the verb.

Use the future progressive tense to describe an action that will be going on at a particular moment in the future.

- We *will be thinking* of you next week on your anniversary.
- The dogs *will be barking* soon if I don't feed them.
- Sharon *will be playing* her new guitar in the recital tonight.

10. **Present Perfect Progressive Tense**—This is the present perfect progressive tense:

- I/you/we/they have been studying
- he/she/it has been studying

Form the present perfect progressive tense by combining the present perfect form of *be* (*have been, has been*) with the present participle form of the verb.

Use the present perfect progressive tense to describe situations that started in the past and are still going on or that have just stopped and have present results.

- It *has been snowing* since last Tuesday evening.
- Mike *has been complaining* about the noise from the new neighbors, but the landlord refuses to do anything about it.
- We *have been watching* late-night television while on vacation.

11. **Past Perfect Progressive Tense**—This is the past perfect progressive tense:

- I/he/she/it/we/you/they had been studying

Form the past perfect progressive tense by combining the past perfect form of *be* (*had been*) with the present participle form of the verb.

Use the past perfect progressive tense to describe a continuous activity in the past that is completed before another action in the past.

- When I received my raise, I *had been working* at the restaurant two months.
- When Carla returned home, she told her sister that she *had been shopping*.
- Paul said that he *had been having* bad dreams, and he blamed them on the huge meals he *had been eating* just before going to bed.

12. **Future Perfect Progressive Tense**—This is the future perfect progressive tense:

- I/he/she/it/we/you/they will have been studying

Form the future perfect progressive tense by combining the future perfect form of *be* (*will have been*) with the present participle form of the verb.

Use the future perfect progressive tense to describe a continuous action in the future that is completed before another action in the future:

■ Jim *will have been working* at the hardware store for seven years next week.

■ Mr. Baylor, my math professor *will have been teaching* for thirty years this June.

■ Tara *will have been studying* the harp for six months tomorrow.

Tips for Choosing the Right Tense

1. Know how to describe an action in the present. Most English verbs have two present tenses. Forms like *I study* and *he works* are called simple present tense. Forms like *I am studying* and *he is working* are called present progressive tense. These two present tenses are used to describe several different kinds of time.

    The simple present tense is usually used to describe permanent situations or things that happen all the time or regularly.

■ Ricardo *plays* goalie on his soccer team.

■ I *drive* downtown to my job five days a week.

■ British Columbia *is* on the west coast of Canada.

The present progressive tense is usually used to talk about temporary continuing actions and events that are going on around now.

■ Richard *is playing* goalie today because the regular goalie was injured last week.

■ I *am driving* to work this week because of the subway strike.

■ Marcella *is looking* for an apartment closer to her job.

a. **Simple Present Tense**—Use the simple present tense in the following situations.

    (1) In summaries of plays, stories, and movies.

■ In Act One, Macbeth *encounters* three witches in the forest. They *tell* him . . .

■ On today's program Margaret *learns* that her real father *is* . . .

    (2) When asking for and giving instructions.

■ How *do* I *enroll* in the exercise class?

■ You *attend* the first session and *fill out* a registration form and *pay* the fee.

    (3) With dependent clauses to refer to the future.

■ I'll be ready when you *call*.

(4) With verbs that cannot normally be used in progressive forms.

- I like the ice cream very much. (**Not:** I *am liking* the ice cream very much.)
- I know his telephone number. (**Not:** I *am knowing* his telephone number.)

Do NOT use the simple present tense in the following situations:

(1) To talk about temporary actions that are going on only around the present.

- The telephone *is ringing.* Shall I get it? (**Not:** The telephone *rings.* Shall I get it?)

(2) To say how long a situation has been going on.

- I *have lived* here since 1990. (**Not:** I *live* here since 1990.)
- I *have been studying* English for two years. (**Not:** I *study* English for two years.)

b. **Present Progressive Tense**—Use the present progressive tense in the following situations.

(1) To describe changing situations.

- Helen *is becoming* more confident in her use of chopsticks.
- Athletes *are growing* taller because of better diets.

(2) To refer to future events in the following constructions.

- Where *are* you *going* on your vacation next week?
- She *is leaving* for Cleveland next month.

Note: When you use the present progressive tense to indicate future action, use a word or phrase like *tomorrow, next week,* and so forth, to indicate time.

(3) To refer to repeated actions if they are happening around the moment of speaking.

- Why *are* you *rubbing* your elbow?
- Fernando *is speaking* to several campus organizations this afternoon.

(4) To describe future events that are decided, or are starting to happen.

- What *is* Phil *doing* this evening? (**Not:** "What *does* Phil *do* this evening?")
- *He's working* on his car. (**Not:** He *works* on his car.)

Do NOT use the present progressive tense in the following situations:

(1) To talk about repeated actions that are not closely connected to the moment of speaking.

- I *ski* once or twice a year. (**Not:** I *am skiing* once or twice a year.)
- Muriel *cries* every time she *sees* that movie. (**Not:** Muriel *is crying* every time she *is seeing* that movie.)

(2) With certain verbs that refer to mental states, to the use of the senses, and to certain other meanings rather than to actions. Rather, such verbs are usually used only in simple present.

- I *realize* now that I was wrong. (**Not:** I *am realizing* now that I was wrong.)
- *Do* you *like* anchovies on your pizza? (**Not:** *Are* you *liking* anchovies on your pizza?)
- I *doubt* that I have enough time to take a nap. (**Not:** I *am doubting* that I have enough time to take a nap.)

Common Verbs Rarely Used in Progressive Tenses			
be	hear	own	seem
believe	imagine	prefer	suppose
belong	know	realize	understand
doubt	like	recognize	wish
feel	love	remember	
hate	need	see	

The common verbs shown in the box are rarely used in progressive tenses. If they are used in progressive tenses, their meaning changes. Notice the difference in meaning in the following pairs of sentences.

- I *feel* we shouldn't try to leave now. (**Not:** I'm *feeling* much better now.)
- I *see* what you mean by that. (**Not:** I'm *seeing* Jo Ann next week.)

2. Learn the difference between the simple past tense and the present perfect tense. Many situations allow us to use either the simple past tense or the present perfect tense.

- I *solved* the problem. *Were* you able to solve it?
- I've *solved* the problem. *Have* you *solved* it?

■ Lisa *saved* one hundred dollars this month. I *saved* fifty.

■ Lisa *has saved* one hundred dollars this month. *I've saved* fifty.

In most situations, however, the meaning of the sentence requires that we choose either the simple past or the present perfect tense.

a. **Simple Past Tense**—Use the simple past tense in the following situations.

   (1) To say when something happened.

   ■ Her parents *came* to this country in 1980.
   ■ I *played* basketball yesterday.

   (2) To describe actions that are not connected with the present.

   ■ Thomas Edison *invented* the lightbulb. (**Not:** *has invented*)
   ■ The United States *was* the first nation to use the atom bomb in war. (**Not:** *has been* . . . .)

b. **Simple Present Perfect Tense**—Use the simple present perfect tense in the following situations.

   (1) To give news of recent events.

   ■ There *has been* a severe earthquake in Japan, according to news accounts.

   (2) With *yet* in questions and negative sentences to show that something is expected to happen.

   ■ *Has* Gerald *arrived* yet?
   ■ Doris *hasn't received* her grades yet.

   (3) With *ever* and *never*.

   ■ I *have* never *been* to Sweden.
   ■ *Have* you ever *been* to Miami?

Do NOT use the simple present perfect to talk about an event that happened at a specific time.

■ There *was* a severe earthquake in Japan yesterday. (**Not:** There *has been* . . . .)

The present perfect always has a connection with the present; the simple past tense only tells us about the past. If we say that something has happened, we are thinking about the past and the present at the same time. Notice the difference in these sentences:

■ My father *worked* as a lifeguard when he was in college.

■ My father *has worked* for the post office for thirty years.

3. Learn the difference between the simple present perfect tense and the present perfect progressive tense. In general, both the present perfect and present perfect progressive tenses can be used to describe recent actions that have results in the present. The present perfect tense, however, suggests completion or a result. The present perfect progressive tense is used to describe or talk about more temporary actions. Notice the difference between these sentences.

■ **Present perfect**
   progressive tense: The artist *has been painting* the portrait all week.

■ **Present perfect tense:** The artist *has painted* over fifty portraits.

a. **Present Perfect Progressive Tense**—Use the present perfect progressive tense to show that an action or event is going on at the time of writing or speaking.

   ■ Charles *has been pulling* weeds and *spraying* the flowers all day.

   ■ I *have been studying* all morning.

   ■ I *have been thinking* about my brother all day.

   ■ *I've been running* on the beach this month.

As you can see, each of the sentences above suggests an emphasis on continued activity.

b. **Present Perfect Tense**—Use the present perfect, on the other hand, to suggest a result or completed activity.

   ■ Charles *has pulled* weeds and *sprayed* flowers all day.

   ■ I *have studied* all morning.

   ■ I *have thought* about my brother all day.

   ■ *I've run* on the beach this month.

Learning to Use Verb Phrases

Most verbs in English consist of only one word. Some verbs, however, consist of two or three words: the main verb and a word like *across, away, down, for, in, off, out, up,* and *with.* Such verbs are called verb phrases or verbal phrases, and their meanings are usually very different from the meanings of their parts taken separately. For example, the verb *run* has a meaning different from that of the verb *run into*.

■ Larry *ran* the mile when he was on his high school track team.

■ I *ran into* an old friend while I was at the library last night.

The verbs *broke* and *broke down* have different meanings, as illustrated by these sentences.

■ Mike *broke* his arm while riding his motorcycle.

■ His motorcycle *broke down* while he was in Phoenix.

The English language has hundreds of these verbs. Make a note of the most confusing ones as you hear them.

Common Two- and Three-Word Verbs and Their Meanings

Verb Phrase	Meaning	Verb Phrase	Meaning
break down	fail or stop	make up	invent
call off	cancel	pick out	select
check into	investigate	put off	delay
clear up	explain	put up with	allow or tolerate
cut down on	reduce	run across	meet by chance
cut off	shut off, stop	run into	collide with or meet by chance
figure out	solve or discover	run out on	betray
fill in	inform	show up	appear, arrive
find out	learn, discover	speak up	express freely, loudly
get off	exit from a vehicle	stand up for	defend
give up	stop trying	straighten out	organize
go over	review	sum up	conclude, summarize
grow up	mature	take back	recover, regain
hand in	submit	try on	test
look after	take care of	try out	compete, apply for
look into	investigate	work out	solve, develop
look out for	take care of, be aware of		

*This is not a complete list. The English language contains many others, and you should learn them as you encounter them.

Sometimes a phrasal verb has an object. In such cases part of the verb phrase can go either after the verb or after the object.

- The referee *called off* the game.
- The referee *called* the game *off*.
- Did you *make up* that story?
- Did you *make* that story *up?*
- We decided to *put off* our vacation until August.
- We decided to *put* our vacation *off* until August.

An exception occurs when the object of a phrasal verb is a pronoun (*me, you, it, him, her, us,* and *them*). In such cases, the pronoun must come before the second part of the verb phrase.

- Please *wake me up* by seven o'clock tomorrow morning. (**Not:** Please *wake up me* by seven o'clock tomorrow morning.)
- You can solve the problem if you *break it down* into its separate parts. (**Not:** You can solve the problem if you *break down it* into its separate parts.)

Learning to Use Adjectives and Adverbs

There are general rules for forming adjectives and adverbs.

1. If an adjective ends in *-e*, add *-r* and *-st* for the comparative and superlative.

   - wide/wider/widest
   - late/later/latest
   - large/larger/largest

2. If an adjective ends in *-e*, keep the *-e* before adding the adverb ending *-ly*.

   - polite/politely
   - extreme/extremely
   - absolute/absolutely

3. If an adjective ends in *-le* (*terrible, probable,* and so forth), leave off the *-e* and add *-y* to form the adverb.

   - terrible/terribly
   - probably/probably
   - reasonable/reasonably

Some adjectives and adverbs have irregular comparative forms.

1. *Good/well* and *better*

   ■ Let me ask him. I know him *better* than you do.

   ■ The car looks *better* since you washed it.

2. *Bad/badly* and *worse*

   ■ Is your headache better? No, it's *worse.*

   ■ The situation was much *worse* than we expected.

Some adjectives are used with particular prepositions. Study these groups of adjectives and the prepositions that follow them. Sometimes other prepositions are possible; a good dictionary will give you more information.

1. *Angry/annoyed/furious* ABOUT something but WITH someone

   ■ Cecilia was angry *about* the results of the election.

   ■ She was angry *with* the voters who supported the tax.

2. *Pleased/happy/disappointed* WITH something

   ■ Jack was disappointed *with* the size of his bonus.

3. *Surprised/amazed* BY something

   ■ Marty was surprised *by* the arrival of his parents.

4. *Married/engaged* TO someone
5. *Good/bad* AT doing something
6. *Aware/conscious* OF something
7. *Jealous/envious/suspicious* OF someone/something
8. *Proud/ashamed* OF someone/something
9. *Afraid/frightened/terrified/scared* OF someone/something
10. *Excited/worried/upset* ABOUT something

The English language contains many pairs of adjectives, one ending in *-ing* and the other in *-ed*.

■ fascinat*ing*/fascinat*ed*	■ astonish*ing*/astonish*ed*
■ amaz*ing*/amaz*ed*	■ shock*ing*/shock*ed*
■ annoy*ing*/annoy*ed*	■ embarrass*ing*/embarrass*ed*

- excit*ing*/excit*ed*
- amus*ing*/amus*ed*
- confus*ing*/confus*ed*
- satisfy*ing*/satisf*ied*

The ending of the adjective—whether it is -*ed* or -*ing*—creates a difference in meaning.

1. Someone is -*ed* if something (or someone) is -*ing*.

    - Kanisha is *exhausted* when she gets home from work because her job is *exhausting*.

2. If something is -*ing*, it makes you -*ed*.

    - Rudolpho was *disappointed* with the movie. The movie was *disappointing*.

Common Expressions

Some commonly used words and expressions can be confusing to students of the English language.

Using *Used To*

Used to when followed by a verb describes past situations that no longer exist or describes actions that happened in the past but no longer happen.

- Sherry *used to smoke*. She *used to smoke* two packs of cigarettes a day. (This sentence means that Sherry smoked regularly in the past but doesn't smoke now.)
- Juan *used to live* in Santo Domingo, but now he lives in Atlanta.
- Connie *used to work* at an electronics store, but now she has her own business.
- San Diego *used to be* a small navy town, but now it is a cosmopolitan city.
- This record shop *used to be* a grocery store.

Used to has no present form. If you wish to describe situations existing in the present, use the simple present tense.

- **Past:** Sherry *used to* smoke.
- **Present:** Sherry *smokes*. (**Not:** Sherry *uses to* smoke.)
- **Past:** Lance *used to* snore when he slept.
- **Present:** Lance *snores* when he sleeps. (**Not:** Lance *uses to* snore when he sleeps.)

To ask questions, use the following form: *did . . . use to . . . ?*

- *Did* you *use to* have a Volkswagen?
- *Did* Marino *use to* play football?

To form the negative, use the following form: *didn't use to . . . .*

- *Didn't* you *use to* have a Volkswagen?
- *Didn't* Marino *use to* play football?

Used to describes things that happened in the past and are now finished. Do not use *used to* to say what happened at a specific past time, or how many times it occurred, or how long it took.

- Charlotte *lost* five pounds last month. (**Not:** Charlotte *used to lose* five pounds last month.)
- Pedro *lived* in Newport News for two years. (**Not:** Pedro *used to live* in Newport News for two years.)
- I *went* to the health club twelve times last month. (**Not:** I *used to go* to the health club twelve times last month.)

Do not confuse *used to* and *to be used to*. If a person *is used to* something, it is familiar or no longer new.

- I *used to be* afraid to drive in heavy traffic. (I was afraid to drive in heavy traffic, but I no longer am.)
- I *am used to* driving in heavy traffic. (I am accustomed to driving in heavy traffic.)

Using *When* and *If*

Be careful not to confuse *when* and *if*. Use *when* for things that are sure to happen.

- *When* we go to lunch today, I think I'll have just a salad.
- *When* you boil water long enough, it turns to steam.

Use *if* for things that will possibly happen.

- *If* he doesn't call me soon, I'll leave for work.
- *If* I buy a new computer, I'll probably get a new monitor with it.
- Please call my brother *if* you go to Cleveland.

Using *Since* and *For*

Use *since* to give the starting points of actions or events, particularly from the point of view of a particular present or past end point.

- Sheila has been married *since* 1998.
- Raul has been studying flamenco *since* his return from Madrid.

Notice that we use *since* when we mention the beginning of the period (*since 1998*, *since his return*, and so forth.).

Use *for* to measure how long something lasts.

- Sheila has been married *for* two years. (**Not:** Sheila has been married *since* two years.)
- Raul has been studying flamenco *for* two months. (**Not:** Raul has been studying flamenco *since* two months.)

Notice that we use *for* when we say the period of time (for *two years*, for *two hours*, for *a long time*, and so forth).

Using *-s* and *-es*

When forming third person singular nouns and pronouns, don't forget that present tense verbs end in *-s* or *-es*.

- **Nonstandard:**   Every day at five o'clock the factory whistle *blow*.
- **Standard:**   Every day at five o'clock the factory whistle *blows*.

- **Nonstandard:**   Roberta *watch* the news on television while working on her math.
- **Standard:**   Roberta *watches* the news on television while working on her math.

If the helping verb *do* or *does* is used, add the *-s* or *-es* to the helping verb, not to the main verb.

- **Nonstandard:**   The whistle *don't* blow at five o'clock.
- **Standard:**   The whistle *doesn't* blow at five o'clock.

Problems with Word Order and Unnecessary Words

Adjectives

When several adjectives come before a noun, they usually have to be ordered in a particular way. For example, we say a *beautiful, small, shiny metal* coin, not a *metal, beautiful, shiny, small* coin. Adjectives like *beautiful* are called opinion adjectives because they tell us what the speaker or writer thinks of the object being described. Adjectives like *small, shiny,* and *metal* are called fact adjectives, and they give objective information about something. Opinion adjectives usually come before fact adjectives when they modify or describe nouns.

opinion	fact
a depressing	rainy day
a glamorous	American actress
a boring	political speech

The rules for adjective order can be very confusing, and there is disagreement among writers and speakers on the rules. Nevertheless, the following list will help you arrange them correctly. In general, adjectives should follow each other in this order before the noun being modified:

1. Opinion (*silly, ugly, intelligent, fascinating,* and so forth)
2. Size (*length, weight, height, width,* and so forth)
3. Age (*old, modern, new, recent,* and so forth)
4. Color (*yellow, red, black,* and so forth)
5. Origin (*British, Western, Oriental,* and so forth)
6. Material (*glass, wood, leather, steel,* and so forth)
7. Purpose (*coffee* table, *racing* car, *water* bottle, and so forth)

Some examples follow. (The numbers correspond to the numbered items in the list above.)

2   3   4   5   6   7
■ a small, ancient, black Japanese wooden cigar box

1   5
■ the impatient German teacher

1   3   5   7
■ a nostalgic old Hungarian wedding song

Adverbs

Adverbs can usually appear in three positions in a sentence. They can appear at the beginning.

■ *Yesterday* a rainbow appeared in the eastern sky.

They can appear in the middle.

■ A rainbow appeared *yesterday* in the eastern sky.

They can appear at the end.

■ A rainbow appeared in the eastern sky *yesterday.*

There are a few situations, however, in which we cannot place adverbs randomly.

1. Do not place adverbs between a verb and its object.

    ■ Maxine plays the piano *beautifully.* (**Not:** Maxine plays beautifully the piano.)

    ■ Laine *often* forgets her new telephone number. (**Not:** Laine forgets often her new telephone number.)

2. Do not place adverbs before *am, is, are, was,* and *were* when the adverbs (*always, never, ever, usually, often, sometimes,* and so forth) say how often something happens.

    ■ Dorothy is *always* on time for her French class. (**Not:** Dorothy always is on time for her French class.)

    ■ Visitors are *sometimes* unaware of the dangers of rip currents. (**Not:** Visitors sometimes are unaware of the dangers of rip currents.)

Repetition of the Subject

Avoid unnecessary repetition of the subject of the sentence.

■ The president *he* gave the State of the Union address last night. (Because *president* and *he* refer to the same person, *he* is unnecessary repetition.)

Other Problems with Grammar, Spelling, and Punctuation

If you have other questions about grammar, spelling, or punctuation, the following list will tell you where you can get help in this book.

	Page
Abbreviations	235
Capitalization	261–265
Comma-splices	198–201
Comparatives and superlatives	296–297
Dangling and misplaced modifiers	211–215
Irregular verbs	95–98; 286
Past and present participles	94–98
Possessives	255–258
Punctuation	234–259

	Page
Run-on sentences	196–197
Sentence fragments	190–196
Spelling	307
Subject-verb agreement	66–81

Additional Reference Books for ESL Students

Irwin Feignebaum. *The Grammar Handbook*. Oxford: Oxford University Press, 1985.

Raymond Murphy. *Grammar in Use*. Cambridge: Cambridge University Press, 2002.

Jocelyn Steer and Karen Carlisi. *The Advanced Grammar Book*. New York: Heinle & Heinle, 1997.

Michael Swan. *Practical English Usage*, 2nd ed. Oxford: Oxford University Press, 1995.

A BRIEF GUIDE FOR AVOIDING ERRORS IN GRAMMAR AND USAGE

Here are the most common errors in grammar and usage that college students make in their writing. For a quick review, turn to the pages cited.

1. **Sentence fragments (incomplete sentences)**

   ■ **Incorrect:** The referee stopped the match. Because of the crowd's rowdy behavior.

   ■ **Correct:** The referee stopped the match because of the crowd's rowdy behavior.

   (See "Prepositional Phrases as Fragments," pages 191–192.)

   ■ **Incorrect:** Her cheering fans encouraged the singer. To sing several encors.

   ■ **Correct:** Her cheering fans encouraged the singer to sing several encores.

   (See "Infinitive Phrases as Fragments, page 192.)

   ■ **Incorrect:** Trying to avoid a head-on collision. Mike pulled off the road and hit a tree.

   ■ **Correct:** Trying to avoid a head-on collision, Mike pulled off the road and hit a tree.

   (See "Participle Phrases as Fragments," pages 192–193.)

   ■ **Incorrect:** A new rule governing offside violations, passed by the referees' association.

   ■ **Correct:** A new rule governing offside violations was passed by the referees' association.

   (See "Noun Phrases as Fragments," pages 194–195.)

- ■ **Incorrect:** All professional boxing fights were contested with bare knuckles until 1892. When John L. Sullivan and James Corbett fought in a bout in which both wore regulation gloves.
- ■ **Correct:** All professional boxing fights were contested with bare knuckles until 1892, when John L. Sullivan and James Corbett fought in a bout in which both wore regulation gloves.

(See "Dependent Clauses as Fragments," pages 195–196.)

Note: Each of the preceding sentence fragments can be corrected in additional ways. Check the appropriate pages.

2. **Run-on Sentences**

- ■ **Incorrect:** The original Social Security Act was passed in 1935 it is administered by the Social Security Administration.
- ■ **Correct:** The original Social Security Act was passed in 1935. It is administered by the Social Security Administration.

(See "Run-on Sentences," pages 196–197, for other ways to correct run-on sentences.)

3. **Comma-Splices**

- ■ **Incorrect:** Machu Picchu is an ancient Inca fortress in the Andes Mountains in Peru, it was built in the mid-fifteenth century.
- ■ **Correct:** Machu Picchu is an ancient Inca fortress in the Andes Mountains in Peru. It was built in the mid-fifteenth century.

(See "Comma-Splices," pages 198–201, for other ways to correct comma-splices.)

4. **Failing to make the subject and verb agree**

- ■ **Incorrect:** Everyone who attended the tryouts were given a number
- ■ **Correct:** Everyone who attended the tryouts was given a number

- ■ **Incorrect:** Across the street was several curious spectators.
- ■ **Correct:** Across the street were several curious spectators.

(See "Making the Subject and Verb Agree," pages 70–81.)

5. **Using the wrong form of the verb**

- ■ **Incorrect:** It was obvious that the tenor had never sang the National Anthem before.
- ■ **Correct:** It was obvious that the tenor had never sung the National Anthem before.

- ▇ **Incorrect:** We were startled to see how much our young nephew had growed since we last saw him.
- ▇ **Correct:** We were startled to see how much our young nephew had grown since we last saw him.

- ▇ **Incorrect:** After running the marathon, Frank laid on the grass and rested.
- ▇ **Correct:** After running the marathon, Frank lay on the grass and rested.

(See "Common Errors Involving Verbs," pages 93–109.)

6. **Using the wrong form of the pronoun**

- ▇ **Incorrect:** Between you and I, Donny's new suit is out of style.
- ▇ **Correct:** Between you and me, Donny's new suit is out of style.

- ▇ **Incorrect:** Who do you intend to vote for in tomorrow's election?
- ▇ **Correct:** Whom do you intend to vote for in tomorrow's election?

- ▇ **Incorrect:** Much to my surprise, my dance partner and myself won a prize in the contest.
- ▇ **Correct:** Much to my surprise, my dance partner and I won a prize in the contest.

(See "Using the Correct Form of the Pronoun," pages 121–134.)

7. **Confusing adjectives and adverbs**

- ▇ **Incorrect:** Laura spoke very modest of her accomplishments.
- ▇ **Correct:** Laura spoke very modestly of her accomplishments.

- ▇ **Incorrect:** Maria's tostadas, based on her mother's recipe, tasted deliciously
- ▇ **Correct:** Maria's tostadas, based on her mother's recipe, tasted delicious.

(See "Confusing Adjective and Adverbs," pages 218–220.)

8. **Misplacing modifiers and participles**

- ▇ **Incorrect:** Snoring loudly, the intruder was not heard by Vince.
- ▇ **Correct:** Snoring loudly, Vince did not hear the intruder.

- ▇ **Incorrect:** After looking over my notes, the biology exam was easier than I had feared.
- ▇ **Correct:** After I looked over my notes, the biology exam was easier than I had feared.

(See "Misplaced and Dangling Modifiers," pages 211–215.)

9. **Misusing commas and other punctuation**

   ■ **Incorrect**: Herbert has lived in this country for fifty years but he still speaks with a heavy accent.

   ■ **Correct**: Herbert has lived in this country for fifty years, but he still speaks with a heavy accent.

   ■ **Incorrect**: In her youth Sheila worked as a waitress, and lab assistant.

   ■ **Correct**: In her youth Sheila worked as a waitress and lab assistant.

   ■ **Incorrect**: Watching television several hours a day, was Hugh's only exercise.

   ■ **Correct**: Watching television several hours a day was Hugh's only exercise.

   (See "Punctuation and Capitalization," pages 234–265.)

10. **Misspelling**

    Proofread your papers carefully, looking closely and carefully for words whose spelling you are uncertain of. You may even find it helpful to have a friend read over you work, since writers are often blind to their own mistakes.

    Keeping a list of troublesome words is another way of pinpointing and reducing the number of misspelled words that can occur in writing.

    Finally, you should own—and use—a college-level dictionary. For suggestions, see page 3 or follow the recommendation of your instructor.

A Glossary
of Usage

This glossary is an alphabetical guide to words that often cause problems for writers. Some entries are labeled "colloquial," and some "nonstandard." A *colloquialism* is a word or phrase more appropriate to informal speech than to writing. Although colloquialisms are not grammatically incorrect, they should be avoided in formal writing, and even in informal writing they should be used sparingly. A *nonstandard* word or phrase is avoided at all times by careful speakers and writers. It is the kind of error sometimes labeled "incorrect" or "illiterate."

If you want to know more about the words in this glossary, consult *Webster's Third New International Dictionary* or a modern college-level dictionary.

accept, except *Accept* is a verb meaning "to receive," and *except* is a preposition meaning "but" or a verb meaning "to exclude or leave out." "I will *accept* your invitation." "Everyone *except* Henry went to Chicago." "We voted to *except* the new members from the requirements."

advice, advise *Advice* is "an opinion you offer"; *advise* means "to recommend." "Her *advice* was always helpful." "The counselor will *advise* you concerning the requirements for that course."

affect, effect To *affect* is "to change or modify"; *to effect* is "to bring about something"; an *effect* is "the result." "The drought will *affect* the crop production." "I hope the treatment will *effect* an improvement in his condition." "The *effect* should be noticeable."

aggravate, annoy These two are often confused. To *aggravate* is "to make a condition worse." "The treatment only *aggravated* his asthmatic attacks." *To annoy* is "to irritate." "The ticking clock *annoyed* Dean as he read."

agree to, agree with You agree *to* a thing or plan. "Mexico and the United States *agree to* the border treaty." You agree *with* a person. "Laura *agreed with* Herb about the price of the computer."

ain't Although *ain't* is in the dictionary, it is a nonstandard word never used by educated or careful speakers except to achieve a deliberate humorous effect. The word should be avoided.

all ready, already *All ready* is an adjective phrase meaning "prepared" or "set to go." "The car had been tuned up and was *all ready* to go." *Already*, an adverb, means "before" or "previously." "The car had *already* been tuned up."

all right, alright The correct spelling is *all right*; *alright* is not standard English.

allusion, illusion   An *allusion* is "an indirect reference to something." "He made an *allusion* to his parents' wealth." An *illusion* is a "false image or impression." "It is an *illusion* to think that I will soon be a millionaire."

among, between   Use *between* for two objects and *among* for more than two. "The hummingbird darted *among* the flowers." "I sat *between* my parents."

amount, number   *Amount* refers to quantity or to things in the aggregate; *number* refers to countable objects. "A large *amount* of work remains to be done." "A *number* of jobs were still unfilled."

anyone, any one   *Anyone* means "any person at all." "I will talk to *anyone* who answers the telephone." *Any one* means a single person. "*Any one* of those players can teach you the game in a few minutes."

anyways, anywheres   These are nonstandard for *anyway* and *anywhere*, and they should be avoided.

awful   Don't use *awful* as a synonym for *very*. It is inappropriate to say or write "The scores of the two teams were *awful* close." It is better to say or write "The scores of the two teams were *very* close."

bad, badly   *Bad* is an adjective; *badly* is an adverb. Use *bad* before nouns and after linking verbs; use the adverb *badly* to modify verbs or adjectives. "Her pride was hurt *badly* (not *bad*)." "She feels *bad* (not *badly*)."

bare, bear   *Bare* is an adjective meaning "naked" or "undisguised." "The baby wiggled out of its diaper and was completely *bare*." *Bear* as a verb means "to carry or support." "The bridge was too weak to *bear* the weight of the trucks."

because of, due to   Use *due to* after a linking verb. "His embarrassment was *due to* his inability to speak their language." Use *because of* in other situations. It is awkward to say or write "The boat struck the buoy in the harbor *due to* the fog." It is better to say or write "The boat struck the buoy in the harbor *because of* the fog."

being as, being that   These are nonstandard forms and should be avoided. Use *since* or *because*.

beside, besides   *Beside* is a preposition meaning "by the side of." "The doctor sat *beside* the bed talking to his patient." *Besides* may be a preposition or adverb meaning "in addition to" or "also." "*Besides* my homework, I have some letters to write."

between you and I   A common mistake. Use *between you and me*.

breath, breathe   *Breath* is the noun. "He tried to conceal the smell of alcohol on his *breath*." *Breathe* is the verb. "The air we *breathe* is often contaminated with pollutants."

can, may   *Can* refers to ability; *may* refers to permission. "After taking only a few lessons, Tom *can* play the trumpet beautifully. Because of the neighbors' complaints, however, he *may* play only in the afternoon."

can't hardly, can't barely   These are double negatives and are to be avoided. Use *can hardly* and *can barely*.

capital, capitol   Capital is "the leading city of a state," "wealth," or "chief in importance." "The *capital* of Nicaragua is Managua." "Lorena lives on the interest from her accumulated *capital.*" "The low interest rate was of *capital* importance in holding down inflation." *Capitol* is the building in which lawmakers sit. "The flag of surrender flew over the *capitol.*"

complement, compliment To *complement* is "to balance or complete." "Kareem's new tie *complements* his suit." To *compliment* is to flatter. As a noun, *compliment* means "an expression of praise." "When anyone *compliments* Bernice, she blushes, because she is unaccustomed to *compliments.*"

conscience, conscious A *conscience* is a "sense of right or wrong." "His *conscience* wouldn't allow him to cheat on the exam." To *be conscious* is "to be aware." "I was not *conscious* of the noise in the background."

consul, council, counsel A *consul* is a "government official stationed in another country." "The American *consul* in Paris helped the stranded New Yorkers locate their family." A *council* is a "body of people acting in an official capacity." "The city *council* passed a zoning regulation." *Counsel* as a noun means "an advisor" or "advice"; as a verb it means "to advise." "The defendant's *counsel* objected to the question." "The *counsel* he gave her was based on his many years of experience." "Saul *counseled* me on my decision."

continual, continuous *Continual* means "repeated frequently," as in "We heard a series of *continual* beeps of an automobile horn." *Continuous* means "without interruption." "I was lulled to sleep by the *continuous* hum of the motor in the deck below."

different from, different than One thing is different *from* another, not different *than*.

discreet, discrete *Discreet* means "tactful" ("*discreet* remarks"); *discrete* means "separate" or "individual" ("*discrete* objects"). "Henry was *discreet* about the source of his funds. He said that he had several *discrete* bank accounts."

disinterested, uninterested To *be disinterested* is "to be impartial." "The judge was a *disinterested* participant in the case." To *be uninterested* is "to lack interest." "It was obvious that Jack was *uninterested* in the lecture because he dozed off several times."

double negatives Unacceptable in formal writing and in most informal situations except for humorous effect. Double negatives range from such obvious errors as "I don't have no paper" to more subtle violations ("I can't scarcely" and "It isn't hardly"). Avoid them.

eminent, imminent *Eminent* means "distinguished" or "famous"; *imminent* describes something about to happen. "The arrival of the *eminent* preacher is *imminent.*"

enormity, enormousness *Enormity* means "atrociousness"; *enormousness* means "of great size." "The *enormity* of the crime shocked the hardened crime reporters." "Because of the *enormousness* of the ship, it could not be docked in the local harbor."

enthused Nonstandard. Use *enthusiastic*. ("He was *enthusiastic* about our plans for next summer.")

farther, further Use *farther* for physical distance ("They live *farther* from town than we do") and *further* for degree or quantity ("Their proposal was a *further* attempt to reach an agreement").

fewer, less Use *fewer* for items that can be counted and *less* for quantity. "*Fewer* jobs are available for young people this summer." "He paid *less* for that car than I paid for mine."

finalize Avoid this term; use *finish*.

flaunt, flout *Flaunt* means "to show off." "To *flaunt* his strength, Carl picked up the coffee table." *Flout* means "to disregard or show contempt for." "*Flouting* the sign posted in front of the store, Mr. Burkett parked in the 'No Parking' zone."

good, well *Good* is an adjective, never an adverb. "She performs *well* (not *good*) in that role." *Well* is an adverb and an adjective; in the latter case it means "in a state of good health." "I am *well* now, although last week I didn't feel very *good*."

hanged, hung Criminals are *hanged*; pictures are *hung*.

hisself Nonstandard. Use *himself*.

if, whether Use *if* to introduce a clause implying a condition. "*If* you go to summer school, you can graduate early." Use *whether* to introduce a clause implying a choice. "I'm not sure *whether* I will go to summer school."

imminent, eminent See *eminent, imminent*.

imply, infer To *imply* is "to hint strongly"; *to infer* is "to derive the meaning from someone's statement by deduction." You *infer* the meaning of a passage when you read or hear it; the writer or speaker *implies* it.

irregardless Nonstandard. Use *regardless*.

is when, is where Avoid these expressions to introduce definitions. It is awkward to write (or say) "A sonnet *is when* you have fourteen lines of iambic pentameter in a prescribed rhyme scheme." It is better to write (or say) "A sonnet is a poem with fourteen lines of iambic pentameter in a prescribed rhyme scheme."

its, it's *Its* is a possessive pronoun meaning "belonging to it." *It's* is a contraction for *it is* or *it has*. See Chapter 6.

kind of, sort of These are colloquial expressions acceptable in informal speech but not in writing. Use *somewhat* or *rather* instead.

leave, let *Leave* means "to go away," and *let* means "to allow." Do not use *leave* for *let*. "Please *let* (not *leave*) me go."

liable, likely, apt *Liable* means "legally responsible" or "susceptible to"; *likely* means "probably"; and *apt* refers to a talent or a tendency. "He is *liable* for the damage he caused." "Those rain clouds indicate it's *likely* to rain this afternoon." "She is an *apt* tennis player."

like *Like* is a noun, verb, adjective, and preposition; do not use it as a conjunction. "He acted as if (not *like*) he wanted to go with us."

loosen, loose, lose *To loosen* means "to untie or unfasten"; *to lose* is "to misplace"; and *loose* as an adjective means "unfastened" or "unattached." "He *loosened* his necktie." "His necktie is *loose*." "Did he *lose* his necktie?"

maybe, may be *Maybe* means "perhaps"; *may be* is a verb phrase. "*Maybe* we'll win tomorrow's game if we're lucky." "It *may be* that we'll win tomorrow."

must of Nonstandard. Write (and say) "must have," and in similar constructions use "could have" (not "could of") or "would have" (not "would of").

myself *Myself* is correct when used as an intensive or reflexive pronoun ("I helped *myself* to the pie," and "I hurt *myself*"), but it is used incorrectly as a substitute for *I* and *me* in the following: "My brother and *myself* were in the army together in Germany" and "They spoke to George and *myself* about the matter."

off of Wordy; use *off*. "Sean jumped *off* (not *off of*) the diving board."

precede, proceed *To precede* is "to go before or in front of"; *to proceed* is "to continue moving ahead." "Poverty and hunger often *precede* a revolution." "They *proceeded* down the aisle as if nothing had happened."

principal, principle *Principal* as an adjective means "main" or "chief"; as a noun it means "a sum of money" or "the head of a school." *Principle* is a noun meaning "a truth, rule, or code or conduct."

quiet, quite, quit Read the following sentences to note the differences. "I wanted to get away from the noise and find a *quiet* spot." "They are *quite* upset that their son married without their permission." "When college starts next fall, he will *quit* his summer job."

raise, rise *Raise* is a verb meaning "to lift or help to rise in a standing position." Its principal parts are *raised, raised,* and *raising. Rise* means "to assume an upright position" or "to wake up." Its principal parts are *rose, risen,* and *rising.*

roll, role *Role* is a noun meaning "a part or function." "The navy's *role* in the war was unclear." *Roll* as a verb means "to move forward, as on wheels"; as a noun, it means "bread" or "a list of names." "The tanks *rolled* down the main street of the town." "Professor Samuals often forgets to take *roll* in class."

set, sit *Set* means "to place something somewhere," and its principal parts are *set, set,* and *setting. Sit* means "to occupy a seat"; the principal parts are *sit, sat,* and *sitting.* See Chapter 5.

shall, will Most authorities, writers, and speakers use these interchangeably. Follow the advice of your instructor.

somewheres Nonstandard. Use *somewhere.* Similarly, avoid *nowheres.*

theirselves Nonstandard. Use *themselves.*

there, their, they're *There* is an adverb meaning "in that place." "Place the packages *there* on the table." *Their* is the possessive form of *they.* "They were shocked to find *their* house on fire." *They're* is a contraction of *they are.* "*They're* usually late for every party."

weather, whether *Weather* is a noun referring to climatic conditions. "If we have warm *weather* tomorrow, let's eat outdoors." *Whether* is a conjunction that introduces alternatives. "It may rain tomorrow whether we like it or not."

who, whom Use *who* when the pronoun is a subject; use *whom* when it is an object. "*Who* bought the flowers?" "To *whom* were the flowers given?"

your, you're *Your* is a possessive form of *you; you're* is a contraction for *you are.* "*Your* dinner is ready." "*You're* the first person to notice that."

A Glossary of Grammatical Terms

This glossary is an alphabetical guide to the grammatical terms used in this book, as well as to other helpful words. Some entries contain references to other terms or to chapters of the text in which they are discussed in detail. For further cross-references, you should consult the index.

abstract noun   A noun that refers to an idea or quality that cannot be identified by one of the senses. Examples are *shame, delight,* and *tolerance.* See also *concrete noun.*

action verb   See *verb* and Chapters 2 and 3.

active voice   See *voice.*

adjective   A word that modifies (limits or describes) a noun or pronoun. "The concert was *long,* but it was *exciting.*" (The adjective *long* modifies the noun *concert,* and the adjective *exciting* modifies the pronoun *it.*) See Chapters 2 and 10.

adjective clause   A dependent clause that modifies a noun or pronoun. "The delegates *who voted for the amendment* changed their minds." (The adjective clause modifies the noun *delegates.*) See Chapter 8.

adverb   A word that modifies (limits or describes) an adjective, a verb, or another adverb. "He cried *softly.*" (*Softly* modifies the verb *cried.*) "They are *extremely* wealthy." (*Extremely* modifies the adjective *wealthy.*) "He left the room *very* hurriedly." (*Very* modifies the adverb *hurriedly.*) See Chapters 2 and 10.

adverb clause   A dependent clause that modifies an adjective, verb, or another adverb. "I think of her *when I hear that song.*" (The adverb clause modifies the verb *think.*) "He became angry *because he had forgotten his keys.*" (The adverb clause modifies the adjective *angry.*) "The band played so loudly *that I got a headache.*" (The adverb clause modifies the adverb *so.*) See Chapter 8.

agreement   The correspondence of one word with another, particularly subjects with verbs and pronouns with antecedents. If the subject of a sentence is singular, the verb is singular ("My *tire is* flat"); if the subject is singular, pronouns referring to it should also be singular ("The *carpenter* forgot *his* hammer"). Plural subjects require plural verbs, and plural pronouns are used to refer to plural antecedents. ("My *tires are* flat." "The *carpenters* forgot *their* tools.") See Chapters 4 and 7.

antecedent   A word or group of words a pronoun refers to. "Jimmy, *who* used to play in a rock group, decided *he* would go back to college to complete *his* degree." (*Who, he,* and *his* all refer to the antecedent *Jimmy.*) See Chapters 2 and 7.

appositive   A word or phrase following a noun or pronoun that renames or explains it. "London, *the capital*, was bombed heavily." "The author *Mark Twain* lived in Connecticut." In the first example, *the capital* is a nonessential appositive because it is not needed to identify the word it follows. In the second example, *Mark Twain* is an essential appositive because it is needed to identify the general term *author*. Only nonessential appositives are set off by commas. See Chapters 6 and 11.

article   *A, an,* and *the* are articles. *A* and *an* are indefinite articles; *the* is a definite article. Articles are usually regarded as adjectives because they precede nouns. See Chapter 2 and "A Checklist for the ESL Writer," pages 278–283.

auxiliary verb   A helping word (or words) used to form a verb phrase. The most common auxiliary verbs are forms of *be* (*am, are, is, have been,* and so on) and *have* (*had, has,* and so on); others include the various forms of *do, can, shall, will, would, should, may, might,* and *must*. See Chapters 2 and 5.

case   The form of a pronoun or noun to show its use in a sentence. Pronouns have three cases: the *nominative* or subject case (*I, he, she, they,* and so on), the *objective* case (*me, him, her, them,* and so on), and the *possessive* (*my, his, her, their,* and so on). Nouns change their spelling only in the possessive case (*Larry's, man's,* and so on). See Chapter 6.

clause   A group of words containing a subject and a verb. A clause may be either independent or dependent. Independent clauses may stand alone as simple sentences. The dependent clause must be joined to an independent clause. "The restaurant was closed by the health department because the chef had hepatitis." (*The restaurant was closed by the health department* is an independent clause; *because the chef had hepatitis* is a dependent clause.) See Chapter 8.

collective noun   A noun that names a group of people or things, such as *army, committee, flock*. Collective nouns usually take singular verbs ("The troop *was* ready to leave") except when the individual members are thought of ("The class *were* arguing among themselves"). See Chapters 4 and 7.

colloquialism   An informal word or expression more appropriate to speech than to writing. See "A Glossary of Usage," pages 308–312.

comma-splice   The misuse of a comma between two independent clauses in a compound sentence. "Herb's sister studied architecture in college, she designed the new office building downtown." Comma-splices can be corrected by substituting a semicolon for the comma or by inserting a coordinating conjunction after the comma. See Chapters 8, 9, and 11.

command   See *imperative sentence*.

common noun   A noun that names a general category or class of people, places, or things: *city, tool, song*. Common nouns are not capitalized except when they begin a sentence. See Chapters 2 and 11.

comparative degree   The "more," "less," or *-er* form of those adjectives that can be compared. See Chapter 10. See also *positive degree* and *superlative degree*.

comparison   A statement about the relation between two (or more) things or the change in the spelling of adjectives and adverbs to show degree. The degrees of comparison in

English are positive (*slowly* and *loud*), comparative (*more slowly* and *louder*), and superlative (*most slowly* and *loudest*). Some modifiers cannot be compared: *round, dead, unique, full,* and so on. See Chapter 10.

complement A word or expression that completes the sense of a verb, a subject, or an object. See *direct object, indirect object, predicate adjective, predicate noun,* and *predicate pronoun.*

complete subject See *subject.*

complex sentence A sentence containing one independent clause and at least one dependent clause. "The grain embargo *that was announced last year* was criticized by the farmers." (The dependent clause is italicized.) See Chapters 3 and 8.

compound Two or more words or word groups linked to form a single unit. For instance, two nouns can form a compound subject. "*Merchants and businesspeople* were united in their opposition to the new tax." Two verbs can function as a compound predicate. "She *danced and sang* in the leading role." See Chapter 3.

compound-complex sentence A sentence containing at least two independent clauses and one or more dependent clauses: "Although the demand for oil has declined, the price of gasoline continues to climb, and the OPEC nations threaten a new price hike." See Chapter 8.

compound sentence A sentence with two or more independent clauses but no dependent clauses. "She wanted to read the book, but someone had previously borrowed it." See Chapters 3 and 8.

compound subject Two or more subjects governed by the same verb. "*You and I* should meet for coffee tomorrow." See Chapter 3.

compound verb Two or more verbs governed by the same subject. "The crowd *threw* beer bottles and *cursed* the referee." See Chapter 3.

concrete noun A noun naming something that can be perceived by one of the senses. Examples are *butter, elevator, scream,* and *buzz.* See also *abstract noun.*

conjugating a verb A way of showing all tenses of a verb. See Chapter 5 and pages 286–290.

conjunction A word that connects words, phrases, and clauses. See also *coordinate conjunction, subordinate conjunction,* and Chapter 2.

conjunctive adverb An adverb that connects independent clauses after a semicolon. "I had looked forward to seeing the movie; *however,* after reading the reviews I changed my mind." See Chapters 9 and 11.

contraction A word formed from the union of two words, with an apostrophe replacing the missing letters: *hasn't (has not), I'm (I am).* See Chapters 6 and 11.

coordinate adjectives Two or more adjectives of equal importance that modify the same noun. "The *tall, scowling* doorman finally let us in." See Chapter 11.

coordinate conjunction A word that connects two or more words, phrases, or clauses of equal rank. The most common coordinate conjunctions are *and, but, so, for, nor,* and *or.* See Chapter 2.

correlative conjunctions Pairs of conjunctions used to join parts of a sentence of equal rank. The most common correlative conjunctions are *either . . . or; neither . . . nor; not only . . . but also;* and *both . . . and.* See Chapters 2 and 10.

dangling modifier   A modifier that has no word in the sentence for it to modify. It is left "dangling" and consequently ends up modifying an unintended word, as in the following: "Raising his bow triumphantly, the violin concerto ended in a crescendo." See Chapter 10.

dangling participle   A participle serving as a modifier that has no word in the sentence for it to modify. "Looking out the window, a car drove by." See Chapter 10.

declarative sentence   A sentence that states a fact or makes a statement. "The capital of Kentucky is Frankfort." See Chapter 11.

demonstrative pronoun   A word used as an adjective or a pronoun that points out an item referred to. The demonstrative pronouns are *this*, *that*, *these*, and *those*. See Chapters 2 and 6.

dependent clause   A group of words containing a subject and verb but unable to stand alone. A dependent clause must be subordinated to an independent clause in the same sentence. "*If you are on the honor roll*, you may be eligible for reduced insurance rates." See Chapters 3, 8, and 9.

direct object   A word that receives the action of the verb. "She helped *him* with the math problem." "I pried the *lid* off the can." See Chapter 6.

elliptical construction   A construction in which one or more words are omitted but understood. "He is heavier than I (*am*)."

essential modifier   A word or group of words necessary for the identification of the object being identified. "The man *with the checkered vest* wants to talk to you." Essential modifiers can be words, phrases, or clauses; they are not separated from the words they modify by commas. See Chapters 8 and 11.

exclamatory sentence   A sentence expressing emotion, usually followed by an exclamation point. "Stop that yelling!" See *imperative sentence* and Chapters 2 and 11.

formal language   Language appropriate to formal situations and occasions, as distinguished from informal language and colloquialisms.

fragment   See *sentence fragment*.

fused sentences   See *run-on sentence*.

gender   The grammatical expression of sex, particularly in the choice of pronouns: *he* (masculine), *she* (feminine), and *it* (neuter), and their related forms. See Chapter 6.

gerund   The "ing" form of a verb when it is used as a noun. "*Jogging* is one of the most popular forms of exercise among Americans." See Chapter 5.

helping/auxiliary verb   See *auxiliary verb*.

imperative sentence   A sentence expressing a command. "Please turn off your motor." See Chapter 11.

indefinite pronoun   A pronoun that does not refer to a specific person or thing. Some of the most common indefinite pronouns include *anyone*, *someone*, *few*, *many*, and *none*. See Chapters 4, 6, and 7.

independent clause   A group of words containing a subject and a verb and capable of standing alone. Also called a *main clause*. See Chapters 3 and 8.

indirect object   The person or thing receiving the direct object, and usually placed in a sentence between an action verb and the direct object: "Jay's lawyer gave *him* several documents to sign." See Chapter 6.

infinitive   The base form of the verb preceded by *to: to hesitate, to think, to start,* and so on. See Chapters 2, 3, and 5.

informal language   Language appropriate to informal situations and occasions. Informal language often uses contractions and colloquialisms.

intensive pronouns   Pronouns that end in *-self* or *-selves* and emphasize their antecedents: *myself, yourself, himself, ourselves,* and so on. See Chapter 6.

interjection   A word or phrase expressing emotion but having no grammatical relationship to the other words in the sentence. Interjections include the following: *Yes, no, oh, well,* and so on. Also called an *exclamation.* See Chapter 2.

interrogative pronoun   A pronoun that is used to form a question: *who, whom, what, which, whose.* "*Who* wants to play softball?" See Chapter 6.

intransitive verb   A verb that does not require an object. "They slept." See also *transitive verb* and Chapter 5.

inverted sentence   A sentence that is not in the usual word order of subject-verb-object. "Angry and dejected was he." See Chapter 3.

irregular verb   A verb that forms its past tense or past participle by changing its spelling: *bring* (*brought*), *think* (*thought*), and *run* (*ran*). See *regular verb* and Chapter 5.

linking verb   A verb that connects a subject in a sentence with another word (usually a noun, pronoun, or adjective) that renames or describes the subject. "The bacon *was* crisp." "You *seem* bored." Common linking verbs are *to be, to seem, to become, to feel,* and *to appear.* See Chapters 2, 3, and 5.

main clause   See *independent clause.*

mass noun   A noun referring to something usually measured by weight, by degree, or by volume rather than by count. Mass nouns are nouns that cannot be counted like *assistance* (we don't say *one assistance, two assistances,* and so on), *money,* and *height.*

misplaced modifier   A word or group of words misplaced in the sentence and therefore modifying the wrong word. "I watched the parade *standing on the balcony.*" See *dangling modifier* and *squinting modifier* and Chapter 10.

modifier   A word or group of words describing or modifying the meaning of another word in the sentence. See Chapter 10.

nonessential modifier   A word or group of words modifying a noun or pronoun but not essential to the meaning of the sentence. Nonessential modifiers are set off by commas. "My father, *who was born in Illinois,* was a metallurgical accountant." Also called *nonrestrictive modifier.* See Chapters 8 and 11.

nonrestrictive modifier   See *nonessential modifier.*

noun   A word that names a person, place, thing, or idea. See Chapter 2.

noun clause   A dependent clause functioning as a subject, direct object, predicate nominative, or indirect object in a sentence. "He told me *what I wanted to hear.*" See Chapter 8.

number   The form of a word that indicates one (*singular*) or more than one (*plural*). See Chapters 4 and 7.

object   A word or group of words receiving the action of or affected by an action verb or a preposition. See *direct object, indirect object,* and *object of preposition.*

object of preposition   A word or group of words following a preposition and related to another part of the sentence by the preposition. "Vince drove his motorcycle across *the United States*." See Chapters 2 and 6.

object pronoun   A pronoun that is used as an object. It may be used as an object of a preposition ("Sit by *me*"); the object of a verb ("Call *us* for more information"); or as an indirect object ("Fiona gave *me* the flowers"). See Chapter 6.

parallel structure   Structure where all items in a series are in the same grammatical form. See Chapter 10.

participle   The "ing" form of a verb (the *present participle*) when it is used as an adjective (a *swimming* pool), or the "d," "ed," "t," or "n" form of a verb (the *past participle*) when it is used as an adjective (the *painted* house). See Chapters 3 and 5.

passive voice   See *voice*.

past participle   See *participle*.

person   The form of a pronoun or verb used to show the speaker (first person: *I am*), the person spoken to (second person: *you are*), or the person spoken about (third person: *she is*). See Chapter 7.

personal pronoun   A pronoun that changes its form to show person: *I, you, he, she, they,* and so on. See Chapter 6.

phrase   A group of words lacking both a subject and a verb. See Chapter 9.

plural   More than one. See also *number*.

positive degree   The form of the adjective or adverb that makes no comparison: *heavy* (positive degree); *heavier* (comparative degree); *heaviest* (superlative degree). See also *comparative degree* and *superlative degree*.

possessive pronouns   Pronouns that show ownership: *my, mine, your, yours, his, her, hers, its, our,* and so on. See Chapters 2 and 6.

predicate   The verb, its modifiers, and any objects in a sentence. The predicate makes a statement about the subject of the sentence.

predicate adjective   An adjective that follows a linking verb and modifies the subject. "We were *happy* to get the news." See Chapters 2 and 10.

predicate noun   A noun that follows a linking verb and names the subject. "Harry is the *captain* of the lacrosse team." See Chapter 6.

predicate pronoun   A pronoun that follows a linking verb and identifies the subject. "My closest friend is *you*." See Chapter 6.

preposition   A word that shows a relationship between its object and another word in the sentence. Common prepositions include *at, by, from, to, behind, below, for, among, with,* and so on. See Chapter 2.

prepositional phrase   A preposition and its object: *on the table, above the clouds, for the evening,* and so on. See Chapter 2.

present participle   See *participle*.

progressive form   A form that expresses action that continues to happen. See Chapter 5.

pronoun   A word that takes the place of a noun or another pronoun. See Chapters 2 and 6.

pronoun antecedent   See *antecedent* and Chapter 7.

pronoun form   The form of a pronoun based on its use. Pronouns change their forms when they are used as subjects or objects or to show possession. See also *case* and Chapter 6.

pronoun reference   See *antecedent* and Chapter 7.

proper adjective   An adjective formed from a proper noun (*Italian* painting, *African* nations, and *Irish* whiskey). Proper adjectives are usually capitalized except in phrases like "china cabinet" or "french fries."

proper noun   A noun referring to a specific person, place, or thing. Proper nouns are capitalized: *Denver, Mr. McAuliffe,* and *Taj Mahal.* See Chapters 2 and 11.

reflexive pronoun   A pronoun ending in *-self* or *-selves* and renaming the subject. Reflexive pronouns are objects of verbs and prepositions. "He perjured *himself.*" "They went by *themselves.*" See Chapter 6.

regular verb   A verb that forms its past tense by adding *-d,* or *-ed: start/started* and *hope/hoped.* See also *irregular verb* and Chapter 5.

relative pronoun   A pronoun that introduces an adjective clause. The relative pronouns are *who, whom, whose, which, that, what,* and *whatever.* See Chapters 6 and 8.

restrictive modifier   See *essential modifier.*

run-on sentence   Two independent clauses run together with no punctuation to separate them: "Her uncle works as a plumber in Des Moines he used to be a professor of philosophy in Boston." The run-on sentence is corrected by placing a semicolon or a comma and coordinate conjunction between the two clauses. See Chapter 9.

sentence   A group of words containing a subject and a verb and expressing some sense of completeness. See Chapters 3 and 9.

sentence fragment   A group of words lacking an independent clause and therefore unable to stand alone. See Chapter 9.

sentence types   Sentences classified on the basis of their structure. There are four types of sentences in English: simple, compound, complex, and compound-complex. See also *complex sentence, compound sentence, compound-complex sentence, simple sentence,* and Chapters 3 and 8.

simple subject   See *subject.*

simple sentence   A sentence containing one independent clause. See Chapters 3 and 8.

slang   An informal word or expression not accepted in formal writing by careful or educated users of the language. Slang is usually short-lived or temporary and should be used sparingly.

split infinitive   An infinitive with a modifier between the *to* and the verb. Split infinitives are avoided by most careful speakers and writers. Examples are *to really want* and *to hardly hear.*

squinting modifier   A modifier that makes the meaning of a sentence ambiguous because it can modify either of two words. "We stood around *nervously* waiting to be introduced." "I asked them *politely* to leave." See Chapter 10.

standard written English   The English of careful and educated speakers and writers. See Chapter 1.

subject   The part of the sentence about which the predicate makes a statement. A *simple subject* does not include any modifiers; a *complete subject* includes modifiers; and a *compound subject* consists of two or more subjects. See also *predicate* and Chapter 3.

subordinate clause   See *dependent clause*.

subordinate conjunction   A word that joins a dependent clause to an independent clause. See Chapters 2, 3, and 8.

superlative degree   The *most*, *least*, or *-est* form of those adjectives and adverbs that can be compared: *most beautiful*, *least valid*, and *greatest*. See also *comparative degree*, *comparison*, and *positive degree*.

tense   The form of a verb that shows the action as being in the past, present, or future times. The most common tenses are simple present, present perfect, simple past, past perfect, simple future, and future perfect. See Chapters 2 and 5 and pages 286–290.

transitive verb   A verb that requires an object in order to complete its meaning: "We *saw* the accident." "They *helped* their neighbors." See also *intransitive verb*.

verb   A part of speech that describes action or a state of being of a subject and thereby tells what a noun or pronoun does or what it is. See Chapters 2 and 5.

verb phrase   A verb that consists of helping verbs and a main verb. "Sal *will* not *arrive* on time." "I *may have lost* your jacket." "We *have won* the lottery!" See Chapters 2 and 3.

voice   Transitive verbs can be either in the *active voice* or in the *passive voice*. When the subject in the sentence performs the action described by the verb, they are in the active voice. "Reverend Jackson performed the ceremony." When the action described by the verb is done to the subject, transitive verbs are in the passive voice. "The ceremony was performed by Reverend Jackson." See Chapter 3.

Answers to
Selected Exercises

Answers are for the editing exercise in Chapter 1 and even-numbered exercises in Chapters 2–11.

Chapter 1

Editing Exercise

1. Sean bought his wife a motorcycle with an electric starter.
2. Because the sidewalk was covered with ice, I walked very carefully to avoid falling.
3. The prospect of moving to a warmer climate delighted his wife and him.
4. Rappelling is a method of descent used by mountain climbers; it employs double ropes rather than picks and shoe cleats. (*Note:* See Chapter 9 for other ways to correct this sentence.)
5. Each of the band members has signed his or her name on the concert program. (*Also:* All of the band members had signed their names on the concert program.)
6. It was an old-fashioned remedy for a cough, made by mixing honey, lemon, and hot water.
7. After running in the marathon, Jackie lay down and rested.
8. As a freshman in college, Mario had broken three records as a member of the basketball team.
9. Osteoporosis is caused by loss of bone mass and strength. It affects twenty-five percent of women over age sixty. (*Note:* See Chapter 9 for other ways to correct this sentence.)
10. Han and I were assigned the task of washing dishes after the dinner.
11. The survivors of the automobile accident said that a heavy downpour of rain had made it really difficult to see the freeway.
12. Football is one of the sports that are becoming popular in Europe.
13. The bankruptcy of many large corporations has frightened many investors. They are afraid of losing their life savings. (*Note:* See Chapter 9 for other ways to correct this sentence.)
14. The president has spoken to the American people and to Congress about his tax reform proposal.
15. Maria was disappointed to learn that whom you know sometimes is as important as what you know in the business world.

16. A piece of the rudder, weighing hundreds of pounds, fell from the airplane as it lifted off the runway.
17. One of the principal agricultural products of Idaho is potatoes.
18. The salesman who sells the most automobiles next month will receive a trip to Hawaii as his prize.
19. The guitar player walked out on the stage and began to play selections from her new album.
20. The mail carrier tried to befriend the dog as it barked loudly and strained at its leash.

Chapter 2

Exercise 2-2   1. 2   2. 1   3. 2   4. 1   5. 3   6. 3   7. 2   8. 3   9. 2   10. 2
Exercise 2-4A   1. Twenty million   2. crash   3. Japanese   4. popular   5. derives   6. stems   7. have   8. famous   9. gross   10. popular
Exercise 2-4B   1. often   2. generally   3. sometimes   4. digitally   5. carefully   6. slightly   7. electrically   8. heavily   9. completely   10. legally
Exercise 2-6   1. and, but   2. and, yet   3. Neither . . . nor   4. and, and, either . . . or   5. but

Chapter 3

Exercise 3-2   1. were   2. was   3. was   4. were   5. were   6. tasted   7. seemed   8. became   9. grew   10. were
Exercise 3-4   1. look   2. are, have   3. is, has been traced   4. has inherited, has   5. carry, suffers   6. clog, cause, damage, cause, supply, are blocked   7. die   8. contain   9. live   10. have
Exercise 3-6   1. life/death   2. affair/Amelia   3. Amelia/she   4. goal   5. Amelia   6. articles/photographs   7. public   8. everyone/airplane/quest   9. flyers   10. message/plane   11. plane/pilots/squads   12. adventurers/scholars/fans   13. rumors   14. some/Earhart/others/she   15. pilots
Exercise 3-8   1. animals/are; others/possess; that/can cause   2. bites/can cause   3. movies/feature; that/frequents   4. bites/can bring   5. people/are   6. reactions/can include   7. victims/are; they/may die   8. bites/cause; others/are   9. spiders/cause; survival/is   10. spider/is called
Exercise 3-10   1. (when the Indian Removal Act was passed in 1830); tribes/were forced; Act/was passed   2. (after settlers heard reports of gold deposits there); President Andrew Jackson/began; settlers/heard   3. (even after many tribes agreed to adopt Anglo culture); Sharing land/was deemed; tribes/agreed   4. (Though some tribes traded their land for tracts out West); tribes/traded; tribes/refused   5. (if any Native American resisted eviction); soldiers/used; Native American/resisted   6. (as they

were marched at gunpoint from their land); Native Americans/left; they/were marched 7. (because they froze or starved to death during the winter march); Hundreds/were buried; they/froze, starved 8. (Because the Native Americans suffered such deep loss and anguish); Native Americans/suffered; journey/is known 9. (When the Cherokee tribe appealed to the Supreme Court for help); tribe/appealed; Court/ruled 10. (Although Andrew Jackson is regarded as an admirable president by many students of history); Andrew Jackson/is regarded; others/hold

Chapter 4

Exercise 4-2 [subject: subject; a] 2. [subject: Goalies; a] 3. [subject: stories; b] 4. [subject: men; b] 5. [subject: results; b] 6. [subject: problem; a] 7. [subject: alarms; a] 8. [subject: outlaws; b] 9. [subject: expectations; b] 10. [subject: reason; b]
Exercise 4-4 1. a 2. b 3. a 4. a 5. a 6. a 7. b 8. b 9. a 10. a 11. a 12. a 13. a 14. b 15. a
Exercise 4-6 1. b 2. b 3. a 4. b 5. b 6. a 7. b 8. b 9. a 10. b

Chapter 5

Exercise 5-2 1. sunk 2. reached 3. nicknamed 4. begun 5. capsized 6. engaged 7. observed 8. flown 9. detected 10. destroyed 11. ordered 12. kept 13. blocked 14. become 15. retained
Exercise 5-4 1. are 2. have slept 3. ate 4. have drunk 5. grew 6. have sat 7. Draw 8. left 9. lay 10. has given
Exercise 5-6 1. lay 2. lain 3. lying 4. lay 5. laid 6. lay 7. laid 8. lie 9. laid 10. lain 11. lay 12. laid 13. lay 14. lying 15. lay

Chapter 6

Exercise 6-2 1. them (b) 2. him (b); me (a) 3. me (c) 4. us (a) 5. you/me (a) 6. me (c); me (a) 7. him (a) 8. us (c); us (a) 9. him/me (a) 10. me (c)
Exercise 6-4 1. b 2. b 3. a. 4. a. 5. a 6. b 7. b 8. b 9. b 10. b

Chapter 7

Exercise 7-2 1. a 2. a 3. a 4. b 5. b 6. b 7. a 8. a 9. a 10. a
Exercise 7-4 Responses will vary.

Chapter 8

Exercise 8-2   1. daily, and   2. (no commas needed)   3. Internet, and   4. (no commas needed)   5. online, for   6. purchases, but   Internet, or   8. online, and   9. (no commas needed)   10. (no commas needed)

Exercise 8-4   Responses will vary.

Exercise 8-6   1. game (that challenges you to score points without losing the ball or tilting the game)   2. technology (which has been added to attract players)   3. components (that are common to all of them)   4. flippers (whose purpose is to keep the ball out of the drain and propel it toward the bumpers and ramps in order to score points)   5. buttons (that are located on either side of the machine)   6. pinball (which weighs 2.8 ounces)   7. ball (that fails to hit a target)   8. ball (that goes down the drain)   9. art (that is carefully crafted to draw the player to a certain machine over any other in the arcade)   10. speaker (that produces musical scores to accompany game play)

Exercise 8-8   1. how a laser beam translates digital data into music   2. Where we spend our honeymoon; how far our ancient Volkswagen can take us   3. where I was when I learned of the *Columbia* space shuttle accident   4. that the life story of Louis Pasteur became a popular film in the 1930s   5. that a bee sting had caused our neighbor's heart attack   6. where you want me to set down this piano   7. how humans will stop or reverse the polluting of Earth   8. who recently paid $ 4 million for a Picasso painting   9. who among my neighbors sings Beyonce songs   dawn each day   10. how my pet cobra can spell out my first name with his body

Chapter 9

Exercise 9-2   1. Sentences 4 and 9 are correct. Responses for the other items will vary.

Exercise 9-4   1. Sentence 6 is correct. Responses for the other items will vary.

Chapter 10

Exercise 10-2   Sentences 5 and 9 are correct. Responses for the other items will vary.

Exercise 10-4   1. I enjoy pizza much more than Garth does.   2. The Tim McGraw CD is more expensive than the Faith Hill CD.   3. Correct   4. Clothes are more fashionable at Tommy Hilfiger than at other stores.   5. We'd rather listen to blues than other kinds of music.   6. The neighbors near our new house in Brownsville are friendlier than the neighbors near our old house in Boston.   7. Sipping coffee with my English instructor is more enjoyable than sipping coffee with a super model.   8. Correct

9. The defense attorney's case is stronger and more interesting than the prosecutor's. 10. Judy's flu has grown worse than it was yesterday.

Exercise 10-6 (*Suggested Revisions*) 1. In computer class, Phuong learned to build Web pages and to use the Internet.   2. Trisha complained that her counselor did not have an understanding of students' problems and he did not like people.   3. Owning a home requires a lot of maintenance, money, and time.   4. Wally's ideas are clever, original, and practical.   5. The ambassador from Iran would neither apologize nor promise to accept the demands of the United Nations.   6. Correct   7. Correct   8. The governor said that his hobbies were fly-fishing and playing video games with his grandchildren.   9. Many people join health clubs for exercise, for relaxation, and for romance.   10. Nicolas Cage is admired as an actor for his dramatic roles as well as for his comedy roles.

Chapter 11

Exercise 11-2   1. difficult, but   2. Correct   3. DVDs, yet/popcorn, carrot coins, or mango slices   4. breakfast, and   5. Correct   6. vegetables, so   7. juice, but   8. soft drinks, diluting juice with water, and   9. serving, and   10. eat out, or

Exercise 11-4   1. Physics, literature, economic science, and   2. No, James   3. Remember, Lakisha, that   4. Hungary, Poland, or Ukraine   5. Michael Jordan, Wilt Chamberlain, Elgin Baylor, and Jerry West   6. men, if you ask me, are record stores, cafes, sports bars, and   7. Correct   8. Tell me, please, how   9. therefore, we   10. China, not

Exercise 11-6   1. 20 Coral Springs Road, Beverly Hills, California   2. Correct   3. champions, not   4. Finkelstein, Ph.D., will   5. Norman, Lois   6. June 26, 2003, the   7. Correct   8. "I don't want to," says Alexa   9. Lopez, D.D.S., said   10. eat, the

Exercise 11-8   1. goal: a tour   2. Correct   3. era: cobbled   4. Correct   5. Correct   6. attractions: sharks   7. of Paul Revere   8. to see tea   9. desk: these   10. treat: a ride

Exercise 11-10   1. noblesse oblige   2. "Hanging Fire," "The Woman Thing," and "Sisters in Arms."   3. Ski Express / Yankee Magazine   4. "My favorite love song," said Darnell, "is 'Just the Way You Are,' as sung by Billy Joel."   5. "to love, honor, and obey"   6. The Van and The Snapper   7. "Faster Than a Speeding Photon," / Discover   8. Aphrodite   9. Field of Dreams   10. Singin' in the Rain / Louisville Herald   11. Frasier   12. The Postman / "Walking Around" / "Leaning into the Afternoons"   13. Stardust / "The Moment" / Giving of the Keys to Saint Peter   14. Titanic / The Titanic   15. Song of Myself

Exercise 11-12   1. twenty   2. *Who's Who in Science*   3. Correct   4. sixty thousand   5. Correct   6. 196,950,711   7. Thirty-one   8. *b*'s and *d*'s   9. you're   10. It's been / its house

Exercise 11-14   1. In 1533, Britain's King Henry VIII—though already married to Catherine of Aragon—married Anne Boleyn and was excommunicated from the Roman Catholic Church by the Pope.   2. If I can't save enough money for tuition next semester, I'll not be able to join my family when they take their vacation to western Canada.   3. One of the most important religious holidays in the Mideast is Ramadan.   4. Every Fourth of July at our company's party, Mr. Dickerson sings "You Give Love a Bad Name" by the hard rock band Bon Jovi.   5. Thanks to their coach's tough training methods, the water polo team from Ukraine won a gold medal at last year's Olympics.   6. The former governor said that her memoir, *Memories of the Mansion*, was factually accurate.   7. We flew Pogo Airlines from West Virginia to western Ireland and then to southern Norway.   8. Jennifer and her husband caught several trout in the Gulf Stream last spring.   9. A politician from the state of Mississippi revealed that he had been a member of the Klan.   10. The oldest university in the United States is Harvard, which was founded in 1636.   11. The Prince of Wales has a country estate at Balmoral Castle.   12. Floods in the northern part of Minnesota damaged the fall crops.   13. Letters written by the explorers of the South Pole were read to our geography class by Professor Brink.   14. Correct   15. Applicants for the sales position were required to pass written examinations in English, Spanish, and Japanese.

Credits

page 35   From "What the Black Man Wants" by Frederick Douglass.

page 36   From *Biology: The World of Life*, 6th ed., by Robert A. Wallace. Copyright 1992 by HarperCollins Publishers, Inc., p. 283.

page 36   From *Psychology: An Introduction*, 3rd ed., by Josh R. Gerow. Copyright 1992 by HarperCollins Publishers, Inc., p. 700.

page 40   From *Native American Voices*, Susan Lobo and Steve Talbot, eds. Copyright 1998 by Addison Wesley Longman, Inc., pp. 266–67. Reprinted with permission.

page 41   From *Management: Leadership in Action*, 5th ed., by Donald C. Mosley, Paul H. Pietri, and Leon C. Megginson. Copyright 1996 by HarperCollins Publishers, Inc., p. 555.

page 68   From *The Kite Runner*, by Khaled Hosseini. Copyright 2003 by Riverhead Press, p. 158.

page 90   From *Cape Cod*, by Henry David Thoreau. Copyright 1987 by Penguin, p. 39.

page 91   From *The Da Vinci Code*, by Dan Brown. Copyright 2003 by Doubleday, p. 78.

page 165   From *I Know Why the Caged Bird Sings*, by Maya Angelou. Copyright 1969 by Random House. New York: Bantam, 1993, p. 146.

Index